Visual Studio Code Distilled

Evolved Code Editing for Windows, macOS, and Linux

Third Edition

Alessandro Del Sole

Apress®

Visual Studio Code Distilled: Evolved Code Editing for Windows, macOS, and Linux

Alessandro Del Sole
Cremona, Italy

ISBN-13 (pbk): 978-1-4842-9483-3   ISBN-13 (electronic): 978-1-4842-9484-0
https://doi.org/10.1007/978-1-4842-9484-0

Managing Director, Apress Media LLC: Welmoed Spahr
Acquisitions Editor: Smriti Srivastava
Development Editor: Laura Berendson
Coordinating Editor: Mark Powers
Copy Editor: Kezia Endsley

Cover designed by eStudioCalamar

Cover image designed by Freepik (www.freepik.com)

Distributed to the book trade worldwide by Springer Science+Business Media New York, 1 New York Plaza, Suite 4600, New York, NY 10004-1562, USA. Phone 1-800-SPRINGER, fax (201) 348-4505, e-mail orders-ny@ springer-sbm.com, or visit www.springeronline.com. Apress Media, LLC is a California LLC and the sole member (owner) is Springer Science + Business Media Finance Inc (SSBM Finance Inc). SSBM Finance Inc is a **Delaware** corporation.

For information on translations, please e-mail booktranslations@springernature.com; for reprint, paperback, or audio rights, please e-mail bookpermissions@springernature.com.

Apress titles may be purchased in bulk for academic, corporate, or promotional use. eBook versions and licenses are also available for most titles. For more information, reference our Print and eBook Bulk Sales web page at http://www.apress.com/bulk-sales.

Any source code or other supplementary material referenced by the author in this book is available to readers on GitHub (github.com/apress). For more detailed information, please visit http://www.apress.com/source-code.

Printed on acid-free paper

To my wonderful wife, Angelica. You are my reason to live.

Table of Contents

About the Author

Alessandro Del Sole is a senior software engineer for a healthcare company, building mobile apps for doctors and dialysis patients. He has been in the software industry for more than 20 years, focusing on Microsoft technologies such as .NET, C#, Visual Studio, and Xamarin. He has been a trainer, consultant, and a Microsoft MVP since 2008 and is the author of many technical books. He is a Xamarin Certified Mobile Developer, Microsoft Certified Professional, and a Microsoft Programming Specialist in C#.

Acknowledgments

Thanks to Smriti Srivastava, Nirmal Selvaraj, Laura Berendson, and everyone else at Apress for the opportunity, renewed trust, and the great teamwork on this book.

Special thanks to the technical editor Damien Foggon, who contributed to the quality and accuracy of the content.

Special thanks to my wife Angelica, for her continuous and strong support.

Introduction

One of the most common requirements in software development today is building applications and services that run on multiple systems and devices, especially with the continued expansion of cloud and artificial intelligence services, and of architectures based on microservices.

Developers have many options for building cross-platform and cross-device software, from languages to development platforms and tools. However, in most cases, such tools rely on proprietary systems, which result in strong dependencies. Moreover, most development tools target specific platforms and development scenarios. Microsoft Visual Studio Code takes a step forward by providing a fully featured development environment for Windows, macOS, and Linux that offers not only advanced coding features but also integrated tools. These tools span across the entire application lifecycle, from coding to debugging to team collaboration. The full tooling is consistent across these languages and frameworks, natively or via extensions, so that developers share the same experience regardless of the technology they use.

With .NET 7 and with .NET MAUI recently released, and with artificial intelligence services becoming part of the modern software implementation, Visual Studio Code becomes even more important to support cross-platform development on multiple operating systems. In this book, developers with any skill level learn how to leverage Visual Studio Code to target scenarios such as web, cloud, and mobile development using the programming language of their choice. This book provides guidance on building apps for any system and any device. This includes managing the application lifecycle, as well as team collaboration.

CHAPTER 1

Introducing Visual Studio Code

Visual Studio Code is not just another evolved notepad with syntax colorization and automatic indentation. Instead, it is a very powerful, code-focused development environment expressly designed to make it easier to write web, mobile, and cloud applications using languages that are available in different development platforms. It supports the application development lifecycle with a built-in debugger and integrated support for the popular Git version control engine.

With Visual Studio Code, you can work with individual code files or with folders containing projects or loose files. This chapter provides an introduction to Visual Studio Code, giving you information on when and why you should use it. It includes details about installing and configuring the program on the different supported operating systems.

Note   In this book, I refer to the product using its full name, Visual Studio Code, as well as its friendly names, VS Code and Code, interchangeably.

Visual Studio Code, a Cross-Platform Development Tool

Visual Studio Code is the first cross-platform development tool in the Microsoft Visual Studio family that runs on Windows, Linux, and macOS. It is a free, open-source (https://github.com/microsoft/vscode), code-centric tool. This not only makes editing code files and folder-based project systems easier, but also facilitates writing cross-platform web, mobile, and cloud applications in the most popular platforms, such

© Alessandro Del Sole 2023
A. Del Sole, *Visual Studio Code Distilled*, https://doi.org/10.1007/978-1-4842-9484-0_1

as Node.js and .NET. It also has integrated support for a huge number of languages and rich editing features such as IntelliSense, finding symbol references, quickly reaching a type definition, and much more.

Visual Studio Code is based on Electron (`https://electronjs.org/`), a framework for creating cross-platform applications with native technologies. It combines the simplicity of a powerful code editor with the tools a developer needs to support the application lifecycle development, including debuggers and version control integration based on Git. Visual Studio Code is therefore a complete development tool, rather than being a simple code editor. For a richer development experience, consider Microsoft Visual Studio 2022 on Windows and Visual Studio 2022 for Mac on macOS, but Visual Studio Code can be really helpful in many situations.

In this book, you learn how to use Visual Studio Code and how to get the most out of it; you discover how you can use it as a powerful code editor and as a complete environment for end-to-end development. Except where necessary to differentiate operating systems, figures are based on Microsoft Windows 10, but typically there is no difference in the interface on Windows 11, Linux, and macOS. Also, Visual Studio Code includes several color themes that style its layout. In this book, figures display the Light (Visual Studio) theme, so you might see different colors on your own screen if you choose a different color theme. Chapter 5 explains how to change the theme, but if you want to be consistent with the book's figures, simply choose File ➤ Preferences ➤ Color Theme and select the Visual Studio 2019 Light Theme. It is worth mentioning that the theme you select does not affect the features described in this book.

When and Why Visual Studio Code

Before you learn how to use Visual Studio Code, explore the features it offers, and discover how it provides an improved code editing experience, you have to clearly understand its purpose. Visual Studio Code is not a simple code editor; rather, it is a powerful environment that puts writing code at its center. The main purpose of Visual Studio Code is to make it easier to write code for web, mobile, and cloud platforms for any developers working on Windows, Linux, or macOS, providing independence from proprietary development environments.

For a better understanding of the nonproprietary nature of Visual Studio Code, let's consider an example based on ASP.NET Core, the cross-platform, open-source technology able to run on Windows, Linux, and macOS that Microsoft produced to create portable web applications. Forcing you to build cross-platform, portable web apps with Microsoft Visual Studio 2022 would make you dependent on that specific integrated development environment (IDE). This also applies to the (free) Visual Studio 2022 Community edition. Conversely, though Visual Studio Code certainly is not intended to be a replacement for more powerful and complete environments, it can run on a variety of operating systems and can manage different project types, as well as the most popular languages. To accomplish this, Visual Studio Code provides the following core features:

- Built-in support for coding in many languages, including those you typically use in cross-platform development scenarios, such as C# and JavaScript, with advanced editing features and support for additional languages via extensibility

- Built-in debugger for Node.js, with support for additional debuggers (such as .NET and Julia) via extensibility

- Version control based on the popular Git version-control system, which provides an integrated experience for collaboration, supporting code commits and branches

In order to properly combine all these features into one tool, Visual Studio Code provides a coding environment based on folders, which makes it easy to work with code files that are not organized within projects and offers a unified way to work with different languages. Starting with this assumption, Visual Studio Code offers an advanced editing experience with features that are common to many supported languages, plus some features that are available to specific languages. As you'll learn throughout the book, Code also makes it easy to extend its built-in features by supplying custom languages, syntax coloring, editing tools, debuggers, and much more via a number of extensibility points. It is a code-centric tool, with primary focus on web, cross-platform code. That said, it does not provide all of the features you need for full, more complex application development and application lifecycle management and it is not intended to be the best choice with some development platforms. If you have to make a choice, consider the following points:

- Visual Studio Code can produce binaries and executable files only if the language you use has support to do so through a command-line interface (CLI), a compiler, and a debugger. If you use a language for which there is no extensive support (e.g., the open-source Go programming language, `https://golang.org`), Visual Studio Code cannot invoke a compiler. You can work around this by implementing task automation, discussed in Chapter 8, but this is different than having an integrated compilation process.

- Except where provided by specific extensions, Visual Studio Code has no designers, so you can create an application user interface only by writing all of the related code manually. As you can imagine, this is fine for some languages and for some scenarios, but it can be very complicated with some kinds of applications and development platforms, especially if you are used to working with the powerful graphical tools available in Microsoft Visual Studio 2022.

- Visual Studio Code is a general-purpose tool and is not the proper choice for specific development scenarios such as building Windows desktop applications.

If your requirements are different, consider Microsoft Visual Studio 2022 or Microsoft Visual Studio 2022 for Mac instead, which are optimized for building, testing, deploying, and maintaining multiple types of applications.

Now that you have a clearer idea of Code's goals, you are ready to learn the amazing editing features that elevate it above any other code editor.

Installing and Configuring Visual Studio Code

Installing Visual Studio Code is an easy task. In fact, you can simply visit `https://code.visualstudio.com` from your favorite browser, and the web page will detect your operating system, suggesting the appropriate installer. Figure 1-1 shows how the download page appears on Windows.

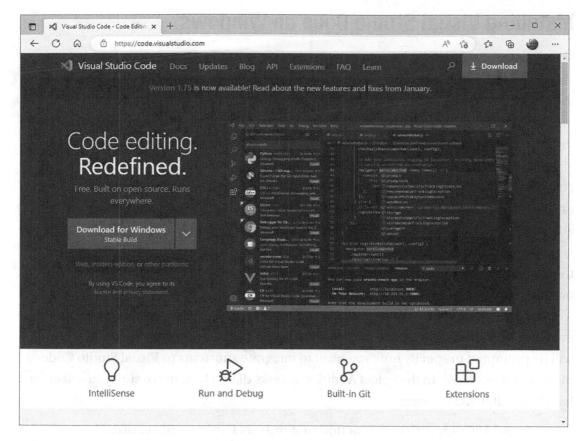

Figure 1-1. *The download page for Visual Studio Code*

Note   Visual Studio Code can also run in Portable Mode, which means that you can create a self-containing folder that can be moved across environments. Since this is a very specific scenario, it isn't covered in this book; you can read the documentation (`https://code.visualstudio.com/docs/editor/portable`) to learn the steps required to generate Portable Mode.

In the following sections, you learn some tips for installing Visual Studio Code on various supported systems.

Note   The latest stable release of Visual Studio Code at the time of this writing is version 1.76.0, released in February 2023.

Installing Visual Studio Code on Windows

Visual Studio Code can be installed on Windows 8, 10, and 11. For this operating system, Visual Studio Code is available with two installers: a global installer and a user-level installer. The global installer requires administrative privileges for installation and makes Code available to all users. The user-level installer makes Code available only to the currently logged-in user, but it does not require administrative privileges.

The user-level installer is the choice I recommend, especially if you work within a corporate environment and you do not have administrative privileges to install software on your PC. The Download for Windows button that you can see in Figure 1-1 will automatically download the user-level installer. If you instead want to download the system-level installer, go to `https://code.visualstudio.com/download` and select the System Installer download that best fits your system configuration (32- or 64-bit, or ARM).

Once the download has been completed, launch the installer and simply follow the guided procedure that is typical of most Windows programs. During the installation, you will be prompted to specify how you want to integrate shortcuts to Visual Studio Code in the Windows shell. In the Select Additional Tasks dialog box, make sure you select (at least) the following options:

- **Add "Open with Code" action to Windows Explorer file context menu**, which allows you to right-click a code file in the Explorer and open a file with VS Code.

- **Add "Open with Code" action to Windows Explorer directory context menu**, which allows you to rightclick a folder in the Explorer and open a folder with VS Code.

- **Add to PATH (available after restart)**, which adds the VS Code's pathname to the PATH environment variable, making it easy to run Visual Studio Code from the command line without typing the full path.

Note   Some antivirus and system protection tools, such as Symantec Endpoint Protection, might block the installation of some files that are recognized as false positives. In most cases, this will not prevent Visual Studio Code from working, but it is recommended that you disable the protection tool before installing Code or, if you do not have elevated permissions, that you ask your administrator to do it for you.

A specific dialog box will inform you once the installation process has completed. The installation folder for the user-level installer is C:\Users\username\AppData\Local\Programs\Microsoft VS Code, while the installation folder for the global installer is C:\Program Files\Microsoft VS Code on 64-bit systems and C:\Program Files(x86)\Microsoft VS Code on 32-bit systems. You will find a shortcut to Visual Studio Code in the Start menu and on the Desktop, if you selected the option to create a shortcut during the installation. When it starts, Visual Studio Code appears as shown in Figure 1-2.

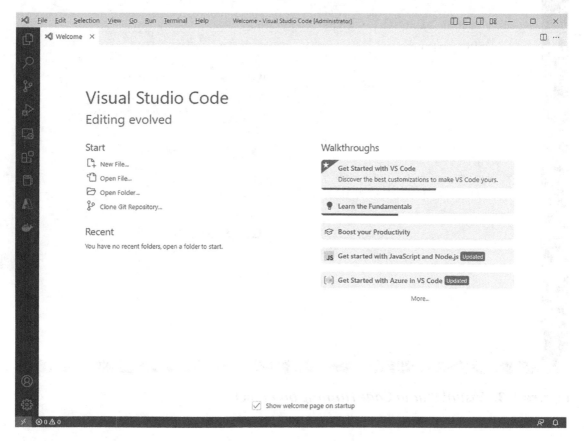

Figure 1-2. *Visual Studio Code running on Windows*

Installing Visual Studio Code on macOS

Installing VS Code on macOS is extremely simple. From the download page, simply click the Download for macOS button and wait for the download to complete. On macOS, Visual Studio Code works as an individual program, and therefore you simply need to double-click the downloaded file to start the application. Figure 1-3 shows Visual Studio Code running on macOS.

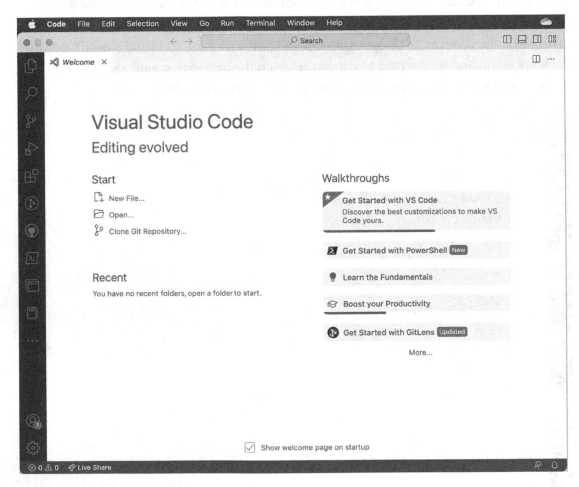

Figure 1-3. *Visual Studio Code running on macOS*

Installing Visual Studio Code on Linux

Linux is a very popular operating system and many derived distributions exist, so there are different installers available depending on the distribution you are using. For the Ubuntu and Debian distributions, you need the .deb installer. For the Red Hat Linux, Fedora, and SUSE distributions, you need the .rpm installer. This clarification is important because, as opposed to Windows and macOS, the browser might not be able to automatically detect the Linux distribution you are using, and therefore it will offer both options.

Once Visual Studio Code is installed, simply click the Show Applications button on the Desktop and then choose the Visual Studio Code shortcut. Figure 1-4 shows Visual Studio Code running on Ubuntu.

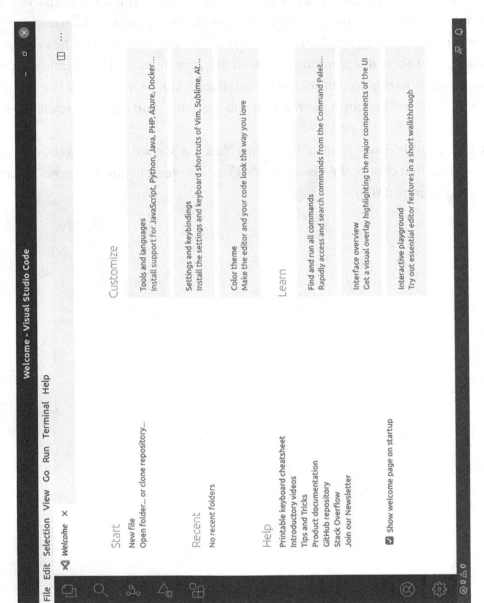

Figure 1-4. Visual Studio Code running on Ubuntu

Note   If you are a Windows user and want to try Visual Studio Code on a Linux distribution, you can create a virtual machine with the Hyper-V tool. For example, you could install the latest Ubuntu version (`https://www.ubuntu.com/download/desktop`) as an ISO image and use it as an installation media in Hyper-V. On macOS, you need to purchase the Apple Parallels Desktop software separately in order to create virtual machines, but you can basically do the same.

Localization Support

Visual Studio Code ships in English, but it can be localized in many other supported languages and cultures. When it's started, VS Code checks for the operating system language and, if it's different from English, it shows a popup message suggesting to install a language pack for the culture of your operating system. The localization support can be also enabled manually.

To accomplish this, choose View ➤ Command Palette. When the text box appears at the top of the page, type the following command:

```
> Configure Display Language
```

You can also just type `configure display` and the command will be automatically listed in the command palette (see Figure 1-5).

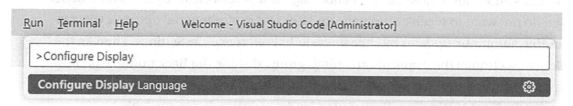

Figure 1-5. *Invoking the command to change the localization*

Note   The Command Palette is discussed thoroughly in Chapter 2.

When you click this command, the Command Palette displays the following options:

- **English (en)**, which allows you to select American English as the culture. This is the default localization and is always available.

- A list of available language packs built by Microsoft.

When you select a language pack, VS Code will download the appropriate package and will show a message saying that a restart is required in order to localize the user interface.

Updating Visual Studio Code

Visual Studio Code is configured to receive automatic updates in the background; Microsoft usually releases monthly updates.

Note   Because VS Code receives monthly updates, some features might have been updated at the time of your reading, and others might be new. This is a necessary clarification you should keep in mind while reading, and it is also the reason that I also provide links to the official documentation, so that you can stay up to date more easily.

Additionally, you can manually check for updates by choosing Help ➤ Check for Updates on Windows and Linux or choosing Code ➤ Check for Updates on macOS. If you do not want to receive automatic updates and prefer manual updates, you can disable automatic updates by choosing File ➤ Preferences ➤ Settings. Then, in the Update section of the Application settings group, disable the Background Updates option. Figure 1-6 shows an example based on Windows. (Obviously, on macOS and Linux, the Enable Windows Background Updates option is not available.)

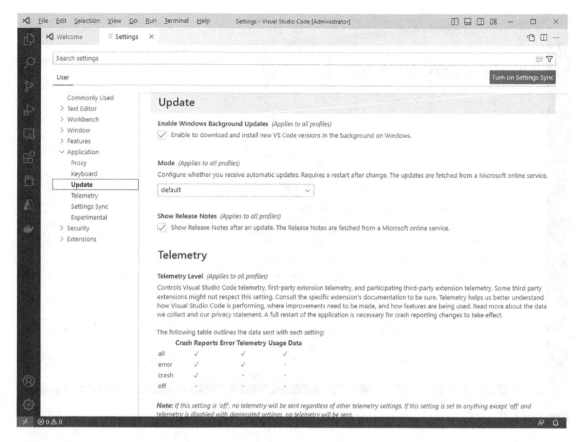

Figure 1-6. *Disabling automatic updates*

You follow the same steps to re-enable updates in the background. Whenever Visual Studio Code receives an update, you will receive a notification suggesting that you restart Code in order to apply the changes. The first time you restart Visual Studio Code after an update, you will see the release notes for the version that was installed, as demonstrated in Figure 1-7.

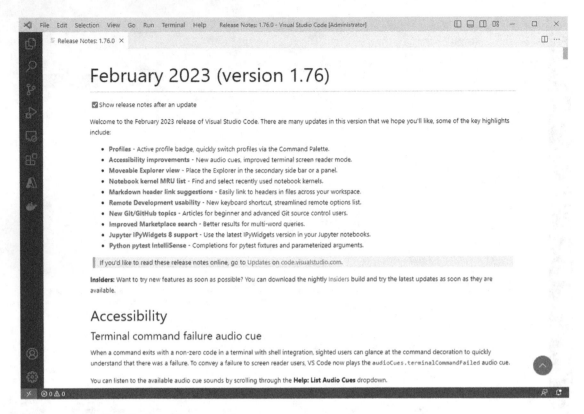

Figure 1-7. *VS Code release notes*

Release notes contain the list of new and updated features, as well as hyperlinks that will open the proper feature page in the documentation. You can recall release notes at any time by choosing Help ➤ Show Release Notes.

Previewing Features with Insiders Builds

By default, the download page of the Visual Studio Code's website allows you to download the latest stable build. However, Microsoft periodically also releases preview builds of Visual Studio Code, called *Insiders builds*. You can download these Insiders builds to look at any new and updated upcoming features before they are released to the general public.

Insiders builds can be downloaded from `https://code.visualstudio.com/insiders`, and they follow the same installation rules described previously for each operating system. They have a different icon color, typically a green icon instead of a blue icon, and the name you see in the application bar is Visual Studio Code - Insiders instead of Visual Studio Code (see Figure 1-8).

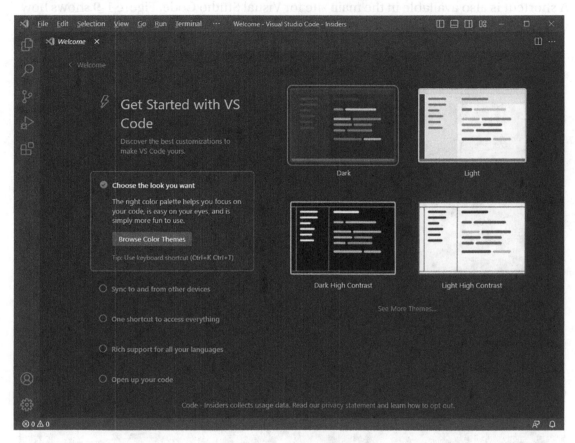

Figure 1-8. *Visual Studio Code Insiders builds*

Insiders builds and stable builds can work side by side without any issues. Because each lives in its own environment, your setting customizations and extensions you installed on the stable build will not be automatically available to the Insiders build and vice versa, so you will need to provide them again.

Insiders builds are a very good way to see what is coming with Visual Studio Code, but because they are not stable, final builds, it is not recommended you use them in production or with code you will release to production.

Visual Studio Code on Web

Microsoft is working on making Visual Studio Code available as a web application running in your favorite browser.

This is currently available as a preview and can be reached at `https://vscode.dev`. A shortcut is also available in the main site for Visual Studio Code. Figure 1-9 shows how VS Code looks in the browser.

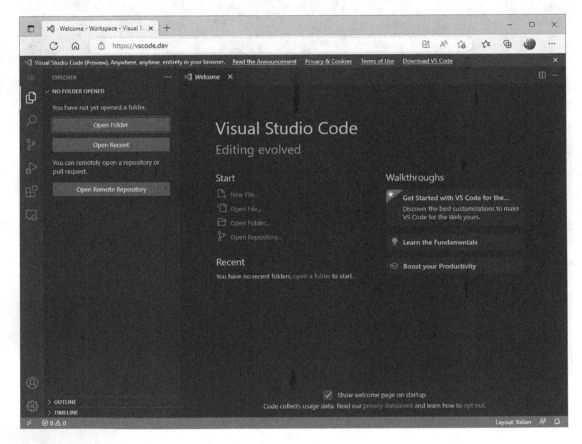

Figure 1-9. *Visual Studio Code as a web app*

When running in the browser, Visual Studio Code offers the same features available on the regular desktop app. You can also fully customize your development environment and experience, and changes will be saved into the local cache. This is a very interesting alternative, but still in preview stage at the time of this writing.

Summary

Visual Studio Code is not a simple code editor, but a fully featured development environment optimized for web, mobile, and cloud development. In this chapter, you saw how to install Visual Studio Code on Windows, macOS, and Linux distributions, learning how to select the appropriate installers and fine-tune the setup process. You also saw how to configure localization and updates. Next, you looked at the Insiders builds, which offer previews of upcoming, unreleased features. Finally, you saw Visual Studio Code running in the browser as a web app, with the same features as the desktop version.

Now that your environment is ready for use, it is time to start discovering the amazing features offered by Visual Studio Code. The next chapter walks through the environment, then in Chapter 3, you learn about all the amazing code-editing features that make Visual Studio Code a rich, powerful crossplatform editor.

CHAPTER 2

Getting to Know the Environment

Before you use Visual Studio Code as the editor of your choice, you need to know how the workspace is organized and what commands and tools are available, in order to get the most out of the development environment.

The VS Code user interface and layout are optimized to maximize the space for code editing, and it also provides easy shortcuts to quickly access all the additional tools you need in a given context. More specifically, the user interface is divided into five areas: the code editor, the Status Bar, the Activity Bar, the Panels area, and the Side Bar. This chapter explains how the user interface is organized and how you can be productive using it.

Note All the features discussed in this chapter apply to any file in any language, and they are available regardless of the language you see in the figures (normally C#). You can open one or more code files via File ➤ Open File to access the editor windows and explore the features discussed in this chapter. Then, Chapter 4 discusses more thoroughly how to work with individual files and multiple files, in one or more languages, concurrently.

The Welcome Page

At startup, Visual Studio Code displays the Welcome page, as shown in Figure 2-1.

© Alessandro Del Sole 2023
A. Del Sole, *Visual Studio Code Distilled*, https://doi.org/10.1007/978-1-4842-9484-0_2

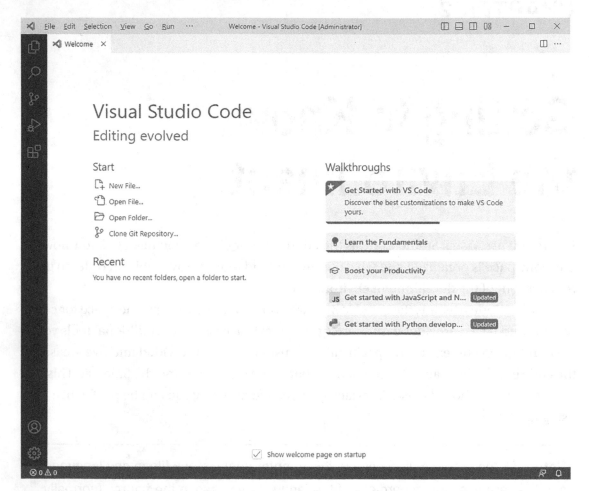

Figure 2-1. *The Welcome page*

On the left side of the page, under the Start group, you find shortcuts for creating and opening files and folders, and for cloning an existing Git repository. Under the Recent group is a list of recently opened files and folders that you can click for fast opening. Under the Walkthroughs group, there are useful links to product documentation, tutorials, cheat sheets, introductory videos, and other learning resources about Visual Studio Code.

By default, the Welcome page is set to appear every time you launch VS Code. To change this default behavior, remove the check mark from the Show Welcome Page On Startup check box. To re-enable the Welcome page on startup, choose Help ➤ Welcome and add the check mark back.

The Code Editor

The code editor is certainly the area where you will spend most of your time in VS Code. The code editor becomes available when you create a new file or open existing files and folders. You can edit one file at a time or edit multiple files side by side concurrently. Figure 2-2 shows an example of the latter.

Figure 2-2. *The code editor and multiple file views*

To do this, you have a couple options:

- Right-click a filename in the Explorer Bar and then select Open to the Side.

- Ctrl-click a filename in the Explorer Bar. This is discussed in the section "The Side Bar" later in this chapter.

- Press Ctrl+\ (or ⌘+\ on macOS) to split the editor into two.

Open editors can also be organized into groups. To accomplish this, you can drag and drop the title of an open editor close to another one and they will be grouped in the same space and the Explorer Bar will show the list of groups. You can quickly switch between editors by pressing Ctrl+1, 2, and so on, until 9. Keep in mind this works with up to nine editor windows. The code editor is the heart of Visual Studio Code and provides tons of powerful productivity features that are discussed in detail in the next chapter. For now, it is enough to know how to open and arrange editor windows.

Reordering, Resizing, and Zooming Editor Windows

You can reorder and resize editor windows based on your preferences. To reorder an editor, click the editor's header (which is where you see the filename) and move the editor to a different position. Resizing an editor can instead be accomplished by clicking the left mouse button when the pointer is on the editor's border, until it appears as a left/right arrow pair.

You can also zoom in and out the environment by clicking Ctrl++ and Ctrl+-, respectively. As an alternative, you can choose View ➤ Appearance ➤ Zoom In and View ➤ Appearance ➤ Zoom Out. You can reset the original zoom factor with Appearance ➤ Reset Zoom.

Note   In Visual Studio Code, the zoom is actually an accessibility feature. As an implication, when you zoom the code editor, everything else will also be zoomed.

The Status Bar

The Status Bar contains information about the current file or folder and provides shortcuts for some quick actions. Figure 2-3 shows an example of how the Status Bar appears.

Figure 2-3. *The Status Bar*

The Status Bar contains the following information, from left to right:

- Git version control information and options, such as the current branch. This is only visible when VS Code is connected to a Git repository.

- Errors and warnings detected in the source code.

- The cursor position expressed in line and column.

- Tab size, in this case Spaces: 4. You can click this to change the indentation size and to convert indentation to tabs or spaces.

- The encoding of the current file.

- The current line terminator.

- The programming or markup language of the open file. By clicking the current language name, you can change the language from a drop-down list that pops up.

- The project name, if you open a folder that contains a supported project system. It is worth noting that, if the folder contains multiple project files, clicking this item enables you to switch between projects.

- The Feedback button, which enables you to share your feedback about Visual Studio Code on Twitter.

- The notification icon, which shows the number of new notifications (if any). Notification messages typically come from extensions or they are about product updates.

It is worth mentioning that the color of the Status Bar changes depending on the situation. For example, it is purple when you open a single file, blue when you open a folder, and orange when Visual Studio Code is in debugging mode. Additionally, third-party extensions might use the Status Bar to display their own information.

The Activity Bar

The Activity Bar is on the left side of the workspace and can be considered a collapsed container for the Side Bar. Figure 2-4 shows the Activity Bar.

Figure 2-4. *The Activity Bar*

The Activity Bar provides shortcuts for the Explorer, Search, Git, Run and Debug, Extensions, Accounts, and Settings tools, each described in the next section. When you click a shortcut, the Side Bar related to the selected tool becomes visible. You can click the same shortcut again to collapse the Side Bar.

The Side Bar

The Side Bar is one of the most important tools in Visual Studio Code, and one of the tools you will interact most with. It is composed of five tools, each enabled by the corresponding icon, described in the following subsections.

The Explorer Bar

The Explorer Bar is enabled by clicking the first icon from the top of the Side Bar and provides a structured, organized view of the folder or files you are working with. The list of active files can be shown in the OPEN EDITORS subview. This can be enabled by clicking the ... button and then selecting Open Editors. It also includes open files that are not part of a project, folder, or files that have been modified. These are instead shown in a subview whose name is the folder or project name. Figure 2-5 provides an example of Explorer.

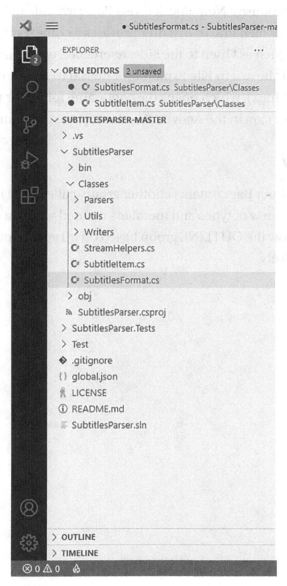

Figure 2-5. *The Explorer Bar*

You must hover your cursor over any file or folder to make the four buttons visible. The subview that shows a folder structure provides four buttons (from left to right): New File, New Folder, Refresh Explorer, and Collapse Folders in Explorer, each of which is self-explanatory. The OPEN EDITORS subview has three buttons (which you get when hovering over with the mouse): New Untitled Text File, Save All, and Close All Editors. Right-clicking a folder or filename in Explorer provides a context menu that offers common commands (such as Open to the Side, referenced earlier in this chapter). A very interesting command is Reveal in File Explorer (or Reveal to Finder on Mac and Open Containing Folder on Linux), which opens the containing folder for the selected item. Notice that the Explorer icon in the Activity Bar also reports the number of unsaved files.

The Outline View

The bottom of the Explorer Bar contains another group, called OUTLINE. This group provides a hierarchical view of types and members defined within a code file or tags. Figures 2-6 and 2-7 show the OUTLINE group based on a TypeScript file and based on an HTML file, respectively.

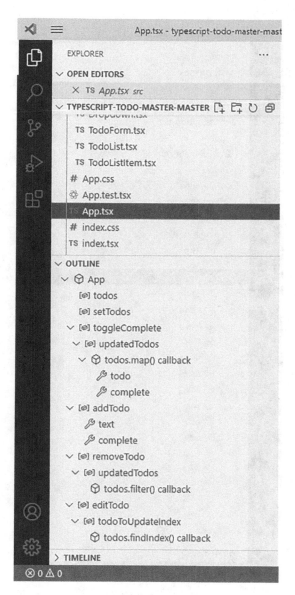

Figure 2-6. *The Outline view on a TypeScript file*

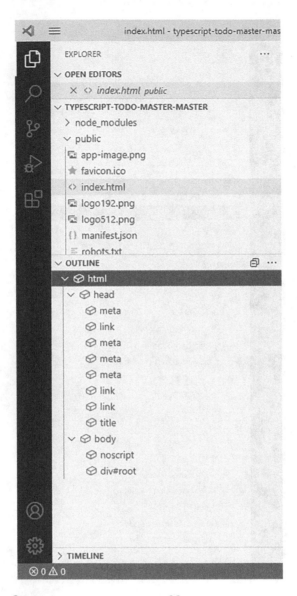

Figure 2-7. *The Outline view on an HTML file*

You can expand types and members defined in a markup file to see what other objects they define, and you can click each item and get the cursor over the selected item definition in the source code. It is worth mentioning that Visual Studio Code highlights with a different color (red in the case of the Visual Studio Light Theme) items that have potential problems and that are highlighted with squiggles in the code editor. Currently, the Outline view is only available to languages such as JavaScript, TypeScript, C#, HTML, Markdown, and JSON. Support for additional languages might be available when installing the appropriate extensions.

The Timeline View

The Timeline view shows the history of local changes made to an individual file. It only works with code for which a local Git repository has been created.

Note   The Timeline view is related to working with Git source control, the topic of Chapter 7, but it is discussed here because it is part of the Explorer Bar. For now, you can click the Source Control button on the Side Bar and then click the Initialize Repository button. This initializes a local Git repository and, consequently, the Timeline feature over individual files.

Figure 2-8 shows an example based on a file called index.html.

Figure 2-8. *The Timeline view showing change history*

In this particular example, the Timeline is showing three changes in the file history: a first local commit, changes saved to disk, and staged changes. This tool is very useful when you work with Git source control, and you want to see a detailed view of the history for each file. Chapter 7 provides detailed explanations about integrated source control features.

The Search Tool

The Search tool, enabled by clicking the Search icon, allows for searching and, optionally, replacing text across files. You can search for one or more words, including special characters (such as * and ?), and you can even search based on regular expressions. Figure 2-9 shows the Search tool in action, with advanced options expanded (files to include and files to exclude), which you enable by clicking the **...** button located under Replace. In the example, search is performed only within .tsx files.

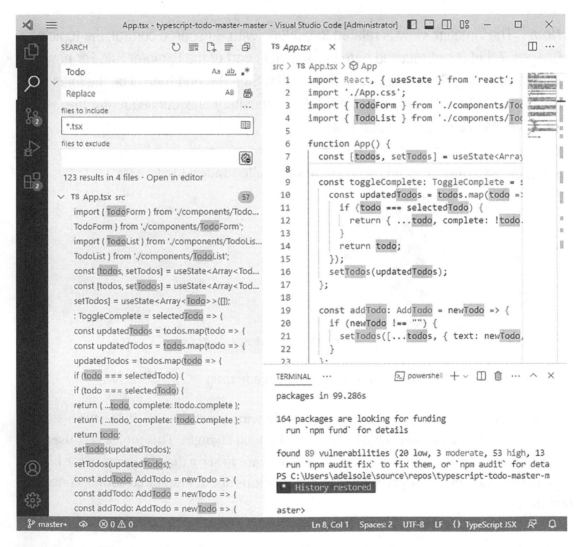

Figure 2-9. *The Search tool*

Search results are presented in a hierarchical view that groups all the files that contain the specified search key, showing an excerpt of the line of code that contains it. Occurrences are also highlighted in both the list of files and in the code editor. You can finally clean up search results by clicking the Clear Search Results button located in the toolbar close to the SEARCH header. If you instead want to replace some text with new text, you can do this by entering the new text into the Replace text box and then clicking the Replace All button.

Searching in the Active File

If you just need to search for contents in the active editor, you can choose Edit ➤ Find. An interactive popup allows you to type the content you want to search, and all occurrences will be highlighted.

With large files and many occurrences of the search result, you can quickly navigate to a specific match by enabling the Command Palette and then typing **Go to Match**. At this point, you can enter the number of a match based on the search result count.

You can also choose Edit ➤ Replace if you need to make replacements in the active editor.

The Git Bar

The Side Bar provides access to Git integration for version control. Git integration is a core topic and is thoroughly discussed in Chapter 7, but a quick look is provided here for the sake of completeness about the Side Bar and because the Timeline view was discussed previously.

The Git Bar can be enabled by clicking the third button from the top of the Side Bar (with a kind of fork icon) and provides access to all of the common source control operations, such as initializing a repository, committing code files, and synchronizing branches. The Git icon also shows the number of files that have been modified locally. Figure 2-10 shows an example. Modified files are listed under the Changes group. Three buttons are available for each listed file: Open File, Discard Changes, and Stage Changes. In Git, as you learn in Chapter 7, the concept of staging changes means keeping changes separate from the main code branch so that a developer can evaluate whether to commit the changes or discard them. Clicking a filename enables a split view that shows the differences between the modified code and the original code; this topic is also more thoroughly discussed in Chapter 7.

Figure 2-10. *The Git Bar*

The Git Bar also provides a popup menu that contains the list of supported Git commands in Visual Studio Code organized into submenus, such as Commit, Push, Pull, and several more you discover later in the book. Click the **...** button in the top-right corner of the Git Bar to open the menu.

The Run and Debug Bar

Visual Studio Code is not only a simple code editor, but also a fully featured development tool that ships with an integrated debugger for JavaScript and .NET. It can be extended with third-party debuggers for other platforms and languages. as well Chapter 9 describes in more detail this important part of Visual Studio Code, but for now note that you can access the debugging tools by clicking the fourth icon from the top of the Side Bar. This opens the Run and Debug Bar, shown in Figure 2-11.

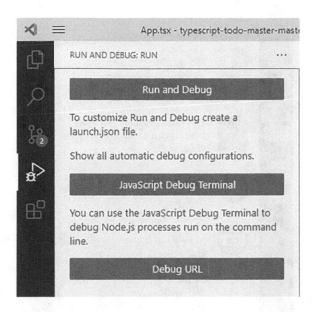

Figure 2-11. *The Run and Debug Bar*

The view varies depending on the platform and programming language. The Run and Debug button, which allows you to start and debug apps, is common to all. In the case of TypeScript or JavaScript files, you will also see the JavaScript Debug Terminal button, which enables a developer console inside the integrated Terminal, and the Debug URL button, which allows you to attach an instance of the debugger to a remote application.

In Chapter 9, you see how to configure the debugging tools and how powerful they are in Visual Studio Code. You also see how easy it is to install additional debuggers.

The Extensions Bar

The Extensions Bar can be enabled by clicking the fifth button from the top in the Activity Bar and allows you to search and install extensions for Visual Studio Code, which include additional languages, debuggers, code snippets, and much more. Extensibility is discussed in Chapter 6, but Figure 2-12 provides an example of how the Extensions Bar appears.

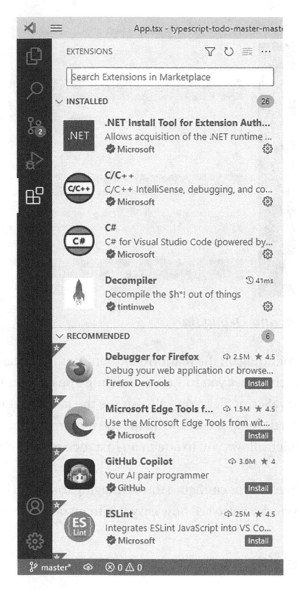

Figure 2-12. *The Extensions Bar*

You not only can search online for extensions, but can also see the list of installed extensions as well as disabled and recommended extensions.

The Accounts Button

One of the biggest benefits of Visual Studio Code is that you can customize it in many ways by arranging the development environment in whichever configuration is most convenient for you. This includes extensions, keyboard shortcuts, general settings, and much more.

If you run VS Code on multiple machines, it would be very useful if you could re-create your environment automatically on all the machines, without the need to set your preferences manually on each machine. Fortunately, this is possible using the Accounts button on the Side Bar.

With this tool, you can sign in with a Microsoft or GitHub account and your settings will be synchronized across all the VS Code installations to which you have signed in with the same account. Following is a list of settings that can be synchronized:

- General settings

- Keyboard shortcuts

- Extensions

- User-defined code snippets

- State of the user interface

You enable settings synchronization by clicking the Accounts button and then choosing Turn on Settings Sync. At this point, VS Code shows a list of settings that you can sync across machines, selecting all of them by default, as shown in Figure 2-13.

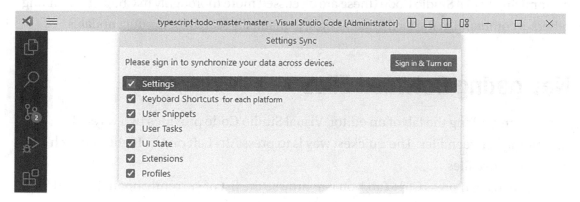

Figure 2-13. *Selecting settings to synchronize*

Select the settings you want to sync, then click Sign In & Turn On. At this point you will be asked to specify which kind of account you want to use, such as Microsoft or GitHub. Obviously, you need to use the same account on all the other Code installations. A browser window opens in which you enter your credentials, and you will quickly get a confirmation message when the sign-in is completed.

> **Note**   On Windows, the Firewall might prompt you with a warning saying that VS Code is trying to open a resource on the web. If this happens, you can safely allow this action.

At this point, Visual Studio Code starts synchronizing all the selected settings, which might take a while. Behind the scenes, settings synchronization is based on two files, `settings.json` and `extensions.json`, which VS Code needs to merge from different installations. If it encounters problems in merging these files automatically, VS Code gives you an option to manually merge settings with the same merging tool used with Git. This is a very useful feature and it will save you a lot of time in getting the same comfortable environment across machines.

The Settings Button

The Settings button is represented with the gear icon, at the bottom of the Activity Bar. If you click it, you will see a popup menu with a list of commands that represent shortcuts for customizing Visual Studio Code (these are discussed more thoroughly in Chapter 5). Among others, a command in the menu enables you to manually search for product updates.

Navigating Between Files

Other than clicking the tab of an editor, Visual Studio Code provides two ways of navigating between files. The quickest way is to press Alt+Left or Alt+Right to switch between active files.

If you instead press Ctrl+Tab, you can browse the list of currently open files and select one for editing, as shown in Figure 2-14.

Figure 2-14. *Navigating between active files*

The Command Palette

Together with the code editor and the Activity Bar and Side Bar, the Command Palette is another very important tool in Visual Studio Code, and it enables you to access Visual Studio Code built-in commands and commands added by extensions via the keyboard. You can open the Command Palette, shown in Figure 2-15, by choosing View ➤ Command Palette or via the Ctrl+Shift+P keyboard shortcut (⌘+P on macOS).

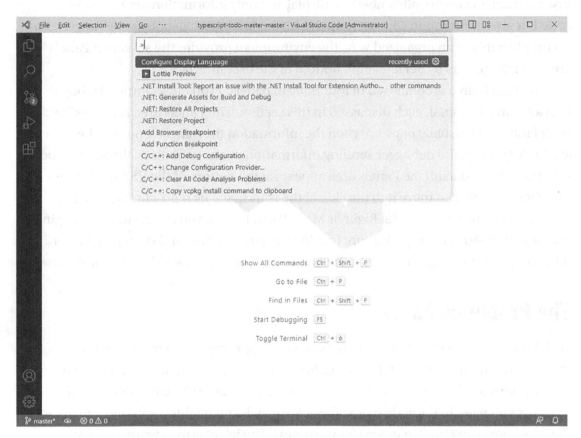

Figure 2-15. *The Command Palette*

The Command Palette is not just about menu commands and user interface instrumentation; it also provides access to other actions that are not accessible elsewhere. For instance, the Command Palette enables you to install extensions as well as restore NuGet packages over the current project or folder. You can simply move up and down to see the full list of available commands, and you can type in some characters to filter the list. You will notice how many of them map actions available within menus and that, for many of them, there is a keyboard shortcut available. Other commands related to extensions, debugging, and Git are discussed in the following chapters, so it is important that you get started with the Command Palette at this point.

The Panels Area

Visual Studio Code very often needs to display not only information about source code but also information coming from the Git engine, external tools, or debuggers. To accomplish this in an organized way, the environment provides the so-called Panels area, which appears by default at the bottom of the user interface.

The Panels area is composed of four built-in panels: Problems, Output, Debug Console, and Terminal, each discussed in this section. The Panels area is not visible by default, and it usually pops up when the information the panels represent becomes available (such as the debugger sending information about symbols in the source code). Additionally, by default the Panels area appears at the bottom of the VS Code's user interface, but you can move it to the side of the workspace by right-clicking a panel and then selecting Move Panel Right or Move Panel Left, or you can restore the original position with Move Panel to Bottom. In addition, you can drag and drop panels in a different position using the mouse. The next sections discuss each panel in more detail.

The Problems Panel

With languages that have built-in enhanced editing support, such as TypeScript (https://www.typescriptlang.org), or for which an extension has been added to provide advanced editing features, such as C#, Visual Studio Code can detect code issues as you type. In the code editor, these are usually highlighted with red squiggles (for blocking errors) and in green (for warnings). The list of errors, warnings, and informational messages is also displayed in the Problems panel. This can be enabled by clicking the number of errors at the bottom-left corner of the Status Bar (see Figure 2-16).

The Problems panel makes it easy to distinguish between errors and warnings due to different icons (a white x over red background for errors and a black exclamation mark over yellow background for warnings). Figure 2-16 shows an example based on some C# code that contains an unused variable (warning) and a syntax error.

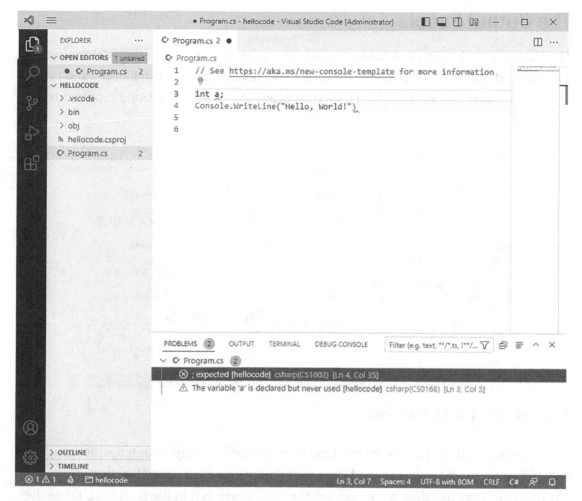

Figure 2-16. The Problems panel

If you have multiple files open, the Problems panel groups problems by filename. Also, for each problem, you can see the folder name and the position within the source code file. Just double-click a problem, and VS Code will move the cursor to the selected item in the code editor.

Note   The code editor also provides a way to quickly fix code issues while typing, but this is not related to the Problems panel and is instead discussed in the next chapter.

The Output Panel

The Output panel is the place where Visual Studio Code displays messages from internal and external tools, such as runtime tools, Git commands, extensions, and tasks. Figure 2-17 shows an example based on the output of Visual Studio Code's main thread.

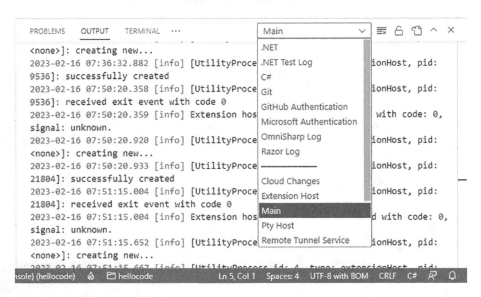

Figure 2-17. *The Output panel*

Because multiple tools might run concurrently during an operation against source code files (e.g., package restore and then compilation) or during the Visual Studio Code lifetime (such as extensions), you can use the drop-down box in the panel to change the view and see the output of each tool. This tool is particularly useful if the execution of external tools fails, and you want to get more information about what happened.

The Debug Console Panel

As the name implies, the Debug Console panel is a specialized panel used by debuggers to display information about code execution. Figure 2-18 shows an example based on the execution of a simple C# application.

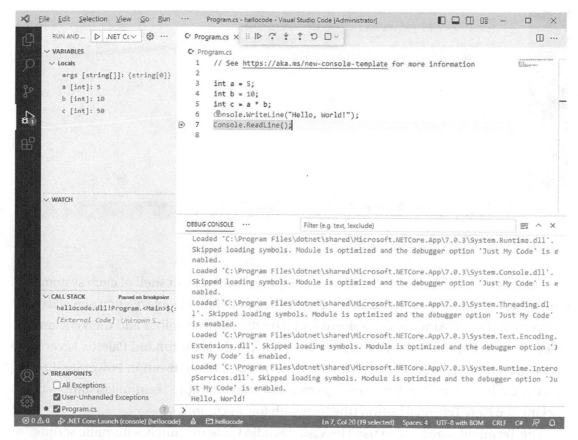

Figure 2-18. *The Debug Console panel*

The Debug Console panel not only shows information about code execution, debug symbols, and any other information a debugger needs to display, but it also acts as an interactive console where you can evaluate expressions. Figure 2-18 shows that a mathematical expression has been manually evaluated using variables defined in the code. Debugging is a very important topic in Visual Studio Code and is thoroughly discussed in Chapter 9, where you find additional information about the Debug Console.

Working with the Terminal

Visual Studio Code allows you to execute commands against the operating system directly from within the development environment. In fact, you can choose the Terminal ➤ New Terminal command to open a new Terminal instance in a panel at the bottom of the work area. Figure 2-19 shows an example based on Windows.

Figure 2-19. *The Terminal panel*

On macOS and Linux, the Terminal tool is based on the bash shell of each system. On Windows, the Terminal is based on PowerShell by default. However, you can select a different tool by clicking the drop-down menu on the panel's toolbar and then clicking Select Default Profile. At this point, you can select, from the Command Palette, several options, including (but not limited to) the Windows command prompt, PowerShell, and the Git bash commandline tool. You can also open multiple Terminal instances by clicking the New Terminal button (the icon with the + symbol).

The Terminal panel is also used by Visual Studio Code to launch automatic scripts and commands against the operating system. For example, when you build a C# application, Visual Studio Code starts the .NET compiler, whose output is displayed in the Terminal panel, as shown in Figure 2-20.

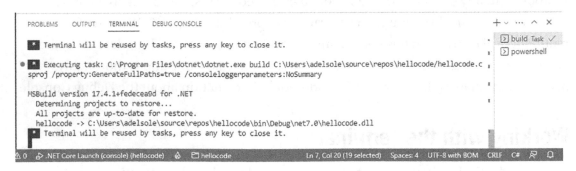

Figure 2-20. *The Terminal panel used for automatic scripting*

Summary

In this chapter, you got an overview of the workspace in Visual Studio Code and of the tools you will interact with frequently. You saw how to take advantage of quick shortcuts in the Welcome page and how you can arrange editor windows.

You saw how the Status Bar provides information about the active file and how the Activity Bar is a collapsed container of shortcuts for the tools contained in the Side Bar: the Explorer Bar, the Search tool, the Git Bar, the Debug Bar, the Extensions Bar, the Accounts button, and the Settings button. You saw how to quickly navigate between files and how the Command Palette provides a way to access commands via the keyboard, both Visual Studio Code commands and extensions' commands. You also walked through another important area in the environment, the Panels area, where you can get information about code issues, get messages from internal and external tools and debuggers, and execute commands and scripts via the Terminal.

Now that you have seen how the environment is organized, it is time to have some fun walking through all the powerful productivity features in the code editor. This is the topic of the next chapter.

CHAPTER 3

Language Support and Code Editing Features

Visual Studio Code is not just another evolved text editor with syntax colorization and automatic indentation. Instead, it is a very powerful codefocused development environment expressly designed to make it easier to write web, mobile, and cloud applications using languages that are available to different development platforms.

With the ambition to provide a powerful, rich development environment, Visual Studio Code integrates a number of editing features that are focused on improving the productivity and quality of your code. This chapter discusses what languages are supported in Visual Studio Code and all the available code editing features, starting from the most basic that are available to all the supported languages to the most advanced productivity tools that are available to specific languages such as C#, JavaScript, and TypeScript.

Note   Keyboard shortcuts used in this chapter are based on the default settings in Visual Studio Code.

Language Support

Out of the box, Visual Studio Code has built-in support for many languages. Table 3-1 groups supported languages by their editing features.

© Alessandro Del Sole 2023
A. Del Sole, *Visual Studio Code Distilled*, https://doi.org/10.1007/978-1-4842-9484-0_3

Table 3-1. *Language Support by Feature*

Languages	Editing Features
Batch, C, C#, C++, Clojure, CoffeeScript, Diff, Dockerfile, F#, Go, HLSL, Jade, Java, Julia, HandleBars, Ini, Lua, Makefile, Objective-C, Objective-C++, Perl, PowerShell, Properties, Pug, Python, R, Razor, Ruby, Rust, SCSS, ShaderLab, Shell Script, SQL, Visual Basic, XML	Common features (syntax coloring, bracket matching, basic word completion)
Groovy, Markdown, PHP, Swift	Common features and code snippets
CSS, HTML, JSON, JSON with Comments, Less, Sass	Common features, code snippets, IntelliSense, Outline
JavaScript, JavaScript React, TypeScript, TypeScript React	Common features, code snippets, IntelliSense, Outline, parameter hints, refactoring, Find All References, Go to Definition, Peek Definition

Visual Studio Code can be extended with additional languages produced by the developer community and downloadable from the Visual Studio Marketplace. This is discussed in more detail in Chapter 6, but, in the meantime, you can look at the available languages out of the box. In addition, support for built-in languages can also be enhanced via extensions in order to leverage all the advanced editing features. This is the case of Python, Julia, C#, and Go. For the purposes of this book, an introduction to C# and C++ is provided for your convenience.

Working with C# and C++

The C# programming language deserves a more detailed introduction, because of its popularity and because it is now a cross-platform language that you can use not only on Windows but also on macOS and Linux. As you can see from Table 3-1, the editing experience that Visual Studio Code offers out of the box for C# is limited to common features.

However, full and rich support for the coding experience with C# is offered via the Microsoft C# free extension (`https://marketplace.visualstudio.com/items?itemName=ms-dotnettools.csharp`). This provides an optimized experience for .NET development and includes all the support and tools you need to build apps with C#, including the necessary support for the .NET debugger. With this extension, you basically get the same experience available to TypeScript, including advanced editing capabilities based on the .NET Compiler Platform (also known as Roslyn) that makes it easier to fix code issues as you type. If you plan to work with C#, I definitely recommend that you install this extension, especially because this chapter discusses some editing features that are available only through the extension.

Extensibility is explained in more detail in Chapter 6, but you can easily install the C# extension without further information by opening any C# code file (`.cs`) and following the instructions shown by Visual Studio Code when it detects that a proper extension is available for that file type.

Similarly, you might want to install the Microsoft C/C++ extension that adds enhanced editing features to the C and C++ languages, plus debugging support for Windows (PDB, MinGW, Cygwin), macOS, and Linux. The extension is available at `https://marketplace.visualstudio.com/items?itemName=ms-vscode.cpptools`, and you can follow the same easy installation steps just described for the C# extension by opening a .c, .h, or .cpp file.

Working with Python

Python is another very popular programming language that has been widely used for data science scenarios especially in the last years.

Out of the box, Visual Studio Code provides basic editing features for Python. However, you can install the Python extension by Microsoft to add editing features such as IntelliSense and code refactoring, plus the debugger.

Due to its importance, Chapter 10 of this book is dedicated to programming with Python in VS Code, but it can be a good idea to start preparing your environment now if you want to discover all the editing features with this language.

Working with Julia

Julia is another programming language that is commonly used for data science scenarios, but it is still a general-purpose programming language.

Out of the box, Visual Studio Code provides basic editing features for Julia, such as syntax colorization, but you can install the Julia extension (`https://marketplace.visualstudio.com/items?itemName=julialang.language-julia`) built by the developers of Julia itself. This will add support for debugging and enhanced editing features, such as IntelliSense, code navigation, a plot panel, and most of the editing features available to languages such as TypeScript.

Obviously, you first need to download and install the Julia binaries on your machine (`https://julialang.org/downloads`).

Working with Go

Go is an open-source, object-oriented, and general-purpose programming language supported by Google. During the past few years, Go has been enhanced to support the most advanced and complex development scenarios, so it has become very popular and used by many important software vendors.

By default, Visual Studio Code offers basic editing support for Go files. However, you can install the official Go extension (`https://marketplace.visualstudio.com/items?itemName=golang.go`), which adds support for IntelliSense, integrated debugging and testing, and enhanced code editing features. If you are a developer working with Go, this extension is needed.

Basic Code Editing Features

Visual Studio Code provides many of the features you would expect from a powerful code editor. This section describes what editing features make your coding experience amazing with this tool. It is worth mentioning that Visual Studio Code provides keyboard shortcuts for almost all the editing features, giving you an option to edit code more quickly. For this reason, keyboard shortcuts are also mentioned for many of the described features.

Note   Features described in this section apply to all the supported languages described in Table 3-1, except where expressly specified.

Working with Text

As you would expect, the code editor in VS Code offers commands for text manipulation and text selection. The Edit menu provides the Undo, Redo, Copy, Cut, Paste, Find, Replace, Find in Files, and Replace in Files commands. These commands are available in every text editor and do not require any further explanation.

The Edit menu also includes the Toggle Line Comment and Toggle Block Comment commands, which add a single-line comment or a block comment, respectively, depending on the language. For instance, in C# the first command would comment a line like this:

```
// int a = 0;
```

By contrast, the block comment tool would add a multiline comment as follows:

```
/* int a = 0;
int b = 0; */
```

The Edit menu also provides a command to work with code snippets, Emmet: Expand Abbreviation. This command is the menu representation of keyboard shortcuts offered by the code editor to add a code snippet. Code snippets are discussed in more detail in the "Reusable Code Snippets" section in this chapter.

The Selection menu not only provides commands for text selection but also provides commands that make it easier to move or duplicate lines of code above and below the current line. The Add Cursor Above, Add Cursor Below, and Add Cursors To Line Ends commands allow working with multicursors, described in the "Multicursors" section in this chapter.

If you click an identifier or a reserved word, or you type name in the editor, you can use the Add Next Occurrence, Add Previous Occurrence, and Select All Occurrences commands. They allow you to quickly select occurrences of the selected word, and occurrences will be highlighted in a different color, which differs depending on the current theme.

Syntax Colorization

For all the languages summarized in Table 3-1, the code editor in Visual Studio Code provides the proper syntax colorization. Figure 3-1 shows an example based on a TypeScript code file.

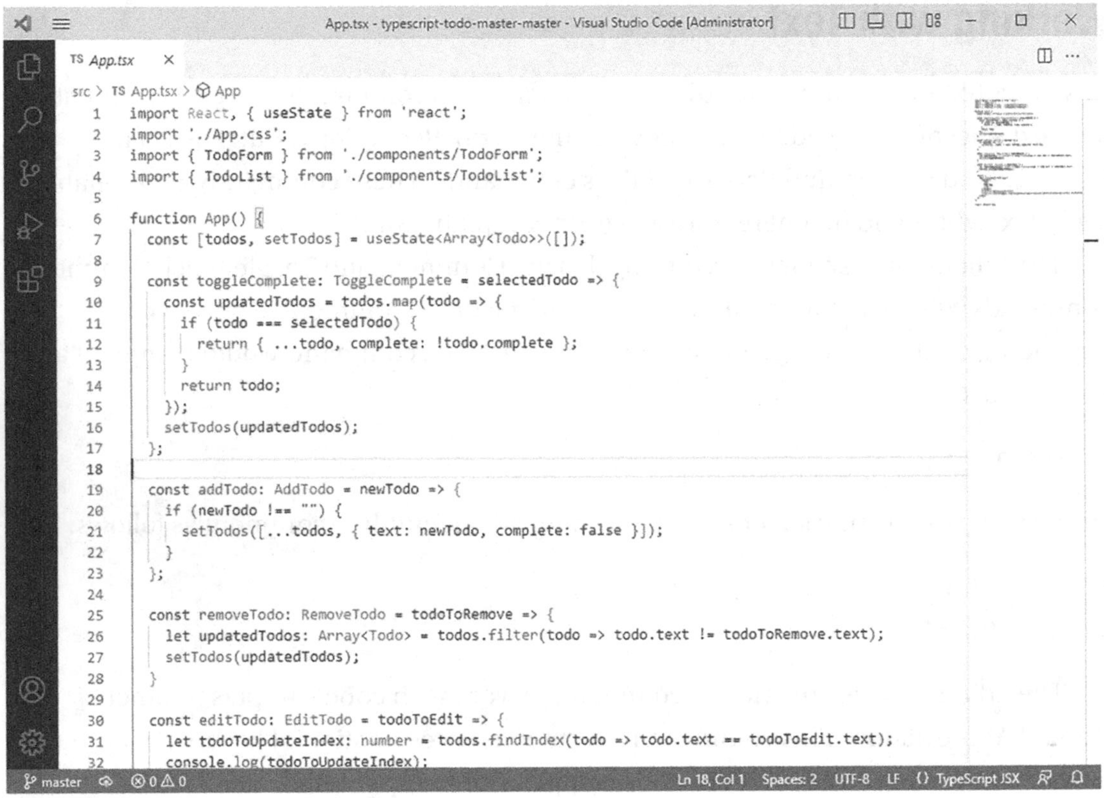

Figure 3-1. *Syntax colorization*

Syntax colorization is available for other languages via extensibility. If you need to work with a language that is not included with Visual Studio Code out of the box, you can check the Visual Studio Marketplace and see if an extension is available to support such a language. See Chapter 6 for information about extensibility. As a side note, syntax colorization is the minimum that an extension must provide to add support for a new language.

Delimiter Matching and Text Selection

The code editor can highlight matching delimiters such as curly braces, brackets, and parentheses (both square and round). This feature is extremely useful to delimit code blocks and is triggered once the cursor gets near one of the delimiters. Figure 3-2 shows an example based on bracket matching in a constructor definition.

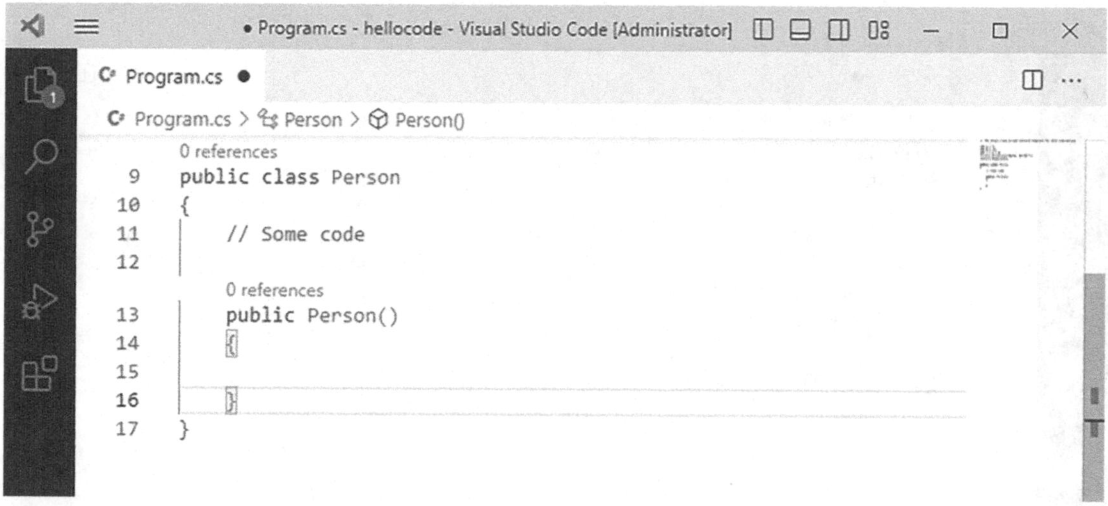

Figure 3-2. *Delimiter matching*

This feature is also very useful when you need to visually delimit nested blocks and with complex and long expressions. It is worth mentioning that you can press Ctrl+D to quickly select a word or identifier at the right of the cursor. You can also quickly select all the text within the delimiters of a code block by pressing Shift+Alt+Arrow Right, and you can quickly deselect the same code block by pressing Shift+Alt+Arrow Left.

Note   With multiple bracket pairs, VS Code now applies bracket colorization so that every pair can be distinguished even more easily. This setting can be managed via the Bracket Pair Colorization option available in the Text Editor settings.

Code Block Folding

The code editor allows you to fold delimited code blocks. Just hover your cursor over line numbers and a symbol representing a down arrow will appear near the start of a code block. Simply click to fold, and you will see the > symbol at this point, which you click to unfold the code block. Figure 3-3 provides an example.

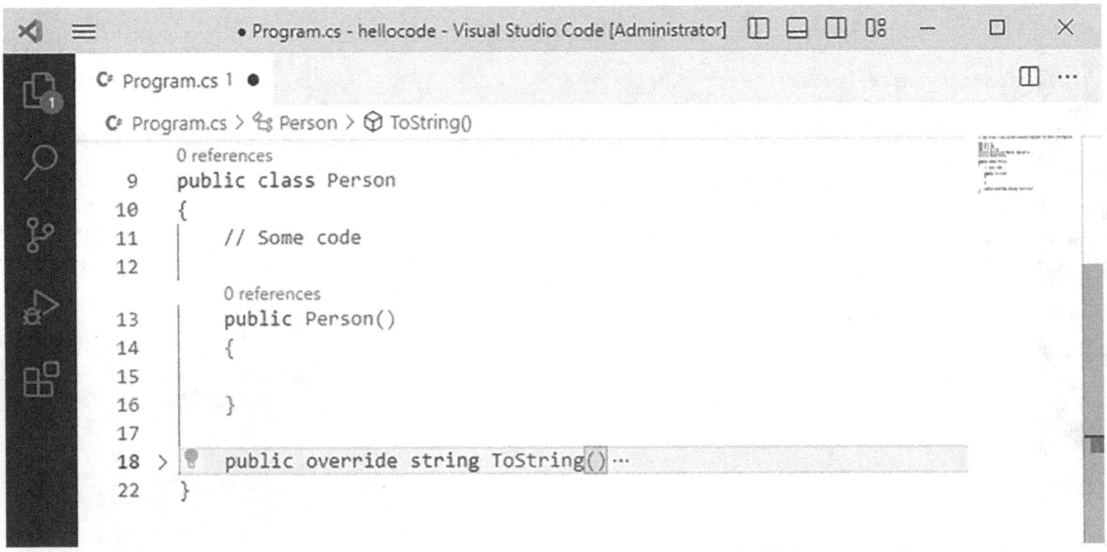

Figure 3-3. *Code block folding*

Note   If code block folding is not enabled in the code editor, open VS Code's Settings. Then in the Text Editor group, enable both the Folding and Folding Highlight options.

Multicursors

The code editor supports multicursors. Each cursor operates independently, and you can add secondary cursors by pressing Alt+Click at the desired position. The most typical situation in which you want to use multicursors is when you want to add (or replace) the same text in different positions of a code file.

Reusable Code Snippets

Visual Studio Code ships with many built-in code snippets that you can easily add by using the Emmet abbreviation syntax and pressing Tab. See Table 3-1 in the "Language Support" section to review which languages support code snippets natively. For instance, in a Swift file, you can easily add a `do..catch` block definition by using the `do` code snippet, as shown in Figure 3-4.

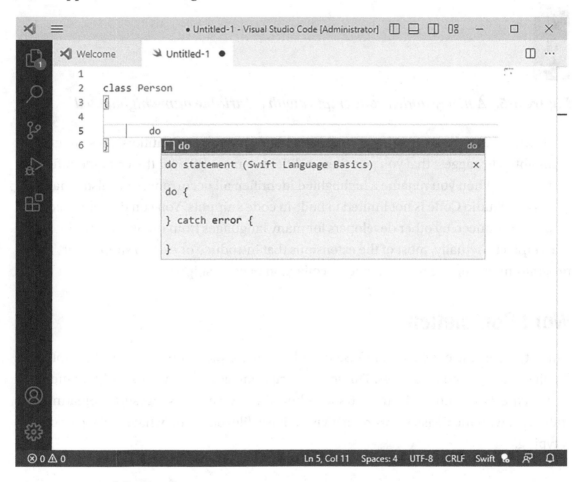

Figure 3-4. *Adding code snippets*

Code snippets are available as you type within the code editor, and you can recognize them by the icon representing a small, white sheet. Notice how a tooltip shows a preview of the code snippet. Pressing Tab over the previous snippet produces the result shown in Figure 3-5.

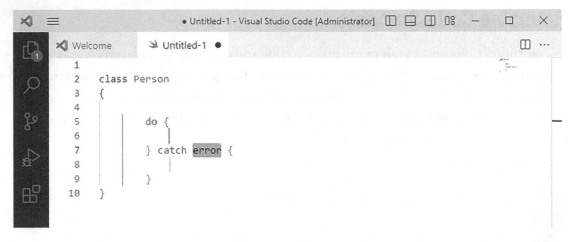

Figure 3-5. *A newly added code snippet with a variable name highlighted*

Notice that if the code snippet contains variable names or identifiers, these might be highlighted to suggest that you give them a different name (like for the error identifier in Figure 3-5). When you rename a highlighted identifier, all occurrences are also renamed.

Visual Studio Code is not limited to built-in code snippets. You can download code snippets produced by other developers for many languages from the Visual Studio Marketplace. Actually, most of the extensions that introduce or extend support for programming languages also include a collection of code snippets.

Word Completion

Out of the box, the code editor in Visual Studio Code implements basic word completion for all the supported languages. This feature helps you complete words and statements as you type. For example, Figure 3-6 shows how the code editor suggests terminating a statement with the `Class` keyword in a Visual Basic file, based on what the developer is typing.

Figure 3-6. *Completing a statement with word completion*

Simply press Enter or Tab to insert the suggested word. The word completion engine learns as you code and can provide suggestions based on variables and member names you declare. For example, Figure 3-7 demonstrates how the editor suggests adding the name of a variable called Test, which was declared previously in the code.

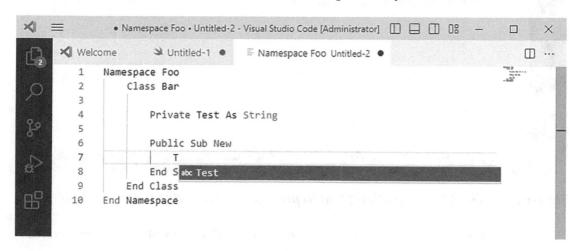

Figure 3-7. *The code editor can suggest identifiers declared in the code*

Minimap Mode

Sometimes it is difficult to find the position of the cursor inside a source code file, especially with very long files. Visual Studio Code provides the Minimap, which is a small preview of the source code file on the code editor's scrollbar. Figure 3-8 provides an example.

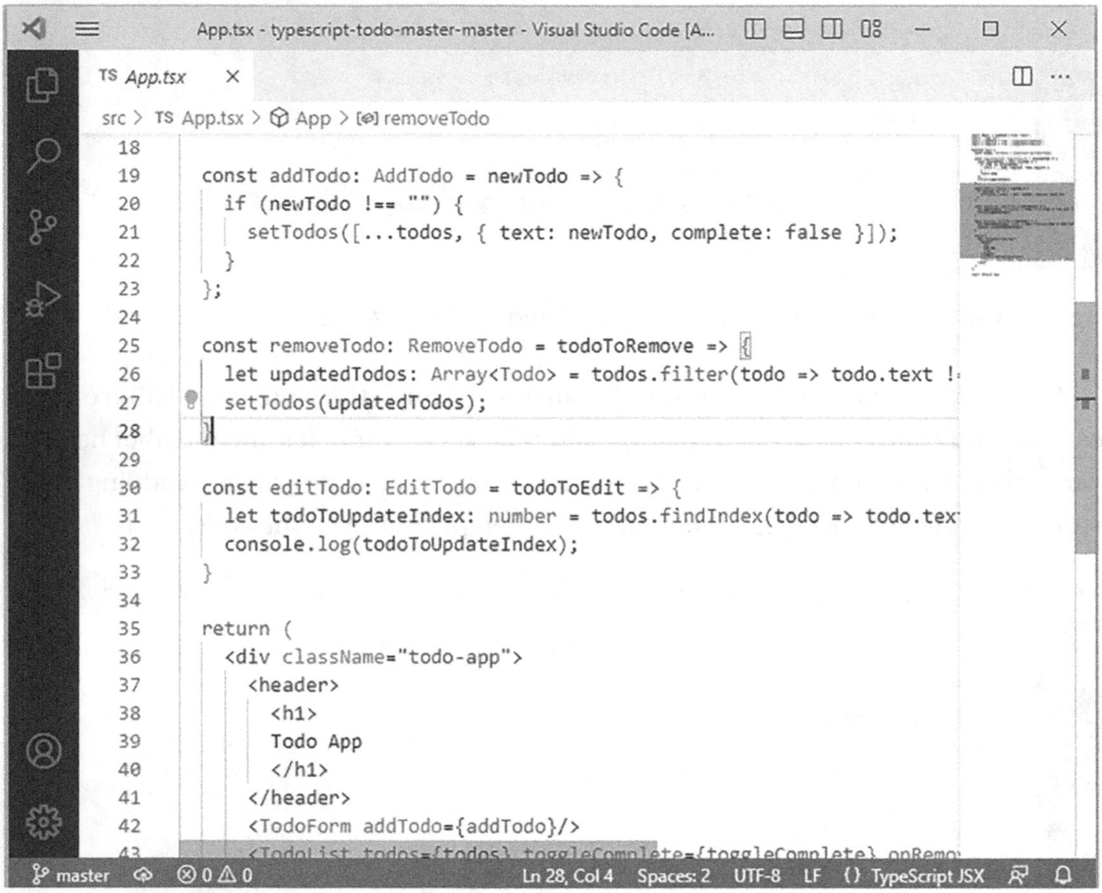

Figure 3-8. *The Minimap allows you to preview source code on the scrollbar*

If you click the Minimap, the portion of source code that is visible in the code editor is highlighted in the scrollbar, so that you can have a better perception of the current position of the cursors. The Minimap can be disabled and enabled using the View ➤ Appearance ➤ Minimap command.

Sticky Scroll

Sticky Scroll allows you to show the nested current scopes during the scroll of the active file at the top of the editor. This feature is not enabled by default.

To enable Sticky Scroll, open the settings and then locate the Sticky Scroll setting within the Text Editor group. You can select the checkbox to enable and disable the feature, and you can specify the number of sticky lines that can be displayed, with a maximum of 5.

Whitespace Rendering and Breadcrumbs

A very common feature with text editors is the option to show light dots instead of white spaces. In Visual Studio Code, this is possible for white spaces within indentations. To accomplish this, choose View ➤ Appearance ➤ Render Whitespace. Figure 3-9 shows an example of how white spaces for indentations are replaced with dots. For this figure, the Solarized Light color theme has been used for better visualization on the paper.

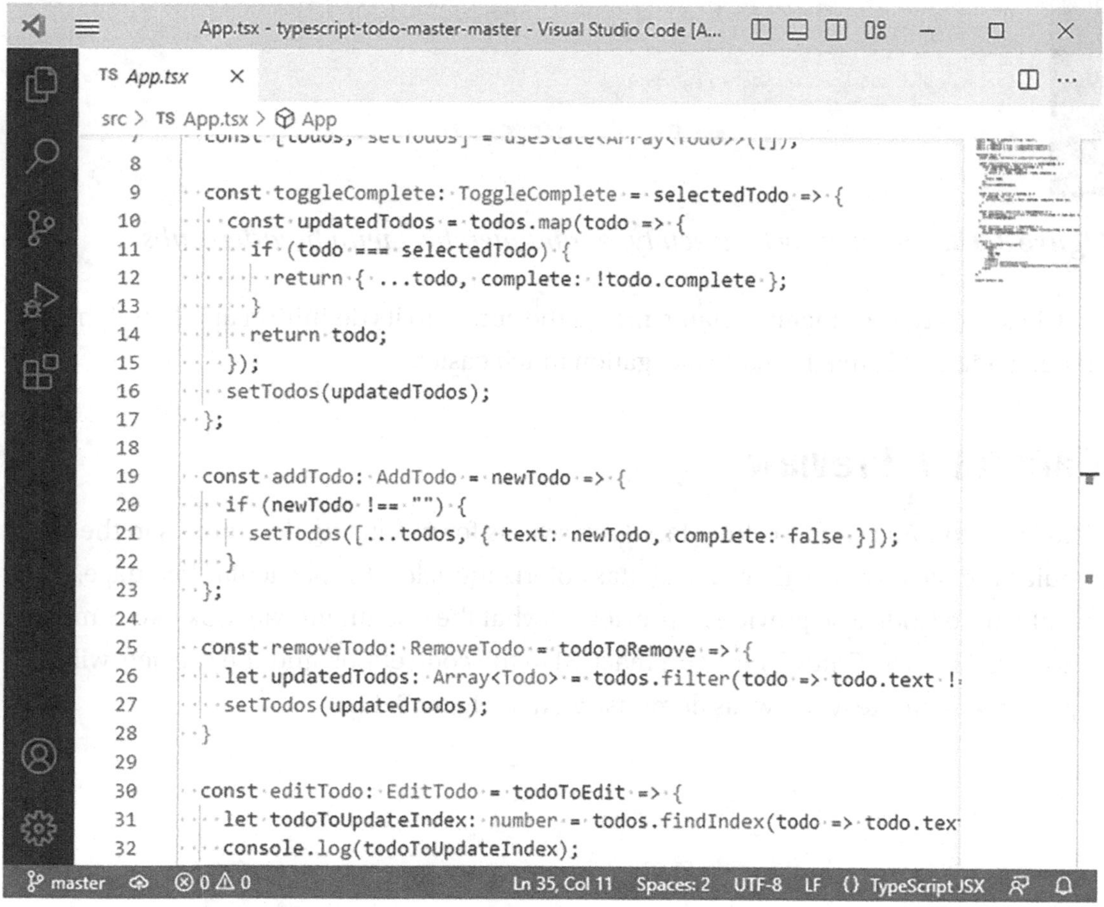

Figure 3-9. *Rendering indentation spaces with dots*

Simply use the same command to return to white spaces. Another very useful command is Breadcrumbs, available in the Appearance submenu. With supported languages, such as JavaScript, TypeScript, and C# with the extension installed, this command shows the list of types and members defined in the current code file at the top of the editor, which you can expand to see their members, as shown in Figure 3-10.

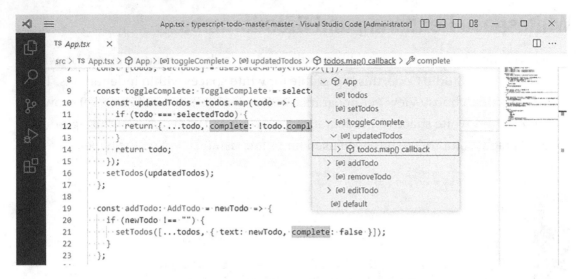

Figure 3-10. *Navigating between types and members with breadcrumbs*

Clicking a type or member name moves the cursor to its definition and highlights the related code block, making code navigation much easier.

Markdown Preview

Visual Studio Code supports the Markdown syntax for producing documents in the very popular .md file format. Other than syntax colorization, for this particular language, Visual Studio Code also provides a preview of what the document will look like. Simply press Ctrl+Shift+V (Cmd+Shift+V on macOS) in the code editor, and the preview will appear in a separate window, as demonstrated in Figure 3-11.

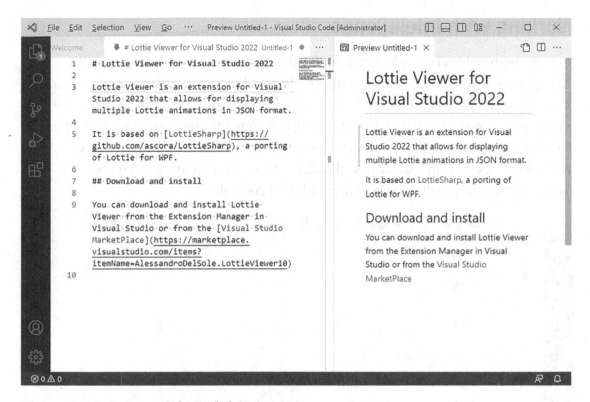

Figure 3-11. *Integrated Markdown preview*

This feature is very useful because it allows you to preview your documents without the need of an external program such as a web browser.

Evolved Code Editing

Visual Studio Code is an extremely powerful code-editing tool and it brings to a cross-platform and multilanguage environment many features that have been available in Microsoft Visual Studio for many years, providing what is called *evolved code editing*. This section explains all the advanced code editing features that are available, out of the box, to languages such as TypeScript and JavaScript and, with the appropriate extensions installed, to languages like C#, C++, and Python.

Working with IntelliSense

IntelliSense provides rich, advanced word completion via a convenient popup list that appears as you type. In the developer tools from Microsoft, such as Visual Studio, IntelliSense has always been one of the most popular features, and the reason is that it is not simply word completion. In fact, IntelliSense provides suggestions as you type, showing the documentation about a member (if available) and displaying an icon near each suggestion that describes what kind of syntax element a word represents. Figure 3-12 shows IntelliSense in action with a C# code file.

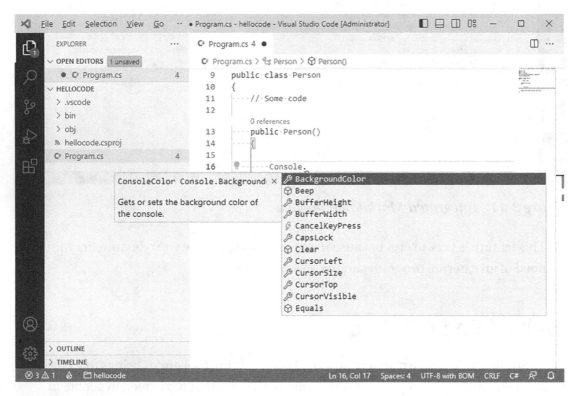

Figure 3-12. *IntelliSense showing suggestions as you type and advanced word completion*

As you can see in Figure 3-12, IntelliSense shows the list of available members as you write, for the given type (in this case, `Console`). When you scroll the list with the keyboard and stop on a word from the completion list, Visual Studio Code shows the member documentation. The little arrow to the right of the dialog can be used to turn the documentation off.

Note   The documentation for a type or member is available only if it has been supplied by the developers. For example, in C#, the documentation for types and members must be provided with XML comments. This enables IntelliSense to display it in a tooltip, as shown in Figure 3-12.

Press either Tab or Enter to complete the word insertion, or simply click. Not limited to this, IntelliSense in Visual Studio Code supports suggestion filtering: based on the CamelCase convention, you can type the uppercase letters of a member name to filter the suggestion list. For instance, if you are working against the System.Console type and you type cv, the suggestion list will show the CursorVisible property, as demonstrated in Figure 3-13.

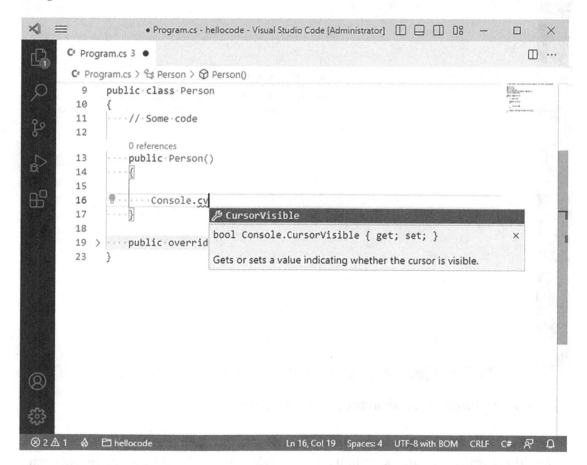

Figure 3-13. *Suggestion filtering in IntelliSense*

IntelliSense also provides the foundation for other advanced features in the code editor that depend on it, as described in the next subsections.

Parameter Hints

When you write a function invocation, IntelliSense also shows a tooltip that describes each parameter. This feature is called *parameter hints* and is available only if the documentation for function parameters has been implemented. An example is visible in Figure 3-14.

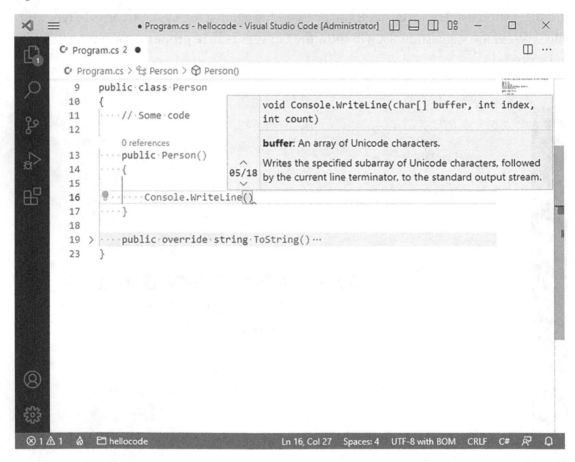

Figure 3-14. *IntelliSense showing parameter hints*

For languages such as C# and TypeScript or, more generally, languages that allow for function overloads, parameter hints show the description for the parameters of each overload. You can also scroll the list of overloads with the up and down arrow keys to select a different overload.

Inline Documentation with Tooltips

If you hover your cursor over types, variables, and type members, Visual Studio Code shows a tooltip that contains the documentation for the selected object. Figure 3-15 provides an example.

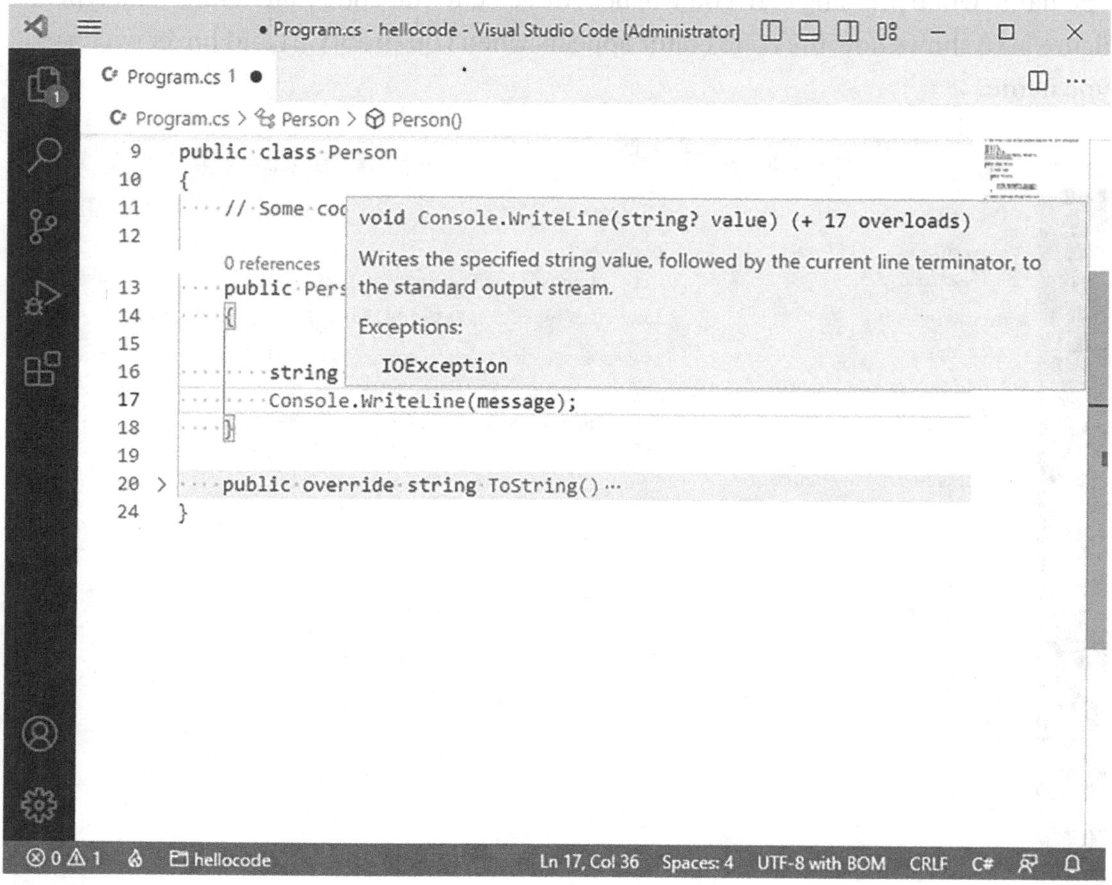

Figure 3-15. *Tooltips provide quick, inline documentation*

Like parameter hints, this feature is available only if the documentation has been implemented.

Note   If you hover your cursor over a variable name, the tooltip shows only the type for the variable.

Go to Definition and Peek Definition

Visual Studio Code provides another interesting feature, called *Go to Definition*. If you hover your cursor over a symbol and press Ctrl (or ⌘ on macOS), the symbol appears as a hyperlink; also, a tooltip shows the code that declares that symbol. If you click the type name while pressing Ctrl, you will be redirected to the code that defines that type. Figure 3-16 shows how the code editor appears when you press Ctrl and hover over a type name.

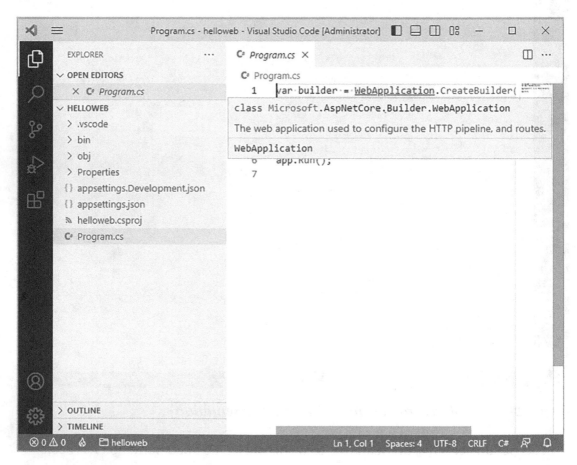

Figure 3-16. *Ctrl+ hovering over a type enables Go to Definition*

The same tool is available if you select a type name and press F12 or if you right-click a type name and then select Go to Definition from the context menu. This is an extremely useful feature that lets you quickly browse between type definitions that are in different code files.

Note   For C#, Go to Definition can also open the definition of a type exposed by the .NET libraries and any NuGet package that includes the type definition information, not just your code.

Now suppose that you have dozens of code files and want to see or edit the definition of a type you are currently using. With other editors, you would search among the code files, which not only can be annoying but also moves your focus away from the original code. Visual Studio Code brilliantly solves this problem with a feature called *Peek Definition.*

You can simply right-click a type name and then choose Peek ➤ Peek Definition (the keyboard shortcut is Alt+F12). An interactive popup window appears, showing the code that defines the type, giving you not only an option to look at the code but also of direct editing. Figure 3-17 shows the Peek Definition window in action. You can press Esc to quickly close the Peek Definition window as an alternative to clicking the Close button.

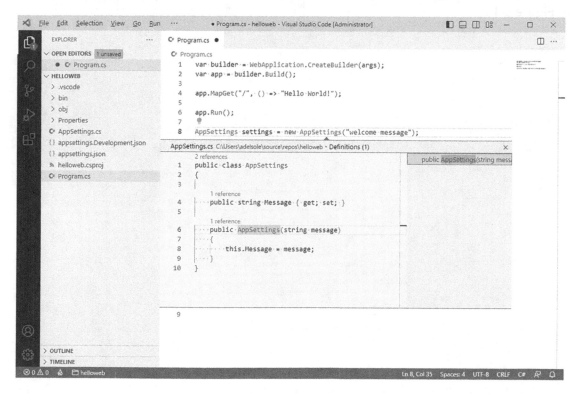

Figure 3-17. *Working on a type defined in another file with Peek Definition*

As you can see, the Peek Definition window is very similar to the Find All References feature, and it still shows the filename that defines the type at its top. Simply click the filename to open the code file in a separate editor.

Go to Implementation and Peek Implementations

Sometimes you might need to understand how many times and where an interface or an abstract class has been implemented.

Though you can accomplish this by finding a type's references (see the next section), Visual Studio Code now offers more convenient ways that work similarly to Go to Definition and Peek Definition, respectively called Go to Implementation and Peek Implementations. You can right-click an interface or abstract class definition and then choose Go to Implementation or Peek ➤ Peek Implementations. Both actions bring up an interactive, nested editor that shows the list of implementations of the selected type on the right, and the code for the first occurrence of the implementation, as you can see in Figure 3-18.

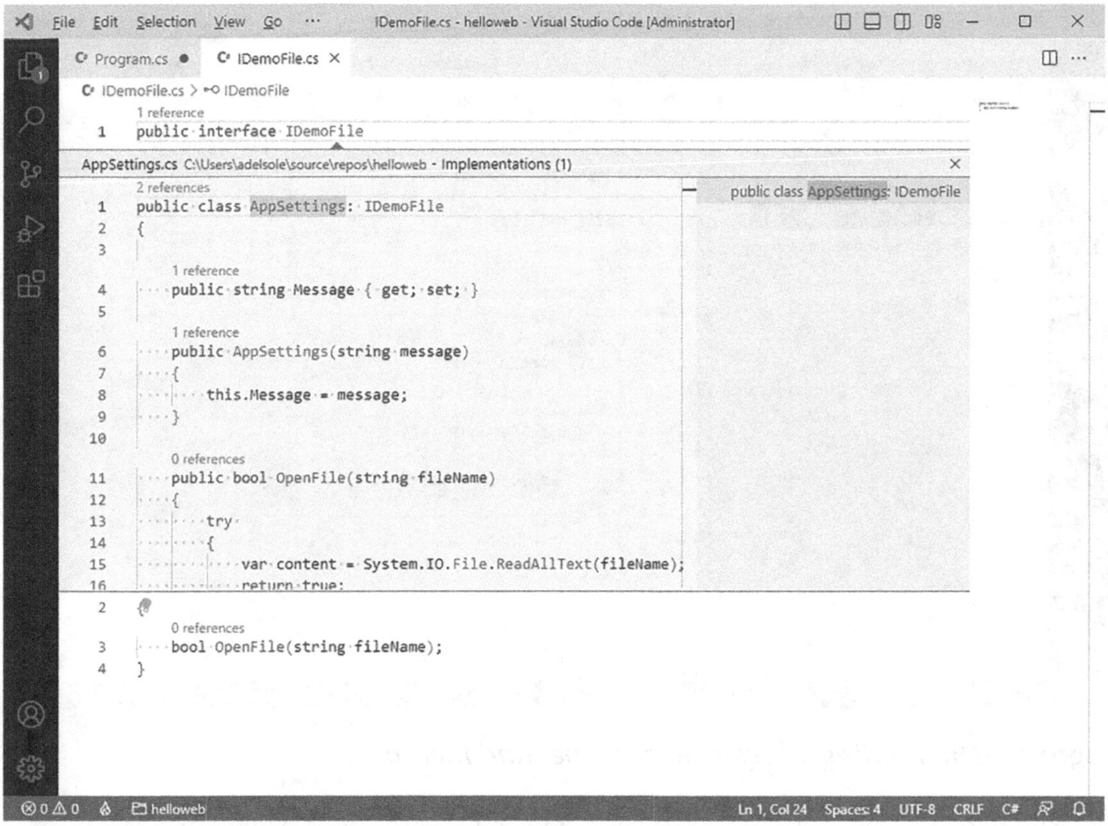

Figure 3-18. *Navigating among type implementations*

The difference between the two actions is the following: with Go to Implementation, when you click an implementation in the list, VS Code opens a new editor window pointing to the file that contains the implementation; with Peek Implementations, when you click an implementation in the list, it is displayed in an interactive popup window similarly to how Peek Definition works.

Finding References

You will often need to know where types or members have been used across your code, and Visual Studio Code provides two nice tools to retrieve references.

The first tool is called Find All References, which you might already be familiar with if you have experience with Visual Studio on Windows. There are different options to run this tool: you can right-click a type or member name and then choose Find All References or you can press Shift+Alt+F12 (Option+Shift+F12 on macOS). Figure 3-19 shows an example based on finding all references of a type called App.

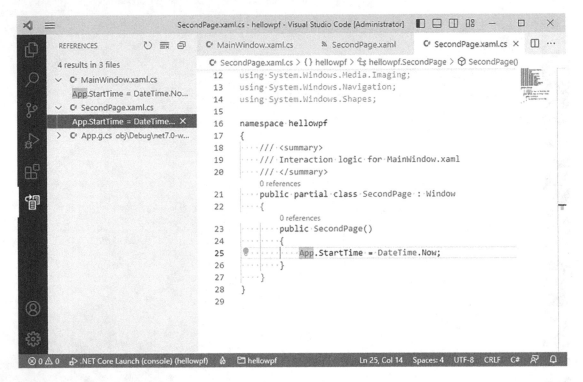

Figure 3-19. *Finding all references of types and members*

The References panel opens on the left side of the screen and shows a list of references grouped by code file, together with the total number of references and of code files involved. It also adds a new entry to the Side Bar that is disabled once you close the References panel. The occurrences are highlighted; when you click one of them, an editor opens on the file that contains the selected occurrence, which is highlighted inside the code.

There is also another tool called Go to References (Shift+F12), which works inside the active editor window. You enable Go to References either by right-clicking the object name and then selecting Go to References or by clicking the number of references at the top of the member definition (see Figure 3-19). You can use the first option anywhere in the code, whereas you can use the second option only when the type or member definition is focused in the code editor.

The user interface for Go to References is the same as for Find All References. Visual Studio Code also provides another useful tool to find type and member references, called Peek References. You can enable this tool by right-clicking an object name and then choosing Peek ➤ Peek References. As the name implies, Peek References displays all the references in the active editor, inside an interactive panel similar to what you saw previously with Peek Definition. Figure 3-20 shows an example, again based on finding all references of a type called App.

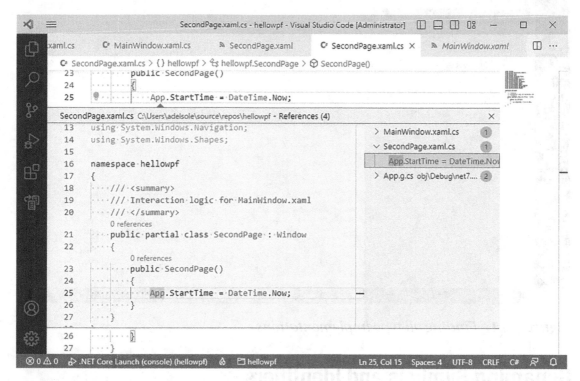

Figure 3-20. *Finding references with Peek References*

If you click an occurrence in the list on the right, the code editor opens a popup window containing the code where that occurrence has been found. It is very important to note that this popup window is interactive, which means that you can edit the code directly without the need to open the containing code file separately. This enables you to keep your focus on the code, saving time. Also, notice that the interactive popup window shows, at the top, the filename that contains the selected reference.

Similar to Find All References is Find All Implementations, which makes it easy to find implementations of an interface or abstract class. Figure 3-21 shows an example where an interface called IPerson is implemented by two classes, Person and Employee. Find All Implementations shows in a tree view all the implementations of the interface and highlights the class definition in the code editor.

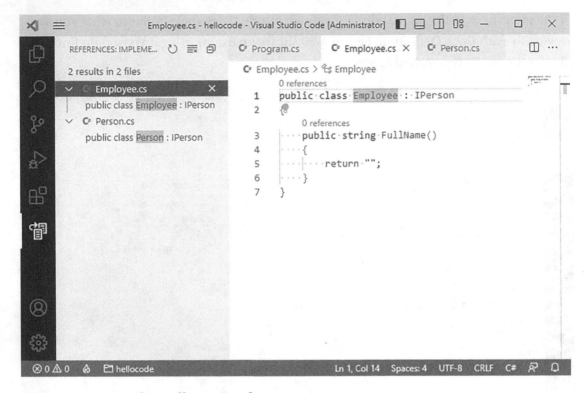

Figure 3-21. *Finding all type implementations*

Renaming Symbols and Identifiers

Renaming a symbol is a frequent task, so Visual Studio Code offers a convenient way to accomplish this. If you press F2 over the symbol you want to rename or right-click and then select the Rename Symbol command, a small interactive popup box appears. There you can write the new name without any dialogs, keeping your focus on the code. Figure 3-22 shows an example based on a symbol called app.

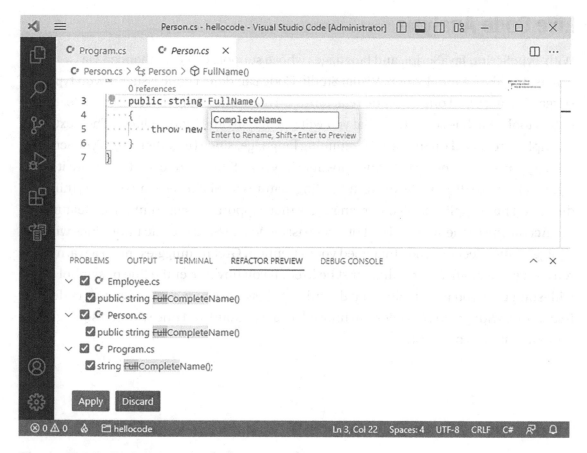

Figure 3-22. *Renaming symbols*

If you press Shift+Enter before renaming, Visual Studio Code shows a preview of how symbols will be renamed (see the REFACTOR PREVIEW tab at the bottom of Figure 3-22). Toolbar buttons in the tab enable you to accept changes (Apply Refactoring button) and reject changes (Discard Refactoring button).

By pressing Enter, all references of that symbol will be renamed accordingly. Additionally, you can rename all the occurrences of an identifier. You simply right-click the identifier, then choose Change All Occurrences (or press Ctrl+F2 on Windows/Linux and ⌘+F2 on macOS). All the occurrences will be highlighted and updated with the new name as you type.

Live Code Analysis

With TypeScript, JavaScript, and languages whose support can be enhanced via extensions like C# and Python, Visual Studio Code can detect code issues as you type, suggesting fixes and offering code refactorings. This is one of the most powerful features in this tool, which is something that you will not find in other code editors. The next examples are based on the C# programming language, since (together with TypeScript) this supports the richest experience possible in Visual Studio Code, and therefore it is a good choice to discuss the powerful coding features available. Of course, everything discussed here applies to all other languages that support the same enhanced features.

According to the severity level of a code issue, Visual Studio Code underlines with squiggles the pieces of code that need your attention. Green squiggles mean a warning; red squiggles mean an error that must be fixed. If you hover over the line or symbol with squiggles, you get a tooltip that describes the issue. Figure 3-23 shows two code issues, one with green squiggles (an unused local variable) and one with red squiggles (a symbol that does not exist).

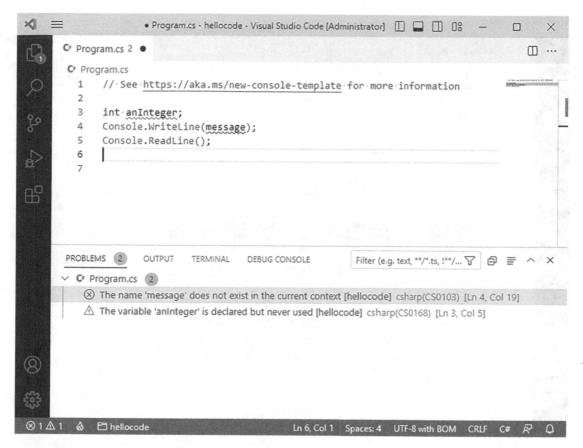

Figure 3-23. *Code issue detection as you type*

Code issues are detected as you type and they are also listed in the Problems panel. Look again at Figure 3-23 and note the icon with the shape of a light bulb. This icon is a shortcut for a tool called Light Bulb. When you click the icon, Visual Studio Code shows possible code fixes for the current context. For example, Figure 3-24 shows the suggestions that the Light Bulb provides to fix the missing symbol underlined with red squiggles.

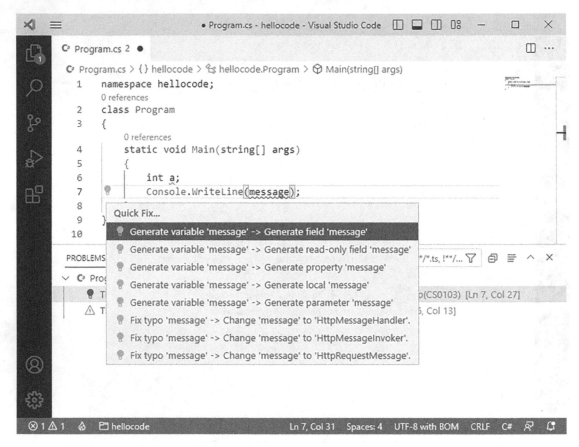

Figure 3-24. *Potential fixes suggested by the Light Bulb*

In this particular case, the editor suggests five options for generating members: create a field, create a read-only field, create a property, create a local variable, or create a parameter. It also offers three options to change the identifier into a different object name, but in this case the goal is generating a new member. Based on the code in Figure 3-24, a field would be created as follows:

```
private static bool message;
```

A property would be generated like this:

```
public static bool Message { get; private set; }
```

Perhaps bool is not the type you would expect here, but Visual Studio Code does not have enough information to infer a different type, so it will generate one based on the type parameter accepted by the first overload of the method, which is bool for

WriteLine. However, when the code contains some information that Visual Studio Code could use to understand the proper type, it generates properties, fields, local variables, and parameters of the expected type. With the Light Bulb, it is also easier to generate types on the fly. Figure 3-25 shows an example based on an object called person, for which a type has not yet been defined. As you can see, for this context the code editor shows a larger list of possible fixes, including generating a new class, either in the current file or in a separate file, including the option of a nested class.

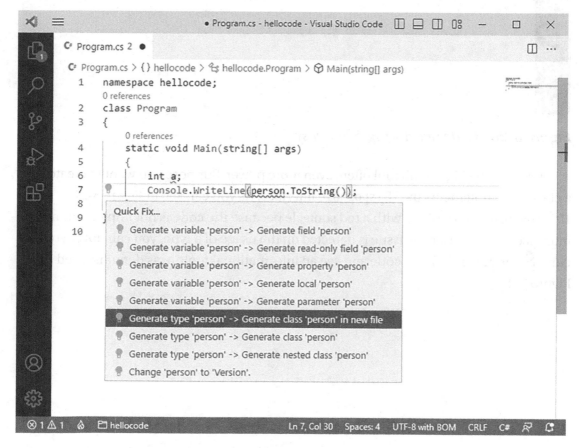

Figure 3-25. *Generating types on the fly*

The Light Bulb can also help you refactor your code and keep it cleaner. For example, you can click any of the using directives (or equivalent in other languages) and, when the Light Bulb appears, you can see how it offers to remove unused code, as shown in Figure 3-26.

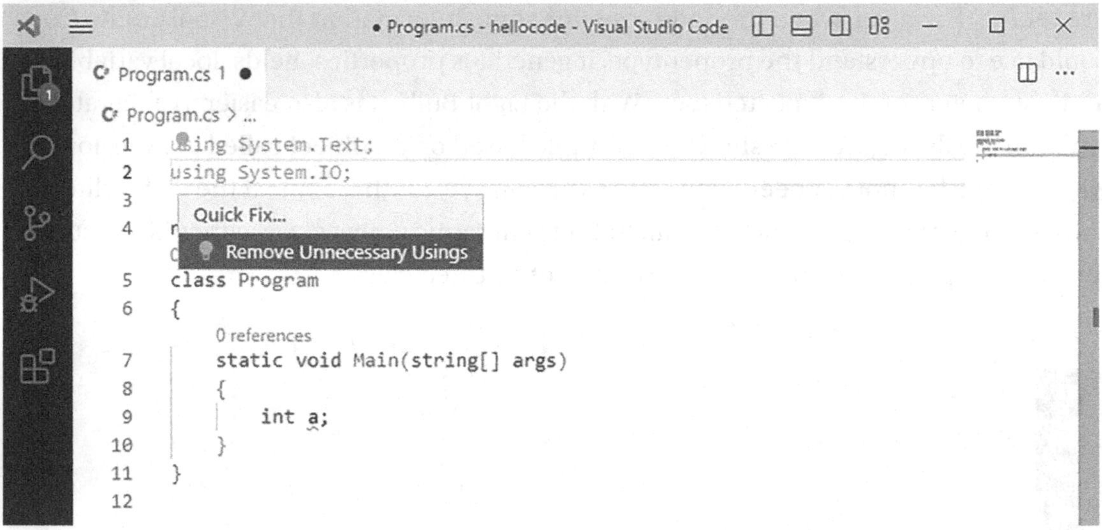

Figure 3-26. *Code refactoring made easy*

Actually, the Light Bulb tool offers even more power. Suppose you want to create a class that implements the IDisposable interface. As you can see in Figure 3-27, IDisposable is underlined with a red squiggle because the code is not implementing the interface yet. When a code issue is detected on the usage of a type, you can hover your cursor over the underlined code and see an informational tooltip, as demonstrated in Figure 3-27.

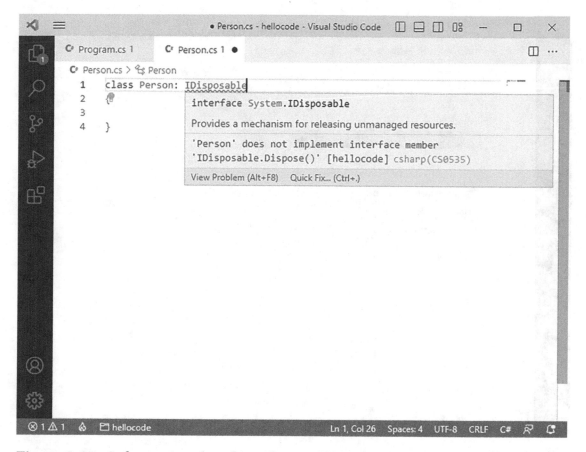

Figure 3-27. *Informational tooltips about code issues*

Tooltips disappear when you move the cursor off the issue, but you can click Peek Problem and dock the error description inside a red box that stays in the code editor. If you still have the Light Bulb enabled, you will see how the code editor suggests potential fixes based on the current context, such as implementing the interface in different ways (see Figure 3-28).

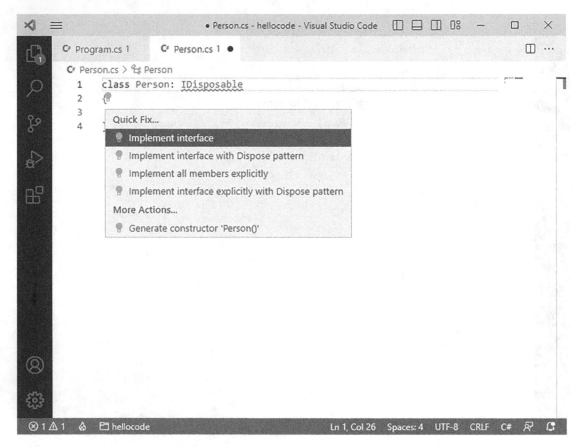

Figure 3-28. *The Light Bulb provides suggestions based on the current context*

Just to give you an idea of the power of this tool, the following code is generated if you choose the Implement Interface with Dispose Pattern option:

```
using System;
public class Person: IDisposable
{
    #region IDisposable Support
    private bool disposedValue = false; // To detect redundant calls
    protected virtual void Dispose(bool disposing)
    {
        if (!disposedValue)
        {
            if (disposing)
            {
```

```
                // TODO: dispose managed state (managed objects).
            }
            // TODO: free unmanaged resources (unmanaged objects)
            // TODO: set large fields to null.
            disposedValue = true;
        }
    }
    // // TODO: override a finalizer only if Dispose(bool disposing) above
    //      has code to free unmanaged resources.
    // ~Person() {
    //    // Do not change this code. Put cleanup code in Dispose(bool
    //        disposing) above.
    //    // Dispose(false);
    // }
    // This code added to correctly implement the disposable pattern.
    public void Dispose()
    {
        // Do not change this code. Put cleanup code in Dispose(bool
            disposing) above.
        Dispose(disposing: true);
        GC.SuppressFinalize(this);
    }
    #endregion
}
```

You will get a similar result, but with different implementation, if you choose one of the other possible code fixes. Although it is not possible to show examples for all the code fixes that Visual Studio Code can apply, what you have to keep in mind is that suggestions and code fixes are based on the context for the code issue, which is a very powerful feature that makes Visual Studio Code a unique editor.

Hints About IntelliCode

For languages such as TypeScript, JavaScript, Java, T-SQL, and Python, the coding experience can be further enhanced with the IntelliCode extension (`https://marketplace.visualstudio.com/items?itemName=VisualStudioExptTeam.vscodeintellicode`).

IntelliCode is an AI-powered code completion engine, whose user interface and user experience is very close to IntelliSense, but it is capable of learning from the way you write code. This includes patterns you use and analysis of the context of your source code. The resulting experience is made of improved suggestions for code completions, based on the context.

Summary

Visual Studio Code is a code-centric tool that supports a wide variety of languages out of the box, offering coding features that are common to all the supported languages, such as syntax colorization, delimiter matching, code block folding, multicursors, code snippets, and code completion.

In addition, languages such as TypeScript and C# provide the so-called evolved code editing experience via integrated tools such as IntelliSense, Go to Definition and Peek Definition, Find All References, and the extremely powerful Light Bulb, which detects code issues as you type and suggests potential fixes based on the context.

Now that you have knowledge of the powerful coding features that Visual Studio Code offers, it is time to see how to use them with individual source code files and structured folders in Chapter 4.

Working with Files and Folders

Being the powerful editor it is, Visual Studio Code provides a convenient way of working with code files and folders containing both loose files and projects. In this chapter, you learn how to work with individual files, with folders containing source code files, and with workspaces. You also learn about VS Code's independence from proprietary project systems as well as its built-in support for a few popular project types.

Visual Studio Code and Project Systems

Visual Studio Code is file and folder based. That means that you can open one or more code files distinctly, but it also means that you can open a folder that contains source code files and treat them in a structured, organized way. When you open a folder, Visual Studio Code searches for one of the following files to organize a structured view of the list of files in the folder:

- `Tsconfig.json`
- `Jsconfig.json`
- `Package.json`
- `Project.json`
- `.sln` Visual Studio solutions and `.csproj` project files for .NET with the C# extension installed

If VS Code finds one of these files, it can organize the file structure into a convenient editing experience and can offer additional rich editing features such as IntelliSense and code refactoring. If a folder only contains source code files, without any of the

81

© Alessandro Del Sole 2023
A. Del Sole, *Visual Studio Code Distilled*, https://doi.org/10.1007/978-1-4842-9484-0_4

aforementioned `.json` or `.sln` files, it still opens and shows all the source code files in that folder, providing a convenient way to switch between all of them. This chapter describes how to work with individual files and with folders in Visual Studio Code, and more details about how it manages projects is provided in the subsection "Working with Folders and Projects."

Working with Individual Files

The easiest way to get started editing with Visual Studio Code is to work with one code file. You can open an existing supported code file with File ➤ Open (Ctrl+O or ⌘+O on macOS). Visual Studio Code automatically detects the language for the code files and enables the proper editing features. In addition, it checks if an extension is available on the Visual Studio Marketplace for the selected language and, if so, offers to install it to improve the editing experience. Of course, you can certainly open more files and easily switch between files by pressing Ctrl+Tab (or ^+Tab on macOS). As you can see in Figure 4-1, a convenient popup box shows the list of open files; by pressing Ctrl+Tab, you can browse files and cycle through the files in the list, and when you release the keys, the selected file becomes the active editing window.

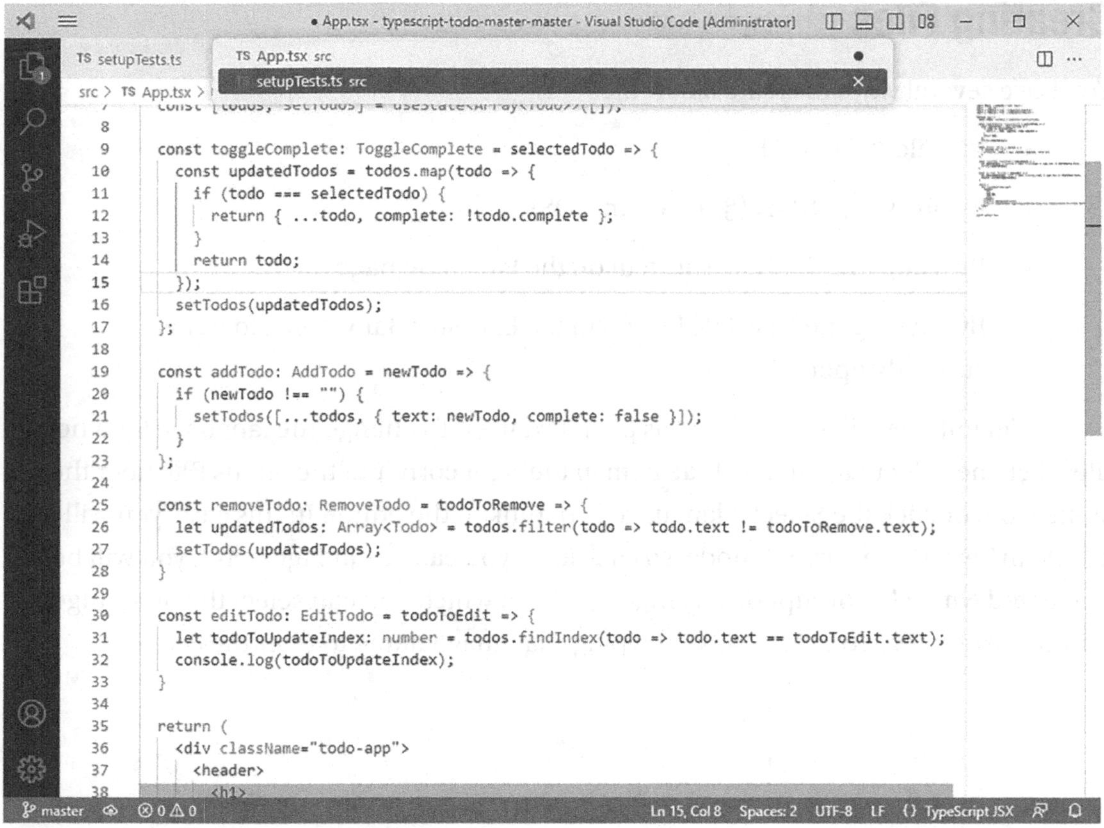

Figure 4-1. *Quickly navigating between open editors*

You can close an editor simply by clicking the Close button in the upper-right corner of each tab, or by using File ➤ Close Editor. You can also quickly close all open editors with the Close All command in the top-right options, under the ... shortcut.

Note   In Visual Studio Code terminology, it is common to refer to open files as *active editors* or *open editors*. This is because editor windows are not limited to code files, but can also display documentation files or provide formatted previews of the content of other types of files (e.g., images and spreadsheets).

Creating Files

You have several ways to create a new file:

- Via File ➤ New File

- By pressing Ctrl+N (⌘+N on macOS)

- By using the New File shortcut on the Welcome page

- By clicking the New File button in the Explorer Bar when a folder is currently opened

By default, new files are treated as plain text files. To change the language for a new file, click the Select Language Mode item in the right corner of the Status Bar, near the smile icon, or click the Select a language hyperlink in the editor. In this case, you will see Plain Text as the current mode, so click it. As you can see in Figure 4-2, you will be presented with a list of supported languages from which you can select the new language for the current file. You can also start typing a language name to filter the list.

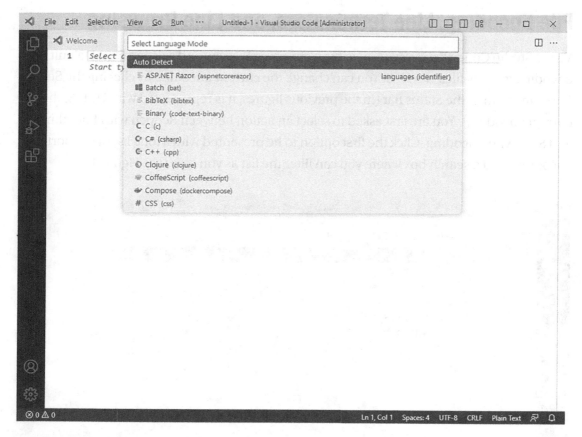

Figure 4-2. *Selecting the language for a new file*

When you select a new language, the Select Language Mode item is updated with the current language, and the editor enables the supported features for the selected language, such as syntax colorization, word completion, and code snippets.

Obviously, you can change the language of any open code file, not just new files.

Language Autodetection

Visual Studio Code can also auto-detect the language in a new code file. For example, if you paste some code from the clipboard into a new file, VS Code will automatically select the appropriate language.

You can also manually select the Auto Detect option from the language selection box.

File Encoding, Line Terminators, and Line Browsing

Visual Studio Code allows you to specify an encoding for new and existing files. Default encoding for new files is UTF-8. You can change the current encoding by clicking the Select Encoding item in the Status Bar (in the previous figures, it is represented with UTF-8, the current encoding). You are first asked to select an action between Reopen with Encoding and Save with Encoding. Click the first option to be presented with a long list of supported encodings and a search box where you can filter the list as you type (see Figure 4-3).

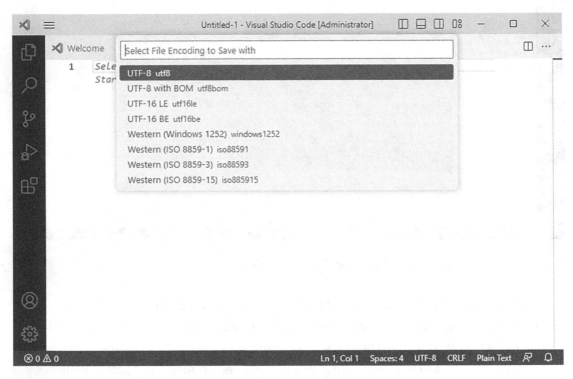

Figure 4-3. *Selecting the file encoding*

Similarly, you can change the line terminator by clicking the Select End of Line Sequence item (in previous figures, it's represented by CRLF). Visual Studio Code supports CRLF (Carriage Return and Line Feed) and LF (Line Feed), and the default selection is CRLF. On Windows, the default sequence is CRLF, while on macOS and Linux it is LF. You can also move fast to a line of code by clicking the Go to Line item, represented by the line number/ column group in the Status Bar. This opens a search box in which you can type the line number you want to go to, and the line of code is immediately highlighted as you type (see Figure 4-4). When you press Enter, the cursor moves to the start of the selected line.

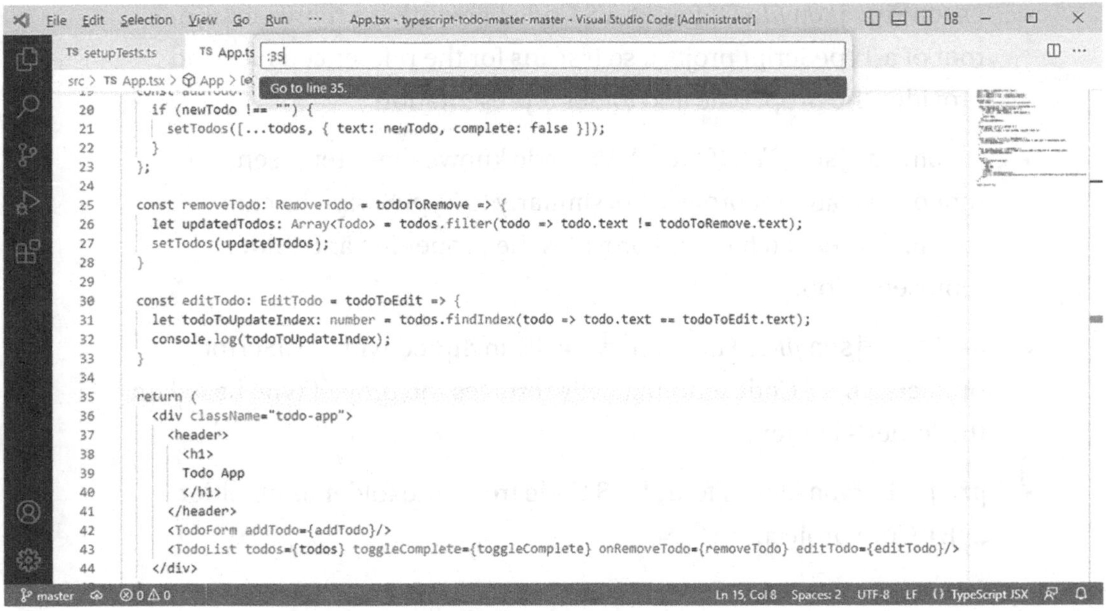

Figure 4-4. *Quickly moving to a specific line of code with Go to Line*

Working with Folders and Projects

Unlike other development environments, such as Microsoft Visual Studio, Visual Studio Code is folder based, not project based. This makes Visual Studio Code independent from proprietary project systems. VS Code can open folders on disk containing multiple code files and organize them the best way possible in the environment, and it also supports a variety of project files. More specifically, when you open a folder, VS Code first searches for the following:

- *MSBuild solution files (*`.sln`*):* In this case, VS Code expects to find a .NET solution made of C# projects, so it scans the referenced projects (*`.csproj` files) and organizes files and subfolders in the proper way. Remember that VS Code needs the Microsoft C# extension installed to properly treat solution files. Note that VS Code can open any `.sln` solution, but full support is currently offered only for .NET 5 and higher. An example of this scenario is provided in Chapter 8.

- `tsconfig.json` *files*: If found, VS Code knows these represent the root of a TypeScript project, so it scans for the referenced files and provides the proper file and folder representation.

- `jsconfig.json` *files*: If found, VS Code knows these represent the root of a JavaScript project. So, similarly to TypeScript, it scans for the referenced files and provides the proper file and folder representation.

- `package.json` *files*: These are typically included with JavaScript projects, so VS Code automatically resolves the project type based on the folder's content.

- `project.json` files: If found, VS Code treats the folder as an older .NET Core project.

Note   Opening a `.sln`, `.csproj`, or `.json` file directly will result in editing the content of the individual file. For this reason, you must open a folder, not a solution or a project file.

Additional project systems might be supported via extensibility. If none of the supported projects is found, Visual Studio Code loads all the code files in the folder as a loose assortment, organizing them into a virtual folder for easy navigation. Now let's explore how to work with folders and supported projects in Visual Studio Code, with corresponding examples.

Opening a Folder

You open a folder by choosing File ➤ Open Folder or choosing the Open Folder shortcut on the Welcome page. You can also drag and drop a folder name from Windows Explorer or macOS Finder onto Visual Studio Code.

Note   On Windows, the VS Code installer also provides an option to enable a shortcut called Open With Code when you right-click a folder or filename in File Explorer.

Whatever folder you open, VS Code creates a structured view in the Explorer Bar, where it shows all files and subfolders that belong to the main folder. Figure 4-5 shows an example based on a TypeScript project.

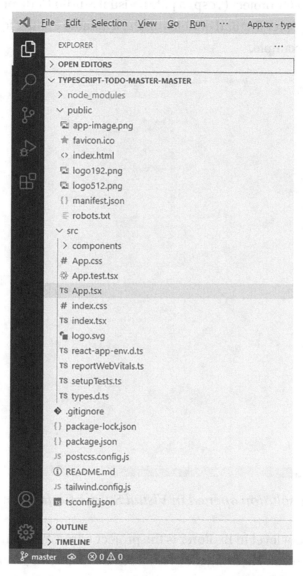

Figure 4-5. *The structured view of files and folders in Explorer*

The root container is the folder name. You see nested files and subfolders, and you can expand each subfolder to browse every file it contains. Simply click a file to open an editor window on it.

Opening .NET Solutions

When you open a folder that contains a .NET solution based on the MSBuild project system (`.sln` file) or a C# project (`.csproj` file), Visual Studio Code organizes all the code files into the Explorer Bar and enables all the available editing features for C#. Figure 4-6 shows an example.

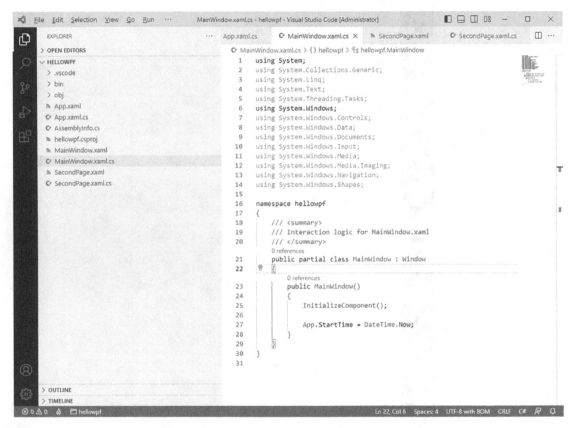

Figure 4-6. *A .NET solution opened in Visual Studio Code*

Notice how the root level in Explorer is the project name. You can browse folders, browse code files, and edit anything that Visual Studio Code can properly recognize. It is worth mentioning that VS Code can certainly open any MSBuild solution, but it is only able to debug applications built with .NET 5 and higher. For instance, .NET 7 allows for creating Windows Presentation Foundation (WPF) and Windows Forms projects; Visual Studio Code and the C# extension support opening this type of solutions as well as running and debugging code. WPF and Windows Forms projects created for the .NET Framework can still be opened in VS Code, and you will still benefit from the structured folder view in the Explorer Bar and the full C# language support, but you will not be able to build, run, and debug the code. Instead, with .NET 7 you also have integrated debugging support, which allows running, debugging, and testing code directly within VS Code. This is discussed in Chapter 9.

Opening JavaScript and TypeScript Projects

Similarly to .NET solutions, Visual Studio Code can manage JavaScript folders by searching for jsconfig.json or package.json files. If found, Code organizes the list of folders and files the proper way and enables all the available editing features for all the files it supports, as shown in Figure 4-7.

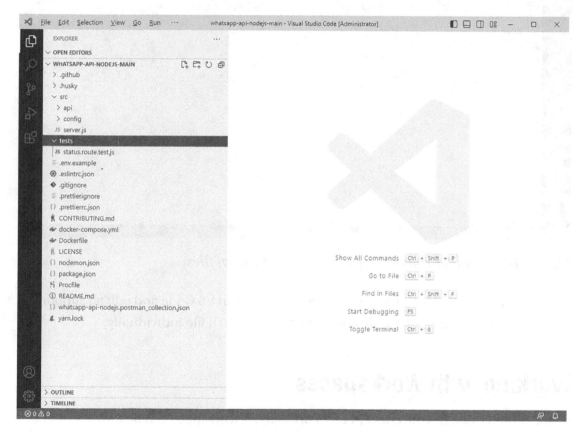

Figure 4-7. *A JavaScript project opened in Visual Studio Code*

TypeScript projects' behavior is the same as for JavaScript, except that Visual Studio Code searches for a file called tsconfig.json as the root.

Opening Loose Folders

Visual Studio Code supports opening folders that contain unrelated, loose assortments of files. VS Code creates a logical root based on the folder name, showing files and subfolders. Figure 4-8 shows an example based on a sample folder called MyFiles that contains files in different languages.

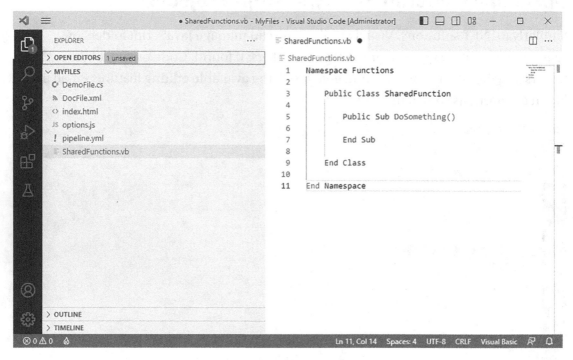

Figure 4-8. *A folder containing a loose assortment of files*

With this option, you can basically open any folder in VS Code and edit all supported files, taking advantage of the code editing features for each file individually.

Working with Workspaces

Visual Studio Code has the concept of a *workspace*. A workspace can be thought of as a logical container of folders. In the latest versions of Visual Studio Code, this feature has also been known as *multi-root workspaces*.

Note   If you have experience with Microsoft Visual Studio, a workspace in Visual Studio Code can be compared to a Visual Studio solution as a container of projects.

Workspaces are extremely useful to organize multiple projects and/or folders into one place. For example, you might have a .NET Web API project, a JavaScript application that consumes such API, and a folder containing documentation. Instead of working on each folder separately, you can put them all under the same workspace and have them all available in Visual Studio Code at the same time. Figure 4-9 shows a workspace, called `SampleWorkspace`, that includes a .NET Web API project, a JavaScript project, and a loose folder.

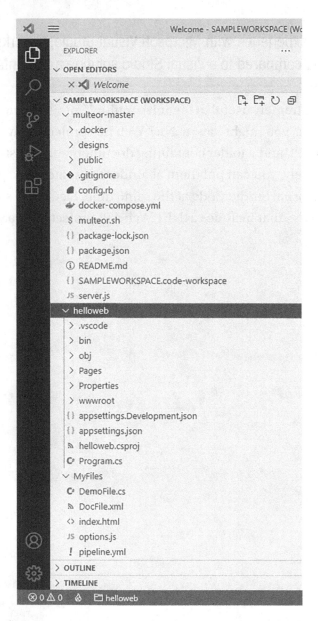

Figure 4-9. *A workspace can group multiple projects and folders into one logical container*

The `multeor-master` folder contains the files for a sample open-source project called Multeor that you can download for instructional purposes from `https://github.com/filidorwiese/multeor`. The Explorer Bar shows the name of the workspace in uppercase together with the (WORKSPACE) literal so that it's easier to recognize it. In the next sections, I explain in more detail how to create and open workspaces and the structure of a workspace file.

Creating Workspaces

You can create a workspace regardless of whether you already have a folder open. If you do have a folder open, choose File ➤ Save Workspace As and VS Code will ask you to specify the location and filename for the new workspace. A workspace is represented by a JSON file with the `.code-workspace` extension, the structure of which is explained shortly.

The workspace name is simply the filename without the `.codeworkspace` extension and is shown in the Explorer Bar (see Figure 4-9). Then you can add other folders to the workspace by choosing File ➤ Add Folder to Workspace. Added folders are displayed in the Explorer Bar under the workspace root.

If you do not have any folders open, you can start either with File ➤ Save Workspace As or with File ➤ Add Folder to Workspace. With the first option, you basically create an empty workspace with a name, and then you add folders as described in the preceding text. With the second option, you instead create an empty, untitled workspace starting from an existing folder. In this case, in fact, the Explorer Bar shows UNTITLED (WORKSPACE) as the new workspace name. When you save the workspace as described in the preceding text, the Explorer Bar shows the new name based on the workspace filename. Remember that workspaces are only logical containers and do not affect the structure or behavior of your projects and folders in any manner.

Note   Folders you add to a workspace can be anywhere on disk; Visual Studio Code will group their content under the workspace root and let you work as if they were in the same location.

Opening Existing Workspaces

You can open an existing workspace by choosing File ➤ Open Workspace. You can also drag and drop a workspace filename from your operating system's file browsing program onto the Visual Studio Code surface. Opening a `.code-workspace` file directly simply results in viewing the file content, not opening the workspace. Similarly, opening a folder that contains a `.code-workspace` file results in opening only the folder, not the workspace. You can only use the specific commands described at the beginning of this paragraph.

Workspace Structure

The information of a Visual Studio Code workspace is stored inside a file with a `.code-workspace` extension. A workspace file is a JSON file with a root element called `folders`. This is an array of `path` elements, each assigned with the name of a folder that is included in the workspace. The following JSON markup represents how the workspace file of the example shown in Figure 4-9 looks on my machine, and it will vary on your computer:

```
{
    "folders": [
        {
            "path": ".\MyFiles"
        },
        {
            "path": "C:\\Source\\helloweb"
        },
        {
            "path": "C:\\Source\\multeor-master"
        }
    ]
}
```

Notice that the full pathname of a folder is provided only if the folder is not in the same location of the workspace file. In this case, the `.code-workspace` file, the `webapp` folder, and the `multeor-master` folders are all in the same location; instead, the `MyFiles` folder is located under a different folder. If you want to see the structure of a workspace file for yourself, you can open it in Visual Studio Code by choosing File ➤ Open File.

Security: Workspace Trust

Visual Studio Code includes interesting security features that allow for safely working with files, folders, and workspaces. These features go under a group named Workspace Trust.

When Visual Studio Code cannot trust the source or author of an individual file, a folder, or a workspace, it will prompt you with different choices such as opening the content as trusted, opening the content in restricted mode, or cancelling the operation. Figure 4-10 shows the warning message.

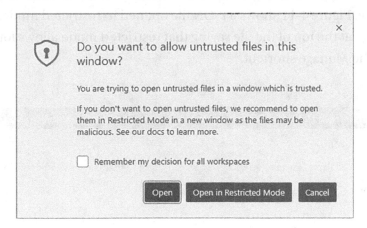

Figure 4-10. *Workspace Trust in action*

Note   The warning message varies if VS Code cannot automatically trust the source or author of the content. Figure 4-10 refers to untrusted files. With untrusted authors, the title of the dialog shows the following message: Do you trust the authors of the files in this workspace? Also, text in the buttons changes accordingly.

If you trust the source or author of the files, folder, or workspace, you can click Open and the content will be opened with no restrictions. If you are not sure, you can click Open in Restricted Mode.

Note   If you select the Remember My Decision for All Workspaces checkbox, your choice will be applied to all files, folders, and workspaces you open from now on and you will no longer be prompted for enabling or disabling restricted mode. However, you can change this preference in VS Code's Settings, as explained shortly.

When you open contents in restricted mode, VS Code only enables code browsing and disables features like debugging, tasks, and some extensions that could work with that content type. Figure 4-11 shows a JSON file opened in restricted mode. Notice the warning message at the top of the file saying that restricted mode allows for safe code browsing, and the Manage shortcut.

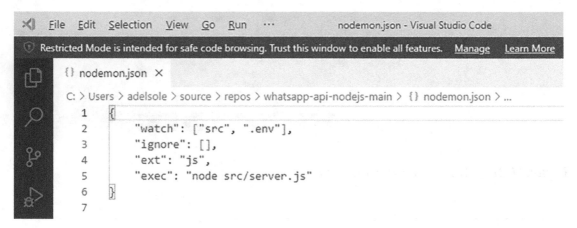

Figure 4-11. *Opening files in restricted mode*

If you click Manage, you can manage the restricted mode for the current file and folder. Figure 4-12 demonstrates this.

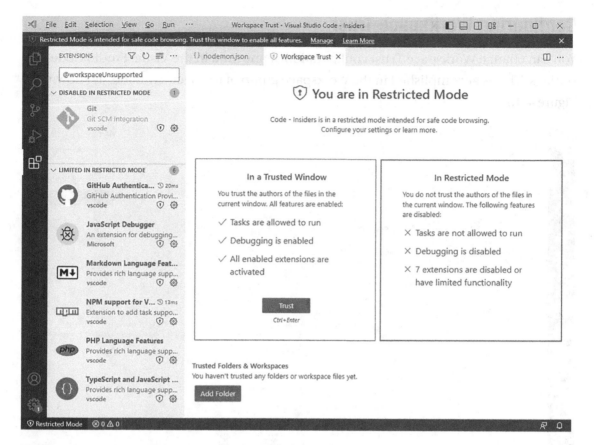

Figure 4-12. *Managing the restricted mode*

The active window, called Workspace Trust, clearly explains the difference between a trusted window and the restricted mode. In a trusted window, debugger, tasks, and extensions are all enabled and running. In the restricted mode, tasks and debugging are disabled, whereas extensions are disabled or have limited functionality. Visual Studio Code decides which extensions must be disabled or partially enabled depending on their target. In Figure 4-12 you can see how, based on my configuration, seven extensions have been disabled. By clicking 7 Extensions, it is possible to see the list of both disabled and limited extensions in the Extensions panel on the left.

Once you have investigated the code, you can click the Trust button to move your file to a trusted window. You can also add specific folders and workspaces to a list of trusted content by clicking the Add Folder button at the bottom of the page.

Configuring Workspace Trust

You can change Workspace Trust configuration at any time in the Visual Studio Code settings. This is accomplished in the Workspace group of the Security node, as shown in Figure 4-13.

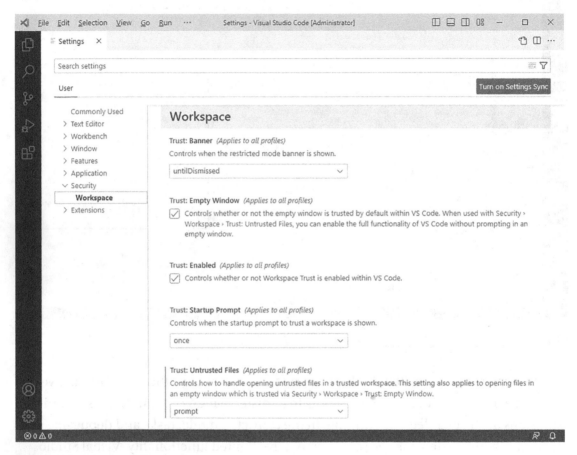

Figure 4-13. *Configuring Workspace Trust*

Note   Figure 4-13 shows how to configure Workspace Trust at the user level. When you open a workspace in restricted mode, you can able configure trust settings per workspace and per folder.

Summary

Visual Studio Code is file and folder based, and it allows for working with individual files as well as with folders that contain source code files. It treats them all in a structured, organized way.

Visual Studio Code also supports a number of project systems such as .NET, TypeScript, and JavaScript, and it allows for creating and managing multi-root workspaces. Workspaces are logical containers of folders that make it easy to have multiple projects and folders under the same visual root. Files, folders, and workspaces can be opened in restricted mode for safe code browsing and moved to a trusted environment once you are sure of the contents. VS Code is not only a very powerful code editor but also a very flexible environment that can be customized in many ways. Customization is the topic of the next chapter.

CHAPTER 5

Customizing Visual Studio Code

Visual Studio Code is an extremely versatile development tool that can be customized and extended in many ways. In fact, you can customize its appearance, the code editor, and key shortcuts to make your editing experience extremely personalized.

Additionally, you can install third-party extensions such as new languages, debuggers, themes, linters, and code snippets. This chapter explains how to customize Visual Studio Code, explaining the difference between customizations and extensions. Then, in the next chapter, you learn how to work with extensions.

Customizations and Extensions Explained

You can personalize the environment of Visual Studio Code with customizations and extensions. The difference is that extensions add new instrumentation or functionalities to a tool or change the behavior of existing functionalities. Implementing IntelliSense for a language that does not have it by default, adding commands to the Status Bar, and adding custom debuggers are examples of extensions.

Customizations are instead related to environment settings and do not add functionalities to a tool. Examples of popular customizations are color themes and key bindings. Table 5-1 summarizes the customizations and extensions in VS Code.

© Alessandro Del Sole 2023
A. Del Sole, *Visual Studio Code Distilled*, https://doi.org/10.1007/978-1-4842-9484-0_5

Table 5-1. *Customizations and Extensions*

Feature	Description	Type
Color themes	Style the environment layout with different colors.	Customization
User and workspace settings	Specify environment preferences.	Customization
Key bindings	Redefine keyboard shortcuts.	Customization
Language grammar and syntax colorizers	Add support to additional languages with syntax colorizers.	Customization
Code snippets	Add TextMate and Sublime Text snippets and type repetitive code faster.	Customization
Debuggers	Add new debuggers for specific languages and platforms.	Extension
Language servers	Implement validation logic for files opened in VS Code.	Extension
Activation	Load an extension when a specific file type is detected or when a command is selected in the Command Palette.	Extension
Editor	Work against the code editor's content, including text manipulation and selection.	Extension
Workspace	Enhance the Status Bar, working file list, and other tools.	Extension
Eventing	Interact with VS Code's lifecycle events such as open and close.	Extension
Evolved editing	Improve language support with IntelliSense, Peek Definition, Go to Definition, and all the advanced, supported editing capabilities.	Extension

In this chapter, you see how to customize Visual Studio Code by changing the existing preferences. Then in the next chapter, you see how to install extensions, including extensions that add new customizations to the development environment, such as themes and key bindings.

Customizing Visual Studio Code

In this section, you discover how easy it is to customize Visual Studio Code by walking through the customization types described in Table 5-1.

Theme Selection

You can select among several themes to give Visual Studio Code a different look and feel. A brief introduction to color themes was given at the beginning of Chapter 1, but now you get more details.

You select a color theme by choosing File ➤ Preferences ➤ Themes ➤ Color Theme or by clicking the Settings button and then choosing Themes ➤ Color Theme. The list of available color themes is shown in the Command Palette, as you can see in Figure 5-1.

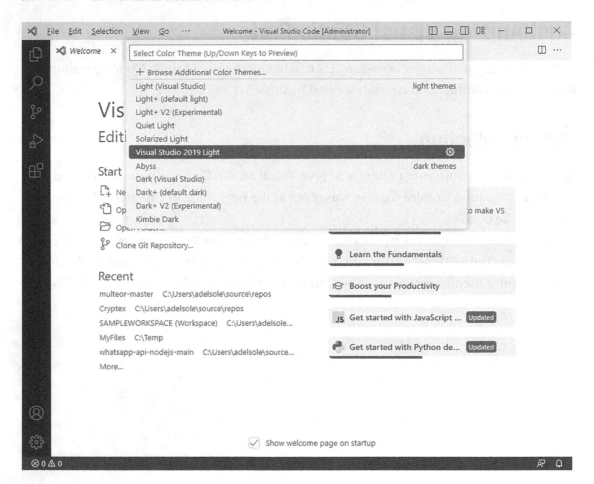

Figure 5-1. *Selecting a theme*

Themes are divided into light themes, dark themes, and high-contrast themes. Once you select a different color theme, it is applied immediately. Also, you can get a preview of the theme as you scroll the list with the keyboard. Figure 5-2 shows the Dark (Visual Studio) theme applied to VS Code, which is a very popular choice; try out the other themes to find one that suits you.

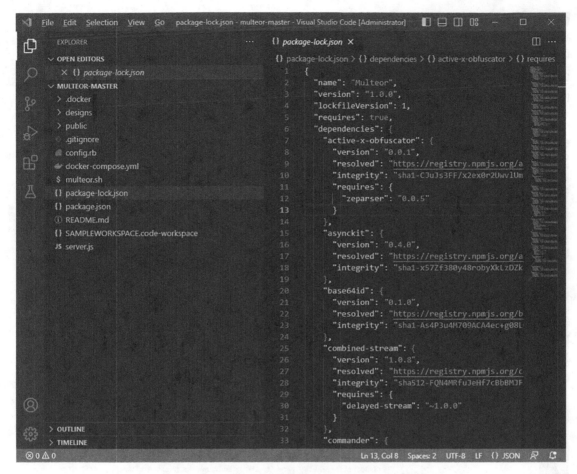

Figure 5-2. *The Dark (Visual Studio) theme applied to Visual Studio Code*

As you might expect, applying a theme also affects the colors used in the code editor so that there is an appropriate brightness and contrast balance. In the next chapter, you see how to install additional themes as extensions.

Customizing the Environment

In most applications, including other IDEs, you set environment settings and preferences via a convenient user interface, and VS Code is no exception. There are two different types of settings: user settings and workspace settings. User settings apply globally to the development environment, while workspace settings only apply to the current project or folder. The following subsections cover both user settings and workspace settings.

Understanding User Settings

User settings globally apply to the VS Code's development environment. Customizing user settings is accomplished by choosing File ➤ Preferences ➤ Settings. When you do this, the Settings editor appears, as represented in Figure 5-3.

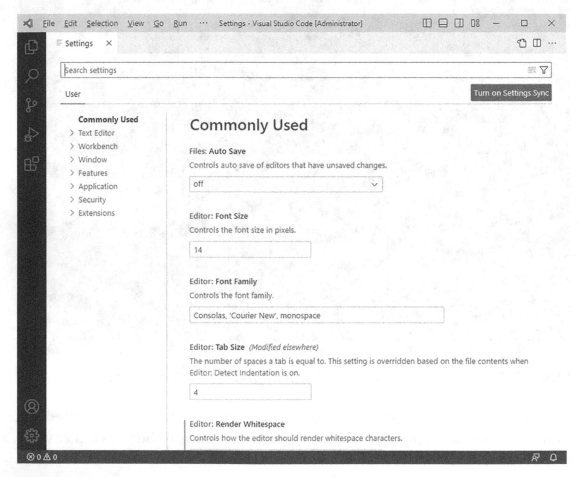

Figure 5-3. *Working with user settings*

On the left side of the editor, settings are grouped by category. In the Search Settings bar, you can quickly search settings based on what you type, and you can also see the number of total settings found, which varies depending on the version of VS Code and on the number of extensions you have installed. You can manually expand setting categories, or you can just scroll the list of settings, and the related category is

automatically highlighted as you scroll. For instance, you could control the behavior of
the Explorer Bar by locating and selecting Explorer under the Features category, and
there you can change the current settings, as shown in Figure 5-4.

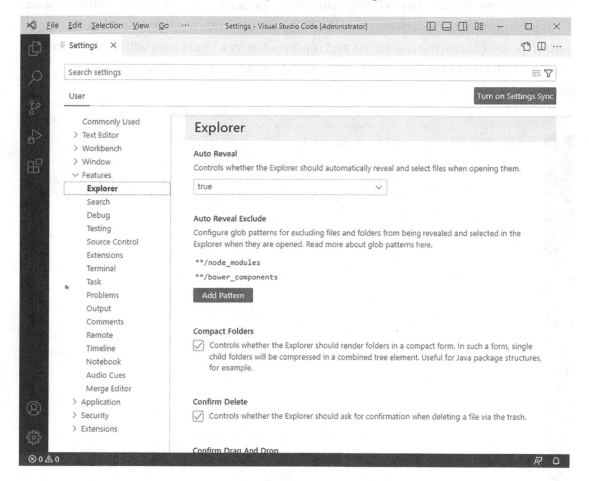

Figure 5-4. *Changing user settings*

Similarly, you can change settings and preferences for the text editor, the whole
application, and extension settings. In fact, extensions that allow for customizing
preferences store their settings in the same place as VS Code does, so that you have a
unique Settings editor. There are hundreds of settings and the number varies depending
on your configuration and installed extensions, so it's not possible to list all settings here.
For more details about available settings, visit the official documentation at https://
code.visualstudio.com/docs/getstarted/settings.

Behind the Scenes: The settings.json File

Behind the scenes, VS Code (and extensions) stores settings inside a file called
`settings.json`. In this file, each key/value pair represents a specific setting and its value.

It is important to understand how this file works, so click the Open Settings (JSON)
button located above the search bar and represented by a sheet icon with a plus symbol
overlayed (the first from left to right). Figure 5-5 shows how the editor appears at
this point.

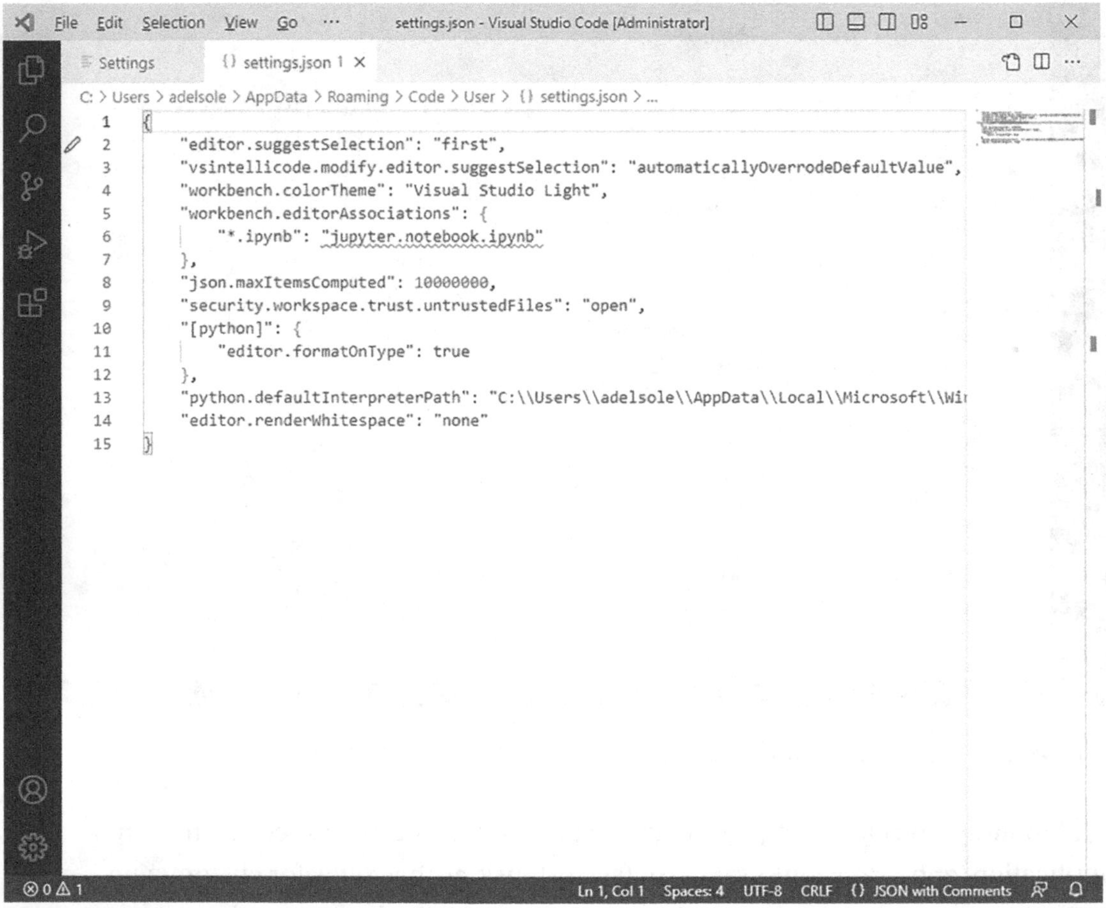

Figure 5-5. *Working with the settings.json file*

As you can see, the editor for `settings.json` allows you to define custom settings by
overriding one or more default settings. It is worth mentioning that changes you do in
this file are at the user or workspace level only, and they do not affect general settings of
VS Code. Also, you will see how IntelliSense helps you choose among available settings

as you type. The code editor also reports errors, such as missing commas or curly braces, as you would expect when editing a JSON file. Within `settings.json`, it is also possible to customize settings for an extension. Every time you modify a setting in the user interface, the related JSON is updated in `settings.json`.

IntelliSense also allows you to get more information about a given setting by clicking the rollover, which shows hints about the setting with a convenient tooltip, exactly as you would expect after learning about IntelliSense's features in Chapter 3. When you are done, do not forget to save `settings.json`; otherwise your changes will be lost.

A Real-World Example: Working with Proxies

If you work for an enterprise, the network probably is behind a proxy server. In this case, you or the system administrator might need to configure Visual Studio Code to work with the proxy. If you do not, you cannot download packages, extensions, and product updates. Visual Studio Code should automatically detect proxies and ask for your credentials, but this does not always happen, so you might need to take some manual steps.

The first thing to do is make sure that the sites described in Table 5-2 are in the allowed applications list of the firewall.

Table 5-2. *Sites Allowed by a Firewall*

URL	Description
update.code. visualstudio.com	Visual Studio Code download and update server
code.visualstudio.com	Visual Studio Code documentation
go.microsoft.com	Microsoft link forwarding service
vscode.blob.core. windows.net	Blob storage for Visual Studio Code
marketplace. visualstudio.com	Visual Studio Marketplace
*.gallery.vsassets.io	Visual Studio Marketplace
*.gallerycdn.vsassets. io	Visual Studio Marketplace
rink.hockeyapp.net	Crash reporting service
bingsettingssearch. trafficmanager.net	In-product settings search
vscode.search.windows. net	In-product settings search
raw.githubusercontent. com	GitHub repository raw file access
vsmarketplacebadge. apphb.com	Visual Studio Marketplace badge service
az764295.vo.msecnd.net	Content Delivery Network (CDN) for Visual Studio Code downloads
download.visualstudio. microsoft.com	Visual Studio download service, which includes dependencies for extensions such as C# and C++

The next step is to configure VS Code to work with the proxy. Actually, if the http_
proxy and https_proxy environment variables have been defined at the system level, VS
Code uses their values. If these variables have not been set, you must provide the proxy
address in the user settings. In the Settings editor, locate Proxy under the Application
category. Then, as you can see in Figure 5-6, enter the proxy address in the Proxy text box.

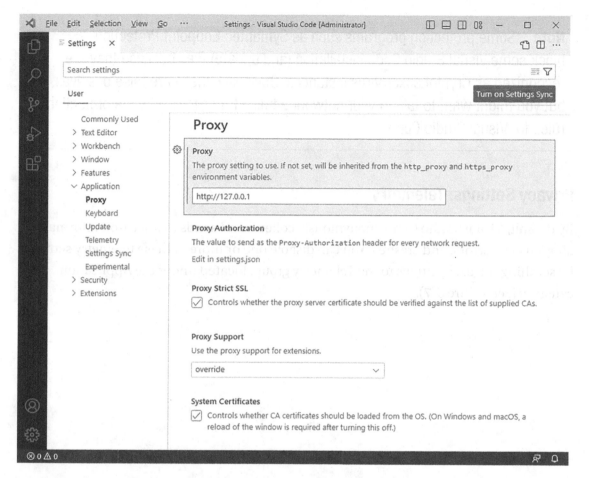

Figure 5-6. *Configuring VS Code to work behind a proxy server*

If your proxy also requires an authorization header, this must be specified in the
`settings.json` file, so you have to click the Edit in settings.json hyperlink and then
enter the value supplied by your network administrator as the value for the `http.`
`proxyAuthorization` key. Also, check the Proxy Strict SSL checkbox if the certificate
should be verified against the list of supplied certification authorities.

Save your changes and check if Visual Studio Code is able to download extensions,
packages, and libraries required by some languages and product updates. If you still
encounter network issues, ask your network administrator to help you configure the
proxy settings.

Note   Some protection programs such as Symantec Endpoint Protection block some Visual Studio Code installation (and update) files because they are recognized as CryptoLocker virus instances. Obviously, these are false positives, but you might want to talk to your network administrator to review the protection rules for Visual Studio Code.

Privacy Settings: Telemetry

By default, Visual Studio Code anonymously collects and sends to Microsoft information about usage, errors, and crashes. You can disable one or more of these telemetry settings by scrolling the user settings to the Telemetry group, located under the Application category (see Figure 5-7).

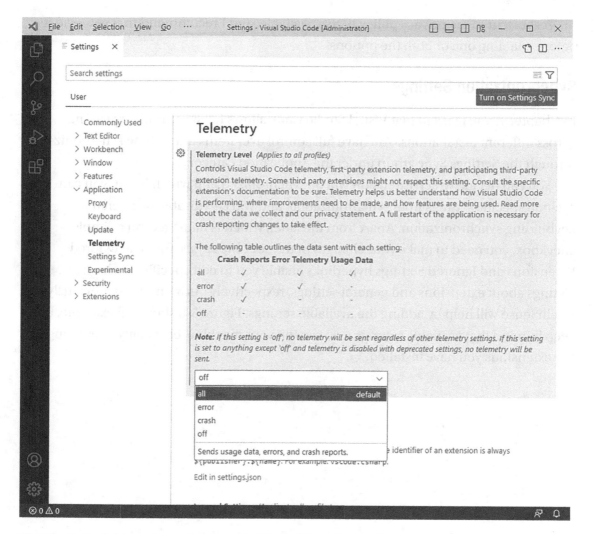

Figure 5-7. *Managing telemetry in Visual Studio Code*

There are four options:

- **All**: When enabled, VS Code collects and sends to Microsoft information about errors and crashes.

- **Error**: When enabled, VS Code collects and sends to Microsoft information about application errors only.

- **Crash**: when enabled, VS Code collects and sends to Microsoft information about application crashes only.

- **Off**: Telemetry is disabled.

A shortcut to the privacy policy is also available, and I recommend that you read it before enabling one or both the options.

Synchronization Settings

In Chapter 1, you learned that Visual Studio Code allows for synchronizing settings across different installations. You have full control over items that can be synchronized through the Settings Sync group under the Application category.

You can decide which extension will be synchronized and which is not, you can exclude specific settings from synchronization, and you can disable or re-enable keybinding synchronization. Apart from the latter, which is managed via a simple checkbox, you need to make your changes in the `settings.json` file. The Ignored Extensions and Ignored Settings hyperlinks enable you to edit specific blocks of settings about extensions and general settings, respectively. As mentioned previously, IntelliSense will help by adding the available settings. Figure 5-8 shows an example, but keep in mind that available settings may vary on your machine, especially depending on the extensions you have installed.

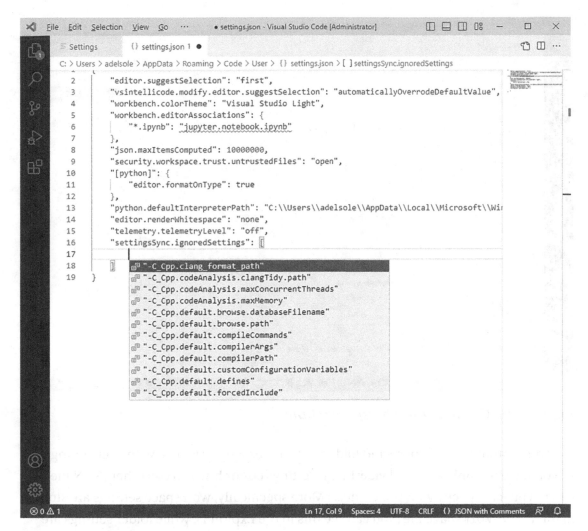

Figure 5-8. *IntelliSense helps manage synchronization settings*

Understanding Workspace Settings

Differently from user settings, which globally apply to VS Code's environment, workspace settings apply to the current workspace and folders in the workspace. As an implication, you first need to open an existing workspace or add an existing folder to a new workspace, to customize workspace settings.

Next you choose File ➤ Preferences ➤ Settings. At this point, the Settings editor shows three tabs: one for user settings, one for workspace settings, and one for individual folders within the workspace, as demonstrated in Figure 5-9.

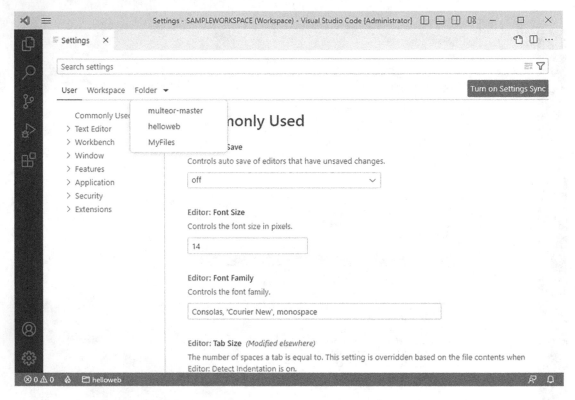

Figure 5-9. *Customizing workspace settings*

You customize workspace and folders settings exactly as you do with user settings, so you have not only a second view in the Settings editor but also two other JSON files where you can specify your preferences. More specifically, workspace settings are stored in the .code-workspace file (you can see this in the Explorer), while folder settings are stored in the settings.json file. The .code-workspace file is saved under the workspace folder, while settings.json is saved under the .vscode subfolder that Visual Studio Code creates inside the opened folder, restricting the settings' availability to the current folder only.

Customizing Keyboard Shortcuts

Visual Studio Code includes a huge number of keyboard shortcuts that you can override with custom values. This is particularly useful if you are used to working with other development tools and you want to have the same keyboard shortcuts in Visual Studio Code.

Note   In the next chapter, you learn how to download ready-to-use keyboard shortcuts that will save you a lot of time, but it's first important for you to know how they actually work.

Like user and workspace settings, keyboard shortcuts are represented with JSON markup, and each is made of two elements: key, which stores one or more keys to be associated to an action, and command, which represents the action to invoke. In some cases, VS Code might offer the same shortcuts for different scenarios. This is the typical case of the Esc key, which targets a number of actions depending on what you are working with, such as the code editor or a tool window. To identify the proper action, keyboard shortcut settings support the when element, which specifies the proper action based on the context. You can quickly get the list of current keyboard shortcuts by choosing File ➤ Preferences ➤ Keyboard Shortcuts. At this point, Visual Studio Code displays a nicely formatted list of commands and shortcuts, as you can see in Figure 5-10.

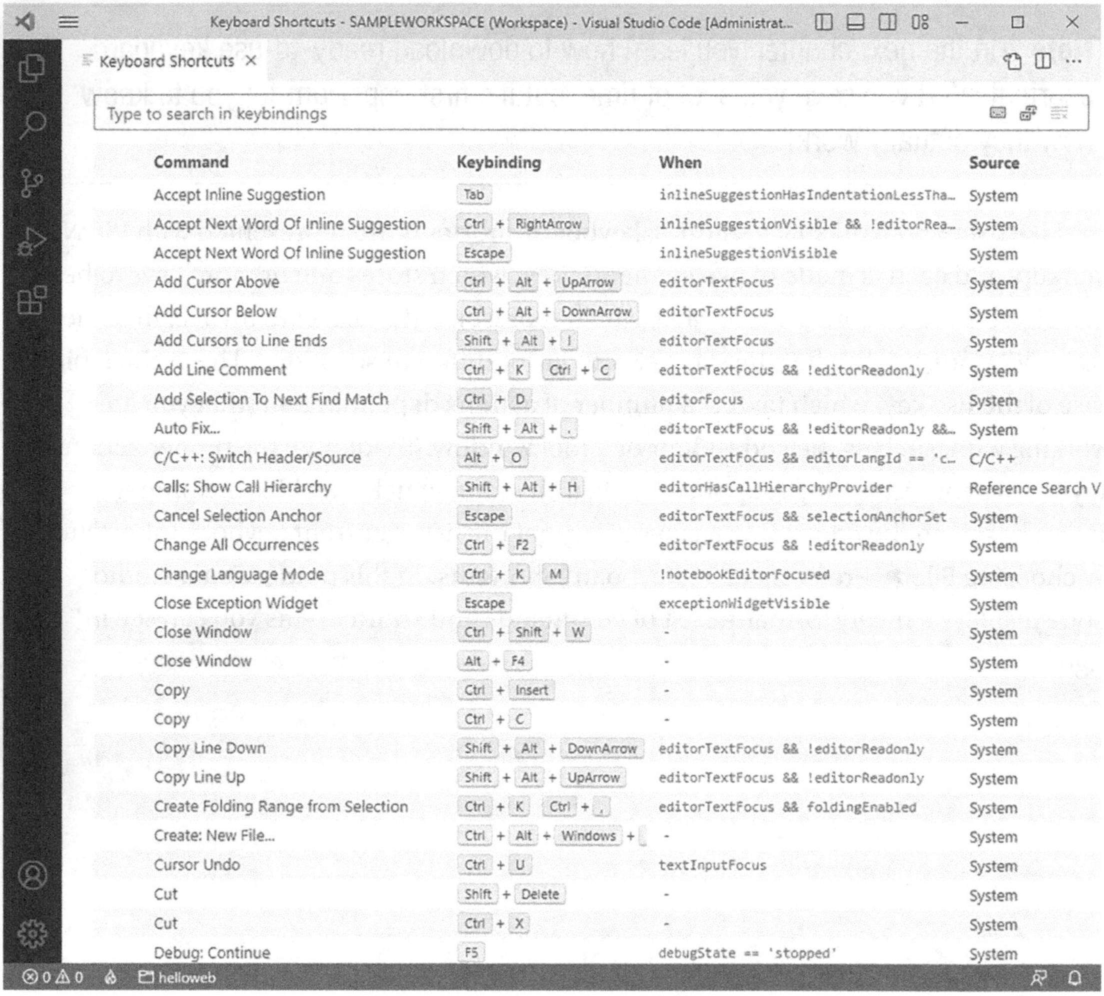

Figure 5-10. *The list of current keyboard shortcuts*

To customize keyboard shortcuts, all you need to do is click the Open Keyboard Shortcuts button, represented by a sheet icon with a plus symbol overlayed, located at the top-right corner of the window. This opens the `keybindings.json` file, where you can override default shortcuts with custom ones (see Figure 5-11).

Note   Remember that Visual Studio Code has (and allows for customizing) different default keyboard shortcuts depending on the operating system it is running on.

You can quickly add a custom keyboard shortcut by clicking the Define Keybinding button or by using the shortcut suggested in the button text (which varies depending on your operating system). When you do this, a popup box appears and asks you to specify the keyboard shortcut, as shown in Figure 5-11.

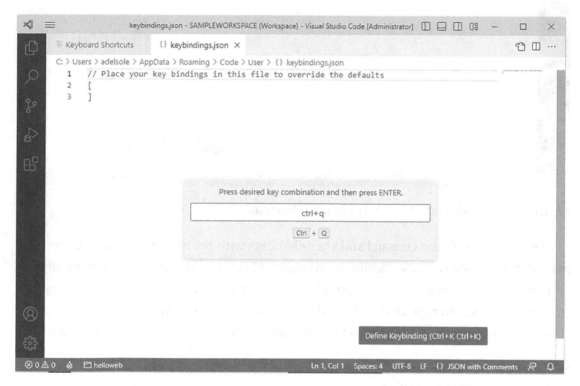

Figure 5-11. *Adding a keyboard shortcut*

When you press Enter, the JSON markup for the new keyboard shortcut is added, as shown in Figure 5-12.

Figure 5-12. *Editing the new keyboard shortcut*

You need to edit the `command` and `when` elements with the command you want to map and for which scenario. Additionally, when editing `keybindings.json` manually, you need to supply the markup for both the old shortcut and the new one. For example, suppose you want to replace the Alt+O shortcut for the C/C++ extension (Switch: Header/Source) with Shift+Alt+O. The markup you need to write looks like the following:

```
{
    "key": "shift+alt+o",
    "command": "C_Cpp.SwitchHeaderSource",
    "when": "editorTextFocus && editorLangId == 'cpp'"
},
{
    "key": "alt+o",
    "command": "-C_Cpp.SwitchHeaderSource",
    "when": "editorTextFocus && editorLangId == 'cpp'"
}
```

Actually, the when element is optional. Save your changes to the `keybindings.json` file to get your new keyboard shortcuts ready.

Creating Reusable Profiles

Suppose you want to use Visual Studio Code for different development scenarios, for example web development with C#, writing documentation with Markdown, or data science development with Python.

For each scenario, you might need specific settings, such as (but not limited to) code snippets, extensions, and keyboard shortcuts that go well with one scenario but that might not be appropriate for another one.

Visual Studio Code allows you to create profiles. A *profile* is a group of customizations that includes extensions, environment settings, code snippets, keyboard shortcuts, UI appearance, and tasks. Profiles can be saved, exported, and shared with others. In order to manage profiles, you click the Settings icon in the Side Bar and then select Profiles. This opens the menu shown in Figure 5-13.

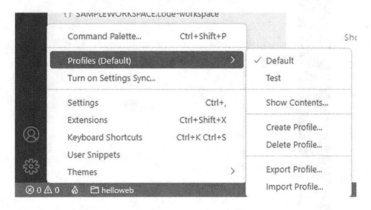

Figure 5-13. *Accessing profile options*

As you can see, there is always a default profile to which current customizations are applied at a global level. Before creating a new profile, you can export the current one for later reuse. With regard to this, click Create Profile. You will be asked to specify if you want to create an empty profile or a new profile from the current one. Select the latter option, then specify a profile name, for example **My Default** (see Figure 5-14).

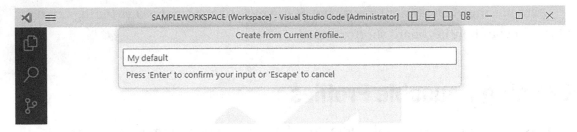

Figure 5-14. *Creating a new profile*

Press Enter when you're ready. At this point, the new profile also becomes the active profile. This can be easily demonstrated by reopening the Profiles menu. If you want to see what is included in the current profile, select Show Contents. Figure 5-15 shows an example of profile contents.

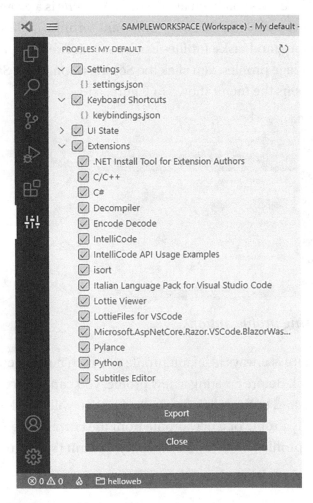

Figure 5-15. *Displaying profile contents*

As you can see, customizations in the profile are grouped by Settings, Keyboard Shortcuts, UI State, Extensions. From here you can also remove one or more customizations from the profile, and you can decide to export the profile for later reuse. Click the Export button. The Command Palette appears and first asks you to specify a profile name, then if the profile should be exported to a remote Gist repository (GitHub option) or to a local file (Local option). Select the second option and choose a target folder and filename. Profile filenames have `.code-profile` extension and are JSON files whose structure represents the profile contents. Exported profiles can be shared with other developers; you can import a profile by selecting the Import Profile command from the Profiles menu (see Figure 5-13).

Note   You do not need to reimport your own profiles every time you switch between existing profiles. You can instead select among installed profiles from the Profiles menu.

Profiles are an easy and convenient way to organize your workspace based on your needs and can really save you a lot of time.

Summary

Visual Studio Code enables you to make several customizations that will help you feel at home, especially if you are used to working with other development tools or code editors. You can select a different color theme from a list, you can customize the environment settings globally or for a specific folder, and you can even create custom keyboard shortcuts.

But the very good news is that customizations can also be downloaded as extensions, as well as new languages, debuggers, and tools. Extensibility is discussed in the next chapter.

CHAPTER 6

Installing and Managing Extensions

Extensibility is one of the key features in Visual Studio Code, because you can add tools, languages, code snippets, debuggers, key bindings, and themes. Extensibility is especially beneficial in the area of languages, because Visual Studio Code enables you to extend the code editor with specific syntax support, which can also include IntelliSense, code snippets, and code refactoring.

This all means that Visual Studio Code has open support for any language and any tool on any platform, opening the possibilities to infinite development scenarios. This chapter explains how to find and install extensions and how to manage extensions on your system.

Installing Extensions

You have two ways of browsing and installing extensions: from the Visual Studio Marketplace and from within Visual Studio Code. The Visual Studio Marketplace is a website that contains extensions for the most popular Microsoft development tools and services, such as Visual Studio, Visual Studio Code, and Azure DevOps. It is available at `https://marketplace.visualstudio.com`, and you need to click the Visual Studio Code tab to see a list of extensions for Visual Studio Code. Figure 6-1 shows the Marketplace for Visual Studio Code.

© Alessandro Del Sole 2023
A. Del Sole, *Visual Studio Code Distilled*, https://doi.org/10.1007/978-1-4842-9484-0_6

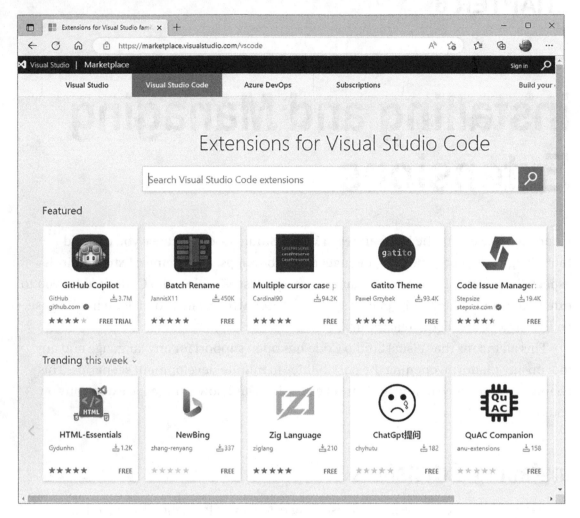

Figure 6-1. *The Visual Studio Marketplace*

You can search for extensions by typing in the search box, or you can browse
the groups below, such as Featured, Trending, Most Popular, and Recently Added. If
you scroll to the bottom of the page, you can also browse extensions by category or
collection. Once you have found an extension of your interest, click its name to see a
detail page. Figure 6-2 shows an example based on the C# extension by Microsoft.

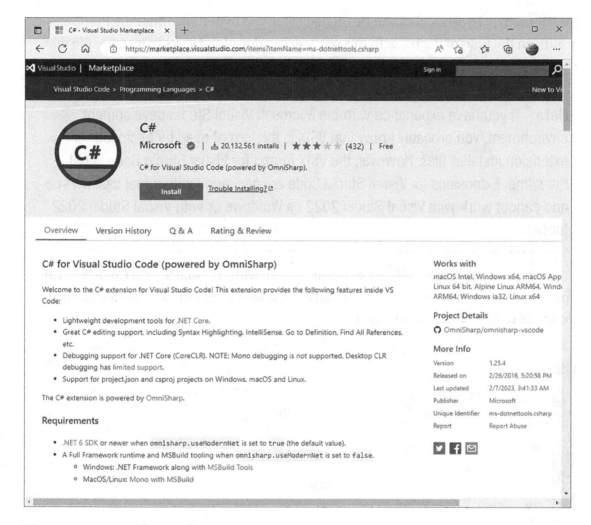

Figure 6-2. *Detail page for an extension*

An extension's page provides a detailed description and guidance about using the extension, often providing links to additional documentation, resources, and the source code (if open-source). I strongly recommend that you read the detail page to get information about what the extension includes, especially with extensions that add language support, because it is important to know if there is support only for a new syntax or also for IntelliSense, code snippets, and debugging.

If you click the Install button, your browser will ask your confirmation to open the download link with Visual Studio Code. When this starts, the extension will automatically be installed. You can also download the offline installer of the extension for later reuse. To do so, click the Download Extension hyperlink under the Resources group, on the right of the page. In this way you can download a `.vsix` installer file that you can then launch manually.

Note   If you have experience with the Microsoft Visual Studio development environment, you probably know that VSIX is the format used by Microsoft for extension installer files. However, the VSIX format for Visual Studio Code is not the same. Extensions for Visual Studio Code are packaged with a tool called `vsce` and cannot work with Visual Studio 2022 on Windows or with Visual Studio 2022 for Mac.

The second way of installing extensions is from within Visual Studio Code. You can open the Extensions Bar and search for an extension and then click a specific extension to get the details, as shown in Figure 6-3.

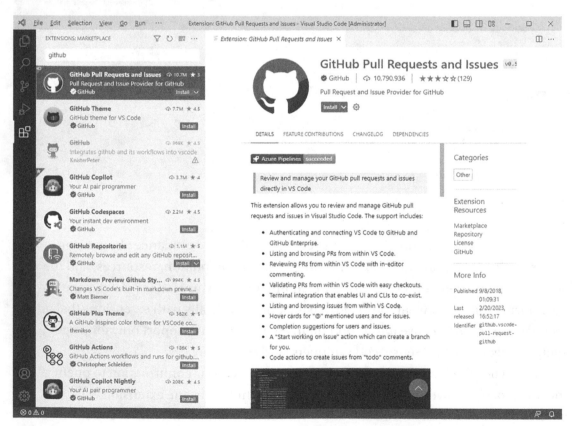

Figure 6-3. *Installing extensions from within Visual Studio Code*

You can click the Install button when you're ready. You need to click the Reload button (that appears once the installation completes) to enable the extension in VS Code. You can also filter the search results; for instance, if you type **category:linters** in the search box, Visual Studio Code will list all the extensions that provide linting support with syntax colorization to specific languages. You can use the same category names you see in the Visual Studio Marketplace.

As an alternative, you can use the Command Palette to download (and manage) extensions. Open the Command Palette and type `extensions`. A list of self-explanatory commands related to extension management will appear. You will typically prefer working with extensions from the Command Palette when you do not want to lose focus on the active editor window; otherwise, using the Extensions Bar's user interface is definitely easier.

Note   Many extensions, especially extensions that provide full language support such as C# and C/C++, rely on additional tools like debuggers and libraries. These additional tools are usually downloaded the first time you use the extension. For example, in the case of the C# extension, required tools and libraries are downloaded the first time you create or open a C# file. These include libraries to support .NET debugging and tools to improve the editing experience via IntelliSense and live static analysis. Also, newly downloaded extensions might need some initial configuration. In this case, a popup box will appear explaining what you need to do to get started.

Extension Recommendations

Visual Studio Code can provide suggestions about recommended extensions based on your activity. When you open the Extensions Bar, you will see a group called RECOMMENDED under the list of installed extensions.

The list of recommended extensions varies on your activity and might be empty the first time you work with Visual Studio Code. As one option, Visual Studio Code can suggest extensions based on the file you open. For example, suppose you open a code file written with the Go language but you do not have installed any Go extension yet. Visual Studio Code has built-in support for the Go language syntax, so the editor provides syntax colorization and basic word completion, but you might want to work with a richer editing experience that includes code snippets, code navigation, and rich IntelliSense support. In this case, VS Code will suggest that an extension is available to help you work with Go files and will offer to install it, as represented in Figure 6-4.

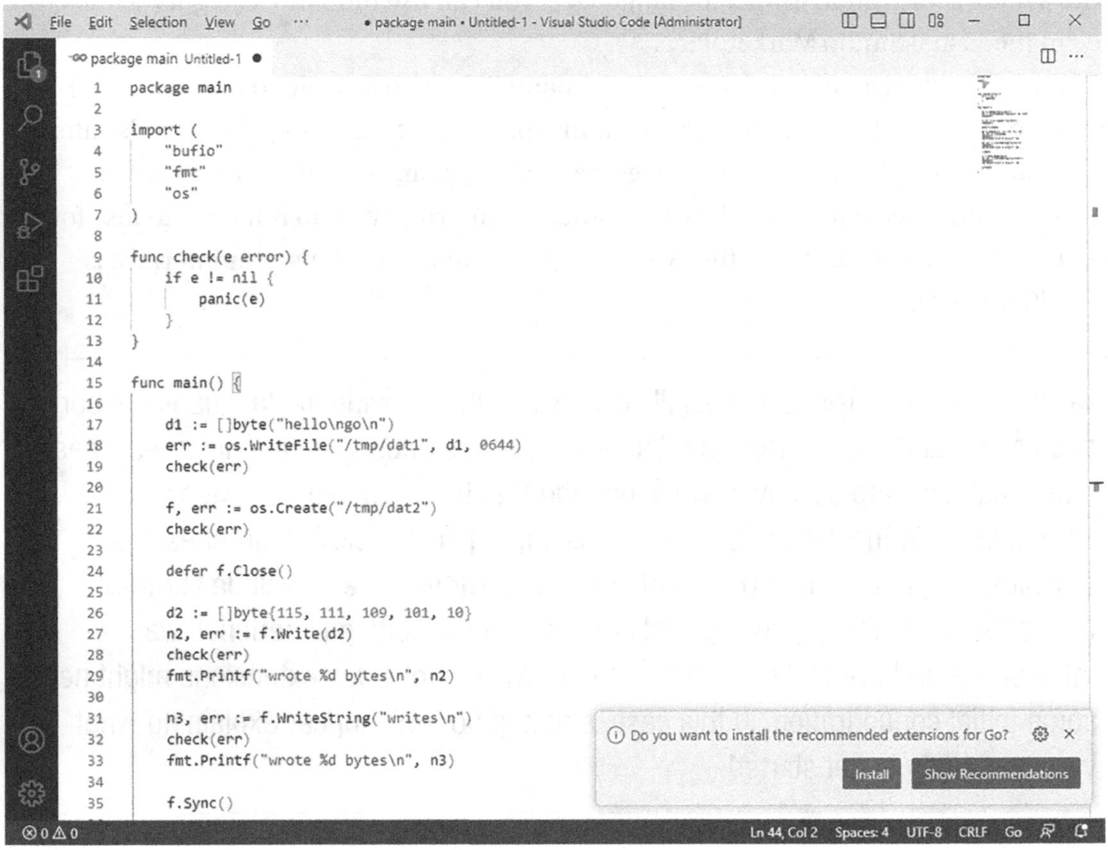

Figure 6-4. *Extension recommendations based on the current file*

You can click Install and Visual Studio Code will automatically install the extension that it thinks to be the most appropriate, or you can click Show Recommendations to see a list of possible extensions. In both cases, the Extensions Bar will open and you will see the list of available recommended extensions, but when you click Install, the proposed extension will be already installing.

Useful Extensions

The Visual Studio Marketplace contains tons of useful extensions, but there is a set that I personally recommend after using Visual Studio Code for a long time in my daily job. Table 6-1 summarizes this set of useful extensions.

Table 6-1. *Recommended Extensions for Visual Studio Code*

Name	Description	Type
C#	C# full language support	Language, debugger, editing
C/C++	C and C++ full language support	Language, debugger, editing
Python	Python full language support	Language, debugger, editing
Language Support for Java	Java full language support	Language, editing
SQL Server (mssql)	SQL Server support	Language, editing, tools
JavaScript Debugger	Node.js debugging with the Chrome browser	Debugger
Debugger for Java	Java debugging support	Debugger
Debugger for Microsoft Edge	JavaScript debugging with the Edge browser	Debugger
.NET Meteor	Mobile development with .NET MAUI	Editing, tools
Node Debug	Debug support for Node.js	Debugger
Visual Studio Keymap	Keyboard shortcuts based on Microsoft Visual Studio	Key binding
Atom Keymap	Keyboard shortcuts based on Atom	Key binding
Notepad++ Keymap	Keyboard shortcuts based on Notepad++	Key binding

(*continued*)

Table 6-1. (*continued*)

Name	Description	Type
Docker	Language support for Dockerfile	Language, editing, tools
vscode-icons	Colored icons for the Explorer Bar	Tools
GitLens	Extend Git integrated features for Visual Studio Code	Tools
PowerShell	PowerShell scripting support	Language, editing, tools
Live Share	Extension for collaborative, real-time development that shares your instance of VS Code with other developers	Tools
Azure Account	Manage your Azure subscription from within VS Code	Tools

As you work with Visual Studio Code on your projects and on the operating system of your choice, you will be able to find and fine-tune extensions that will help you be more productive.

Managing Extensions

The Extensions Bar allows you to quickly manage extensions. It shows the list of installed extensions, as shown in Figure 6-5. Then, for each extension, the button with the gear icon opens a popup menu that contains commands for disabling or uninstalling an extension.

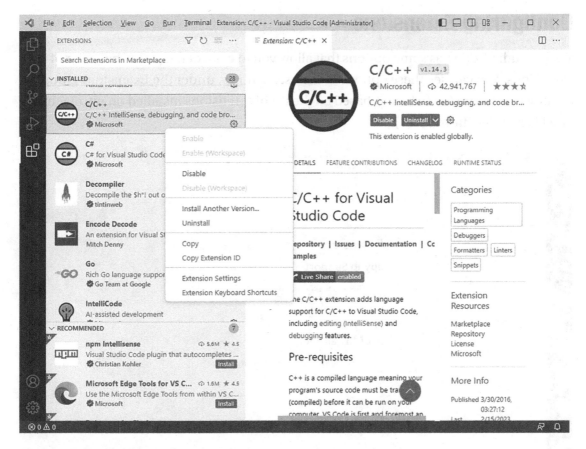

Figure 6-5. *Shortcuts for extension management*

You can also click an extension name, and the detail page will show the Disable and Uninstall buttons. Notice that when you disable or uninstall an extension, in most cases you will need to click a button called Reload (that appears when the extension has been disabled or uninstalled) to refresh the development environment. It is worth mentioning that you can change the default view of the Extensions Bar (displaying the list of installed extensions) by clicking the ... button at the top of the EXTENSIONS group and choosing the Views submenu. You then can choose among different options, such as viewing popular extensions, checking for extension updates, and installing extensions from .vsix files.

Note   Shortcuts for extension management are also available in the Command Palette.

Configuring Extensions

Visual Studio Code has some options that allow you to control the global behavior of extensions. You can see these options in the user settings, under the Extensions group, as shown in Figure 6-6 (which is based on the list of extensions installed on my machine and likely differs from yours).

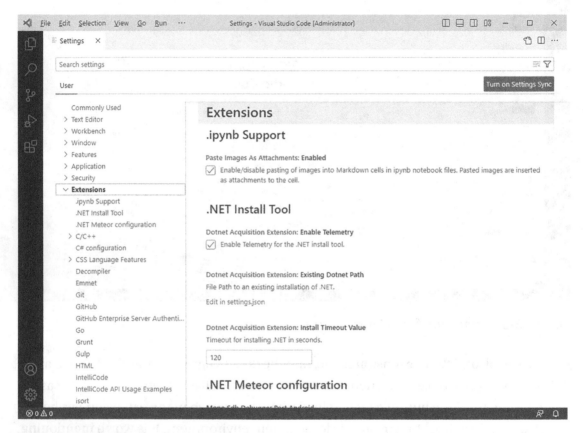

Figure 6-6. *Customizing options about extension management*

There are detailed comments that explain what each option is about. Each extension allows for customizing its own behavior in the user settings and edits can also be done in the well-known `settings.json` file. For instance, suppose you have the C# extension installed. If you look in the user settings, you will find a group called C# Configuration. If you expand this group, you will see the full list of options about the C# extension, which include options for code editing and for tools the extensions add. Figure 6-7 shows these options.

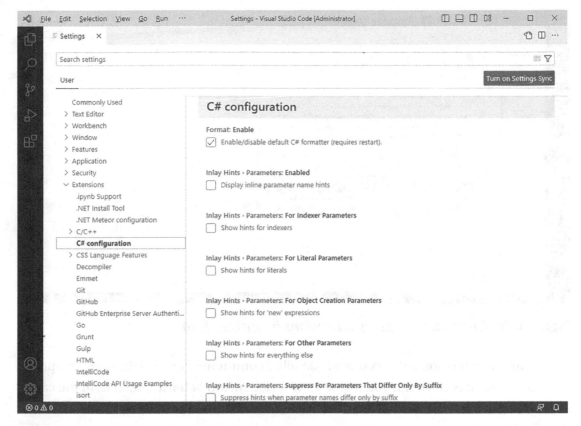

Figure 6-7. *Customizing extension options*

If you want to instead edit extension settings in the `settings.json` file, IntelliSense will simplify your work by showing setting names and a tooltip with the setting description when you scroll the list. Figure 6-8 shows an example where IntelliSense is showing some settings for the C# extension, identified with the `csharp` literal.

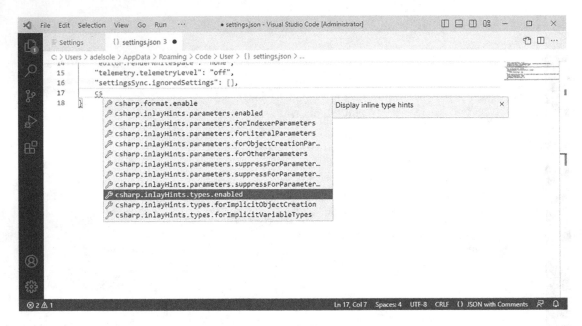

Figure 6-8. *Customizing extension options in settings.json*

Normally, extension authors provide detailed comments that explain what an option is about so that it is easier for you to fine-tune an extension behavior, such as in the case of the C# extension.

Writing Your First Extension

You can build extensions for Visual Studio Code and share them through the Visual Studio Marketplace. You can basically build any type of supported extension, such as language support, editing features, themes, code snippets, debugger adapters, and key bindings. You also need to register as a publisher on the Marketplace, which requires you to have a Microsoft account.

Extensions are usually written with TypeScript and, for most of them, you can use an extension generator such as the Yeoman tool on Node.js. As you can imagine, extension authoring is a complex task and, due to the large number of extension types, it is not possible to provide full guidance in this chapter. However, here you learn how to create your first extension to share custom code snippets. In this way, you learn how to set up the development environment to build extensions and learn the extensibility basics.

Setting Up the Environment

You create Visual Studio Code extensions via special TypeScript and JavaScript projects, and the project structure differs depending on the extension type. As a prerequisite, you need to install Node.js (`https://nodejs.org`), if you have not already done so.

Once Node.js is installed, the simplest way for getting started is installing an extension generator, such as Visual Studio Code Extension Generator tool, also known as Yeoman. Either in a command prompt or in the Terminal, run the following command line:

```
> npm install -g yo generator-code
```

Once installed, create a new folder called `codesnippetsdistilled` and move into the new folder. This will be the location for the new extension project. Then, run the following command:

```
> yo code
```

This will start the Visual Studio Code Extension Generator, as shown in Figure 6-9.

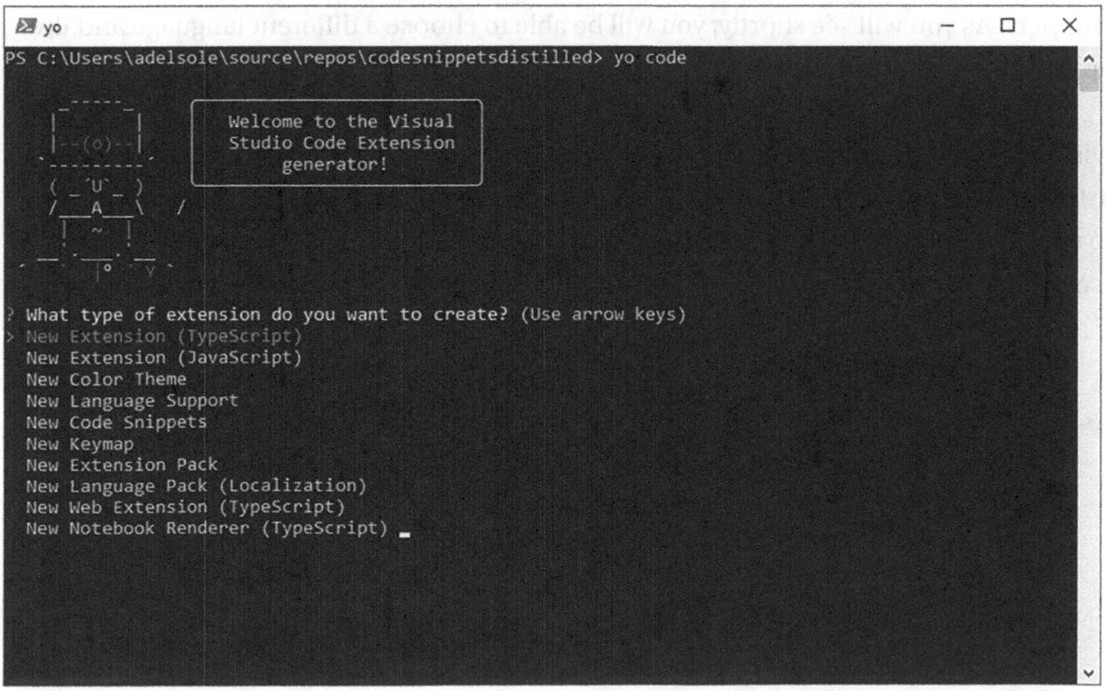

Figure 6-9. *The start options of the Visual Studio Code Extension Generator*

As you can see, the tool allows for creating any type of VS Code extension. You will likely use it at least until you get familiar with the VS Code extensibility API and with the specific project structure.

Fixing PowerShell Script Problems

Depending on your system configuration, launching the Yeoman tool might result in the following PowerShell error: ".ps1 is not digitally signed. The script will not execute on the system."

If this is the case, you can change the script execution policy to be bypassed for the current PowerShell session with the following command line:

```
> Set-ExecutionPolicy -Scope Process -ExecutionPolicy Bypass
```

This is a temporary change and only affects the current session.

Creating an Extension

You will now create an extension that allows for packaging and sharing reusable C# code snippets. As you will see shortly, you will be able to choose a different language and the approach is still the same.

Building an extension of this type is the simplest option and fits well in a book of the Distilled series. If you look at Figure 6-9, you can see a list of extension types. With the arrow keys, move to New Code Snippets and press Enter. At this point, the tool asks you to specify if you want to import existing TextMate or Sublime code snippets from disk (see Figure 6-10).

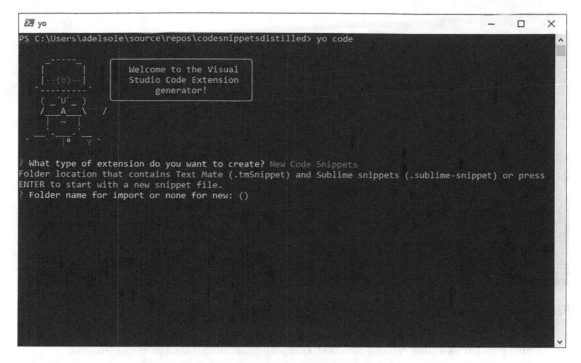

Figure 6-10. Specifying new or existing snippets

This is not mandatory, and you can press Enter to start with a blank code snippet, which is also a good idea for a better understanding of a snippet's structure. You will now get a sequence of questions, and you can answer by keeping Figure 6-11 as a reference.

- For the What's the name of your extensions? question, enter SnippetsDistilled.

- For the What's the identifier of your extension? question, enter snippetsdistilled if it's not automatically entered.

- For the What's the description of your extension? question, enter Reusable C# Code Snippets.

- As the Language id, enter csharp. This is also where you specify a different identifier if your snippets target another language.

- Choose to not initialize a Git repository, also because working with Git is the topic of the next chapter.

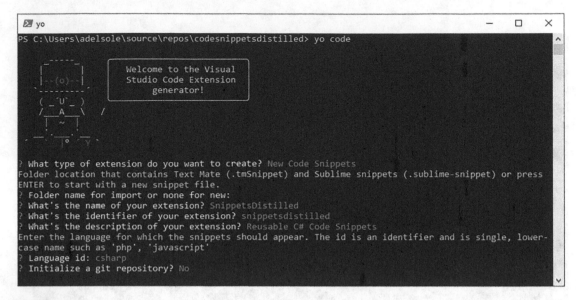

Figure 6-11. The steps required to create the extension

When you press Enter, Visual Studio Code will generate the extension project.

Developing the Extension

Open the extension folder in Visual Studio Code, as you would do any other folder. Figure 6-12 shows how it appears.

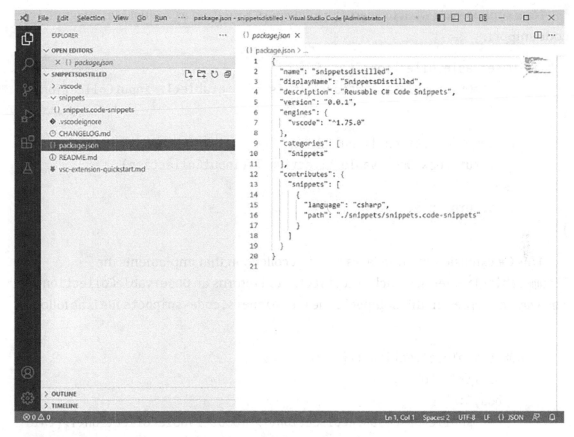

Figure 6-12. *The extension project opened in VS Code*

Following is a summary of the relevant points:

- The package.json file contains the extension metadata and the
  information about the included code snippets and their source.

- The README.md file is a Markdown file that you will likely upload as
  the extension documentation.

- The CHANGELOG.md file is a Markdown file where you can write any
  changes with the previous version.

- The vsc-extension-quickstart.md file is a Markdown file that
  provides useful information for the extension development and testing.

- The snippets subfolder contains a file called snippets.code-
  snippets and is the place where you enter your reusable code
  snippets.

Now suppose you want to share the following C# method as a reusable, integrated code snippet:

```
public ObservableCollection<T>
        ToObservableCollection<T>(this IEnumerable<T> inputCollection)
{

    if (inputCollection != null)
        return new ObservableCollection<T>(inputCollection);
    else
        return null;
}
```

This C# extension method takes an input collection that implements the IEnumerable<T> interface, such as a List<T>, and returns an ObservableCollection<T>. The way you represent this snippet inside the snippets.code-snippets file is as follows:

```
{
    "ToObservableCollection": {
        "prefix": "obs",
        "body": [
            "public ObservableCollection<T> ToObservableCollection<T>(this
            IEnumerable<T> ${0:inputCollection}) {",
            "\tif (${0:inputCollection} != null)",
            "\t\treturn new ObservableCollection<T>(${0:inputColle
            ction});",
            "\telse",
            "\t\treturn null;",
            "}"
        ],
        "description": "Convert to ObservableCollection"
    },
}
```

ToObservableCollection is the snippet identifier. The prefix, with value obs, represents the keyboard shortcut that you type in the editor to generate code based on the snippet. The body element contains the actual code snippet, and it requires the following explanations:

- You can associate variable tags so that the code editor highlights occurrences of the same variable or identifier. In the previous code, this is represented by the ${0:inputCollection} tag. Tags can be added as sequences (e.g., ${0}, ${1}, ${2}, and so on).

- Indentation is represented with the \t escape sequence.

- The body of each code snippet is an array of strings. This is why there is a string for each line of the snippet itself.

If you create your code snippets with a dedicated editor such as TextMate or .Sublime, you can create snippet extensions more easily and with fewer manual steps.

Running the Extension

You can quickly test your extension by choosing Run ➤ Start Debugging.

Note   Debugging in Visual Studio Code has not been explained yet; however, you do not need to know the details right now. At the moment, you simply need to know that you start debugging the extension to see how it works in an isolated instance and that you will be able to use all the TypeScript and JavaScript debugging tools that you learn about in Chapter 9.

This will start a new instance of Visual Studio Code. A new C# file should be automatically generated. If this does not happen, create a new text file and select C# as the language. At this point, you can immediately use your extension by typing the snippet prefix, as you can see in Figure 6-13.

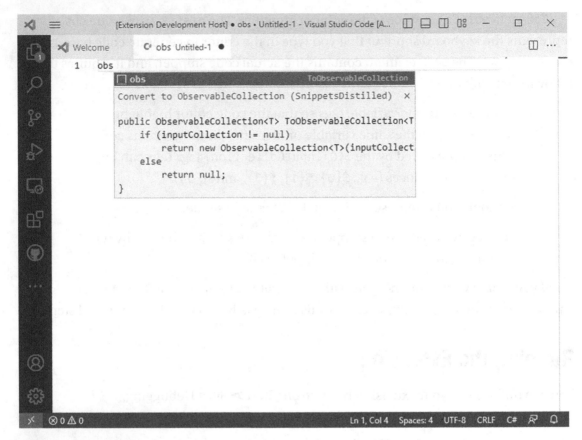

***Figure 6-13.** Previewing the new code snippet via IntelliSense*

You can press Tab and the code snippet will be added to the editor, as demonstrated in Figure 6-14.

***Figure 6-14.** Adding the snippet to the code file*

Notice how the occurrences of the `inputCollection` identifier have been highlighted because of the tags you added to the JSON previously. This also makes the developer quickly understand which identifiers can be renamed.

Packaging Extensions

When you have completed the extension development and testing, you can share your work. The appropriate way to do this is by generating a VSIX installer package that can be shared or published to the Visual Studio Marketplace.

You package extensions via the Visual Studio Code Extensions tool, often referred to as `vsce`. This tool must be installed with the following command line:

```
> npm install -g @vscode/vsce
```

Now you can package your extensions, but you first need to edit the `README.md` file in your extension project. You need at least to remove the following line:

```
This is the README for your extension "snippetsdistilled".
```

The reason is that the packaging tool wants to prevent you from shipping the extension with the auto-generated documentation. This is obviously arguable, but it is the way it works. At this point you can type the following command inside an instance of the Terminal. Make sure that the current folder is the project folder:

```
> vsce package
```

Figure 6-15 shows the `vsce` output (as well as the `README.md` file with the changes mentioned previously).

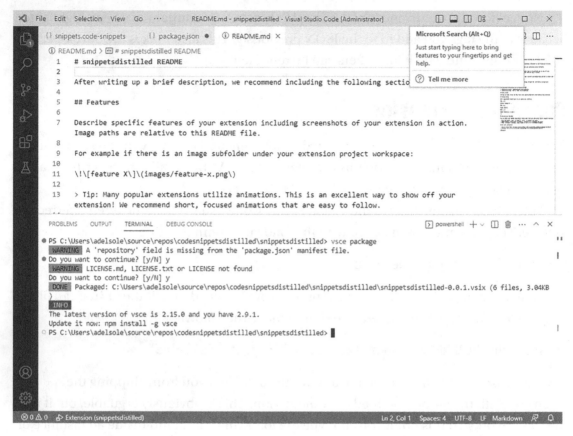

Figure 6-15. *Packaging the VS Code extension*

The vsce tool has generated a .vsix package inside the project folder. This file can either be installed manually or published to the Visual Studio Marketplace. Publication requires setting up an account plus access tokens and other support tasks, so this is not covered here. You can refer to the Publishing Extension page of the documentation (https://code.visualstudio.com/api/working-with-extensions/publishing-extension), but at least you have your package ready.

Extension Development Summary

There is much more about extension development, but there are steps and concepts that are common to all the extension types, such as:

- Generating a project via Yeoman, the Visual Studio Code Extension Generator.

- Debugging and testing with the integrated tools.

- Generating packages via the `vsce` tool.

In addition, building extensions like custom languages, commands, and other integrated tools requires knowledge of the extensibility points, thoroughly described in the Extension API page of the documentation (`https://code.visualstudio.com/api`). This should be your starting point if you want to discover more about building sophisticated extensions.

Summary

Extensibility is a key feature in Visual Studio Code, because it allows you to add power to the development environment. Extensions can add new languages (with or without rich editing support), debuggers, keyboard shortcuts, themes, code snippets, and tools. You can install extensions from the Visual Studio Marketplace or from within Visual Studio Code, through the Extensions Bar or the Command Palette.

Visual Studio Code can also provide extension recommendations based on the context, such as when you open a file written in a language for which there is no built-in support. Visual Studio Code makes also makes managing extensions simple, with shortcuts to disable and uninstall extensions and the capability to configure extensions' behavior via the user settings file. In the last part of the chapter, you learned how to start developing and publishing extensions, using the Visual Studio Code Extension Generator tool. In the next chapter, you see how to leverage extensions to add features to Visual Studio Code to another core feature that makes it a step forward compared to its competitors: version control with Git.

CHAPTER 7

Source Control with Git

Writing software often involves collaboration. This is true whether you are part of a development team, are involved in open-source projects, or are an individual developer who has interactions with customers. Microsoft strongly supports both collaboration and open-source, so Visual Studio Code provides an integrated source control system that is based on Git and can be extended to other providers.

This chapter describes not only all the integrated tools for collaboration over source code from within Visual Studio Code that are available out of the box, but also explains how to use extensions that you will find very useful on the job. These extensions will help you better review your code and push your work to services based on Git, such as Azure DevOps and GitHub. Notice that the source control and version control terms are used interchangeably.

Source Control in Visual Studio Code

Visual Studio Code supports different source control providers via extensibility, but it offers integrated support for Git. Git (`https://git-scm.com/`) is a very popular distributed, cross-platform version control engine that makes collaboration easier for small and large projects. One of the reasons for its popularity is that Git is open-source, and therefore it has always been loved by large open-source communities.

Visual Studio Code works with any Git repository, such as GitHub or Azure DevOps, and it provides an integrated way to manage your code commits.

Note that this chapter is not a guide to Git; rather, it is a place to learn how Visual Studio Code works with it, so for further information, visit the Git official page. Also, remember that Visual Studio Code requires the Git engine to be installed locally, so make sure it is available on your machine or download it from `https://git-scm.com/downloads`. To demonstrate how Git version control works with Visual Studio Code, I use a small TypeScript project called Greeter, available in the TypeScript Samples

151

© Alessandro Del Sole 2023
A. Del Sole, *Visual Studio Code Distilled*, https://doi.org/10.1007/978-1-4842-9484-0_7

repository from Microsoft (`https://github.com/Microsoft/TypeScriptSamples`). This is marked as archived but it is good for the purposes of this chapter. You can download the repository on your system as a `.zip` file by clicking the Code button in the repository page, and then clicking the Download ZIP shortcut. When you're ready, you can extract the Greeter subfolder on your disk. Obviously, you are free to use another example or another project of your choice, regardless of the language, but to follow along with the examples in this chapter, you'll need Greeter. At this point, open the Greeter project folder in Visual Studio Code to start collaborating over the source code.

Downloading Other Source Control Providers

As I mentioned earlier, VS Code supports additional source control managers, also referred to as SCM, via extensibility. You can open the Extensions Bar and type **SCM providers** in the search box to find third-party extensions that target other source control engines. Figure 7-1 shows an example of selecting an extension that adds support for the Subversion engine (`https://subversion.apache.org`).

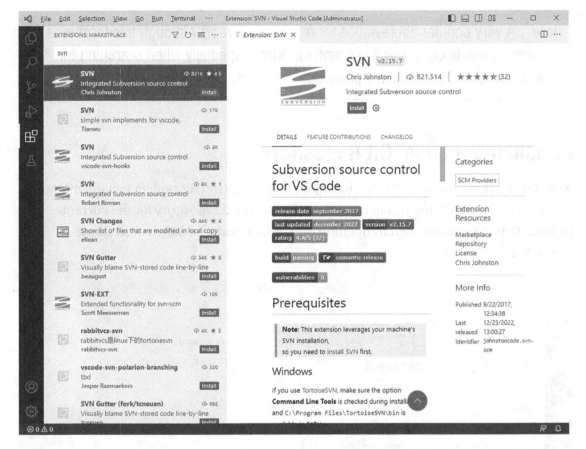

Figure 7-1. *Installing additional source control providers*

Because VS Code provides in-the-box support only for Git, other source control providers are not discussed in this chapter. If you want to install SCM extensions, make sure you refer to the documentation provided by the producer.

Managing Repositories

With Git, version control supports both a local repository and a remote repository to work. This section explains how to create both, supplying information that you will not find in the documentation, especially for remote repositories.

> **Note**   A very popular abbreviation for repository is *repo*. Although this term is not used in this book, you will encounter it often, especially when searching for information about open-source projects.

Initializing a Local Git Repository

As a starting point for the following examples, open the Greeter project you downloaded previously. The first thing you need to do is create a local repository for the current project. This is accomplished by opening the Git tool from the Side Bar, as shown in Figure 7-2.

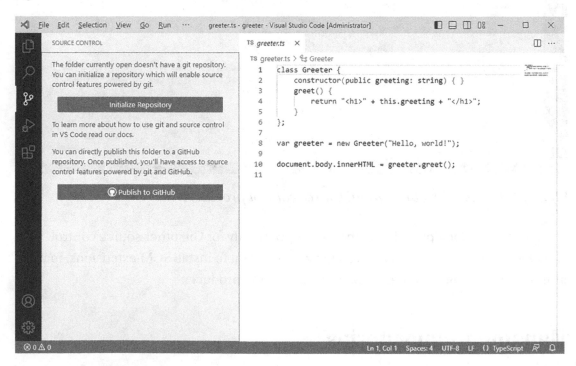

Figure 7-2. *Ready to initialize a local Git repository*

Clicking the Publish to GitHub button allows you to initialize a local repository and publish to GitHub at the same time, but because it is important to understand how the flow works and how to properly authorize VS Code to GitHub, the steps here are split into creating a local repository first and then publishing to the remote one. Click the

Initialize Repository button at the top (see Figure 7-2). Visual Studio Code will initialize the local repository and show the list of files that now are under version control but not committed yet (see Figure 7-3).

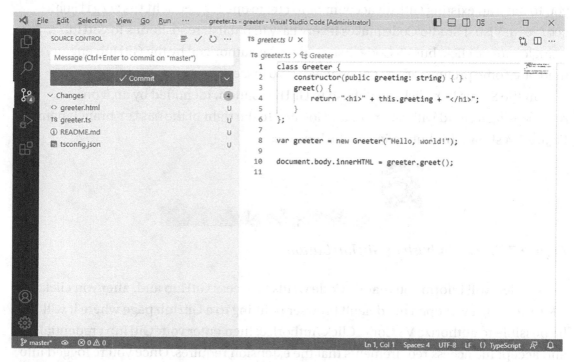

Figure 7-3. *Files are under version control but not committed yet*

Notice how the Git icon shows the number of pending changes. This is an important indicator that you will always see anytime you have pending, uncommitted changes. Write a commit description and then press Ctrl+Enter. You will see a warning message saying that there are no staged files at the moment, and you will be offered to stage and commit all files directly. Staging is discussed in the next section, so for now click Yes. At this point, files are committed to the local repository, and the list of pending changes will be cleaned. Now there is a problem: you need a remote repository, but the official documentation does not describe how to associate one to VS Code. The next section explains how to accomplish this.

Creating a Remote Repository

Visual Studio Code works with any Git repository. There are plenty of platforms that use Git as the version control engine, but probably the most popular platforms are GitHub, Atlassian Bitbucket, and Microsoft Azure DevOps. This section shows you how to create a remote repository on GitHub. I chose GitHub not only because of the popularity of the platform but also because Visual Studio Code includes a built-in extension called GitHub that is expressly designed to simplify the workflow against GitHub itself. This requires you to have an existing GitHub account or to create one for free at `https://github.com/join`. Visual Studio Code makes it very easy to publish repositories to GitHub with a single mouse click, but VS Code first needs to be authorized by the GitHub engine, so there are some preliminary steps you need to do just once.

On the Status Bar, click the Publish to GitHub button, identified by an icon representing a cloud with an arrow and located to the right of the `master` branch name. Figure 7-4 shows this button inside the blue box.

Figure 7-4. *The Publish to GitHub button*

An alert will inform you that VS Code wants to access GitHub and, after you click OK to accept, it will open the default browser pointing to a GitHub page where it will be possible to authorize VS Code. Click Authorize, then enter your GitHub credentials and accept the access requirements that the extension requires. Once you're logged into GitHub, the browser will ask for your confirmation to open Visual Studio Code.

VS Code will ask your permission to open an URL passed by the browser and that is required to log in from the development environment. Allow this, so that Visual Studio Code can complete the authentication process automatically. At this point VS Code is enabled to access GitHub. As I mentioned previously, the steps required to authorize Visual Studio Code need to be done only once.

Because the project folder has been created from a web source (you downloaded the sample code), Visual Studio Code marks the repository as unsafe, as shown in Figure 7-5.

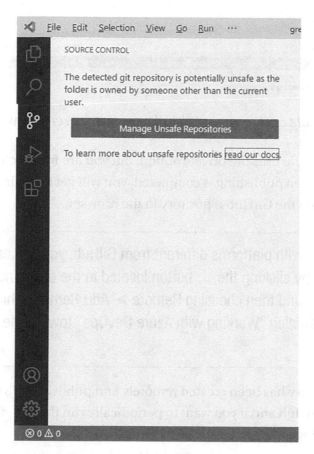

Figure 7-5. *VS Code detects an unsafe repository*

According to the documentation, Visual Studio Code marks a repository as unsafe when it resides in a folder that is owned by multiple users. However, this can also happen with downloaded files. You can click Manage Unsafe Repositories and, from the Command Palette, select the name of the repository you want to mark as safe (greeter in this case).

At this point you need to click the Publish to GitHub button again on the Status Bar. VS Code shows a text box containing the repository name; by default, this is based on the current folder name, but you can write a different name. It also provides two options to publish the repository to GitHub based on the folder name, as you can see in Figure 7-6. One option is to publish to a private repository, and the other option is to publish to a public repository.

Figure 7-6. *Available options to publish the repository remotely*

The current example uses the private option, but you are free to choose whichever option you prefer. When publishing is completed, you will get a confirmation message and an option to open the GitHub repository in the browser.

Note   If you work with platforms different from GitHub, you can easily associate a remote repository by clicking the … button located in the upper-right corner of the Source Control Bar and then choosing Remote ➤ Add Remote. This is explained in practice in the section "Working with Azure DevOps" toward the end of this chapter.

Once the repository has been created remotely and published, VS Code will ask if you want to open GitHub and if you want to periodically run the `git fetch` command to pull any remote changes automatically (see Figure 7-7).

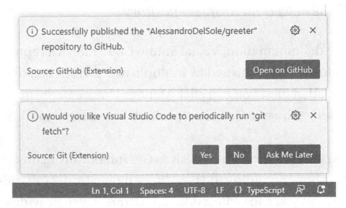

Figure 7-7. *VS Code offers to open GitHub and to run git commands*

You are free to open GitHub and to click Yes on the second prompt. If you are not sure and want to get more information, you can always click Ask Me Later.

Handling File Changes

Git locally tracks changes on your code files, and the Git icon in VS Code shows the number of files with pending changes. This number is actually updated only after you save your files. In VS Code, handling file changes is very straightforward. In Figure 7-8 you can see how the number of pending changes is highlighted in the Git icon but also how files that have changes are marked with a brown M (where M stands for Modified), whereas deleted files are marked with a red D (where D stands for Deleted). Note that these markers are also visible in the Explorer Bar, and the total number of changes appears on the Git icon of the Explorer Bar.

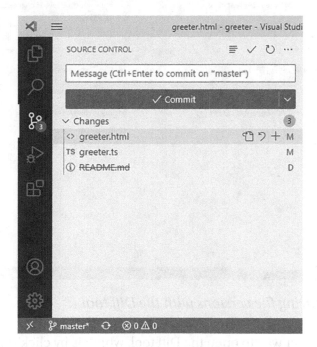

Figure 7-8. *Identifying the number of pending changes*

By clicking a file in the list, you can see the differences between the current and previous versions of the file with the Diff tool. Figure 7-9 shows an example.

The left side shows the old version and the right side shows the new one. The line highlighted in red represents code that has been removed, whereas the line highlighted in green represents new code. Specific changes inside the lines of code are represented with darker shades of red and green, as you can see for the words `world` and `developers` in Figure 7-9. This is a very important tool when working with any version control engine.

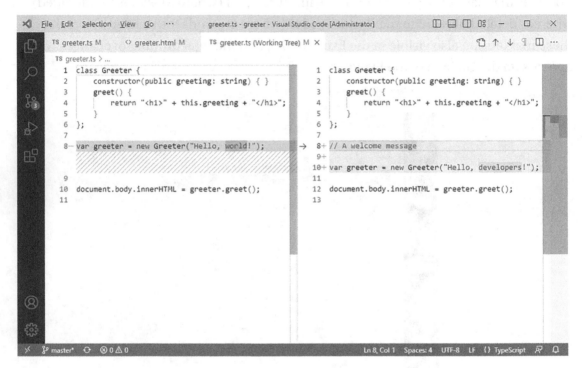

Figure 7-9. *Comparing file versions with the Diff tool*

There is also another way to open the Diff tool, which is by clicking the Open Changes button at the upper-right corner of the active editor. This button is only available when the file has tracked changes.

Staging Changes

You can promote files for staging, which means marking them as ready for the next commit. This is actually not mandatory, as you can commit directly, but it is useful to have a visual representation of your changes. You can stage a file by simply clicking the + symbol near its name, or you can stage all files by right-clicking the Changes title and then choosing Stage All Changes or clicking the plus icon on the bar. Visual Studio Code organizes staged files into a logical container, as you can see in Figure 7-10. Similarly, you can unstage files by clicking the – symbol.

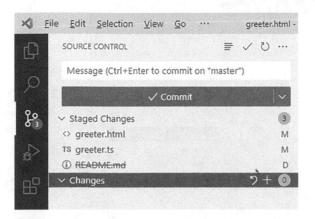

Figure 7-10. *The view of staged and unstaged changes*

The workflow based on staging is very convenient, because if you no longer want to commit a file, you can simply unstage it before the code gets committed to the repository.

Managing Commits

The ... button provides access to additional actions, such as Commit, Sync, Pull, Stash, and Pull (Rebase). Figure 7-11 shows the full list of built-in Git synchronization commands available in VS Code. Notice that some of them are grouped into submenus, such as the Pull, Push submenu, which you can see in Figure 7-11.

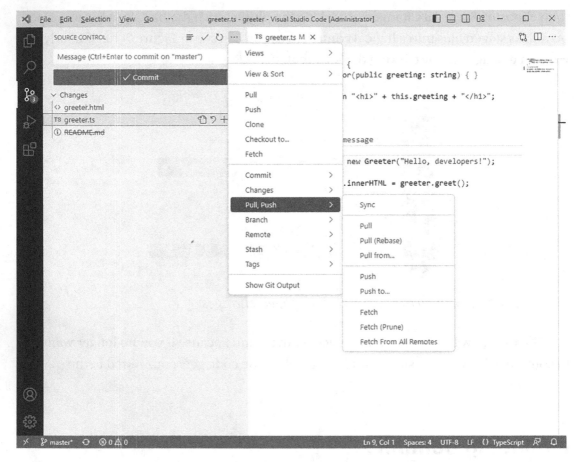

Figure 7-11. *Shortcuts to commit and synchronize changes*

When you are satisfied with your work on the source code, you can choose the Commit ➤ Commit All command to commit your changes. Remember that this action commits files to the local repository. Also, before you commit, you might want to check staged and nonstaged changes so that the code is committed without missing any files. You have to use the Push command to send changes to the remote repository.

You also have an option to undo the last commit and revert to the previous version with the Commit ➤ Undo Last Commit command. Pull and Pull (Rebase), both in the Pull, Push submenu, allow you to merge a branch into another branch; **Pull** is nondestructive and merges the history of the two branches, while Pull (Rebase) rewrites the project history by creating new commits for each commit in the local branch. The Sync command in the same submenu performs a Pull first and then a Push operation, so that both the local and remote repositories are synchronized.

There is also a command called Stash, which allows you to store modified tracked changes and staged changes in a cache, so that you can switch to another branch while having unfinished work on the current branch. Then, with the Pop Latest Stash and Pop Stash commands, under the Stash submenu, you can retake the latest version of your unfinished work or a specific version of the unfinished work, respectively.

Every time you work with Git commands, such as Commit and Push, Visual Studio Code redirects the output of the Git command line to the Output panel. Figure 7-12 shows an example.

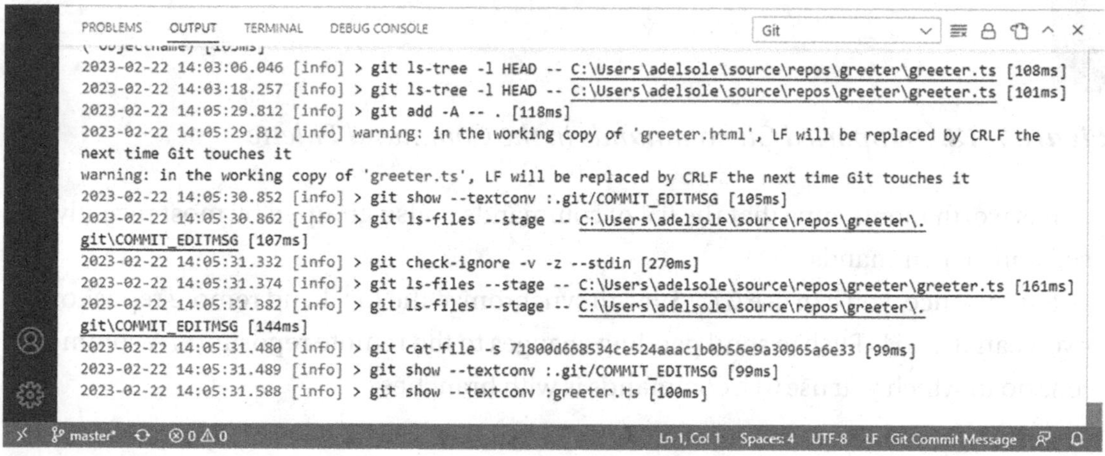

Figure 7-12. *Messages from the Git command line are shown in the Output panel*

You need to select Git from the drop-down menu in the Output panel in order to see the Git output. You can also open the Output panel using the Show Git Output command from the popup menu shown in Figure 7-11.

Working with the Git Command-Line Interface

The Command Palette has support for specific Git commands that you can type as if you were in a command-line terminal. Figure 7-13 shows a partial list of available Git commands, displayed by typing **Git** in the Command Palette. The full list of commands is quite long and cannot be totally included in Figure 7-13, but you can type **Git** on your own computer and scroll the list to see all available commands.

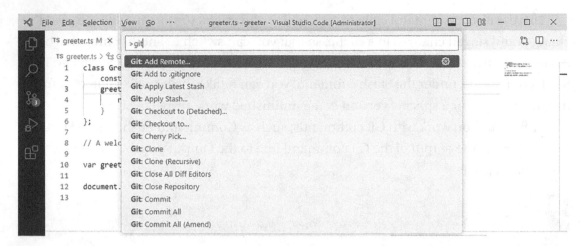

Figure 7-13. *Supported Git commands in the Command Palette*

It is worth mentioning that the list of commands is also grouped by most recently used and all commands.

For instance, you can use `Git Sync` to synchronize the local and remote repositories, or you can use `Git Push` to send pending changes to the remote repository. A common scenario in which you use `Git` commands is with branches.

Creating and Managing Branches

For a better understanding of what a branch is, suppose you have a project that, at a certain point of its lifecycle, goes to production. You need to continue the development of your project, but you do not want to do it over the code you have written so far.

You can create two histories by using a branch. When you create a repository, you also get a default branch called `master`.

Note   There have been changes in GitHub, as well as in Azure DevOps, so if you first create a remote repository on this platform directly, the main branch is no longer called `master`, but instead is called `main`. This change is specific to GitHub, so if you create a Git repository either locally or on other platforms, you still get the `master` branch.

Continuing with the example, the master branch could contain the code that has gone to production, and now you can create a new branch, such as development, based on master but different from it. In Visual Studio Code, you have different options to create a new branch: The first option is to create a branch from the Command Palette by typing **Git branch**, selecting the Git: Create Branch option, and specifying a new branch name, such as develop.

Note   develop is a shortening for development. Creating a branch named develop is intentional because it is how a development branch is called in the so-called GitFlow (http://datasift.github.io/gitflow/ IntroducingGitFlow.html) approach. If you join a team that uses GitFlow, you will likely work on the develop branch.

This creates a new branch locally, based on master. The second option is to click the current branch name in the Status Bar (master in this case) and then click the Create New Branch command (see Figure 7-14). Enter the new branch name and press Enter.

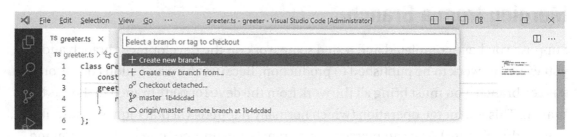

Figure 7-14. *Creating a branch*

In addition, you can use the Create New Branch From command to create a new branch from a branch that is not the active one. When a new branch is created, the Status Bar shows it as the active branch; when you are ready, you can publish the new branch to the remote repository with the Publish Branch button, represented by the cloud icon (see Figure 7-15).

Figure 7-15. *The new branch is set as active and ready to be published*

Switching to a Different Branch

Switching to a different branch is very easy. Simply click the name of the active branch in the Status Bar, and VS Code displays the list of branches, as shown in Figure 7-16. If the repository already has a remote branch, it will also be visible in the list and recognizable by the origin/ prefix.

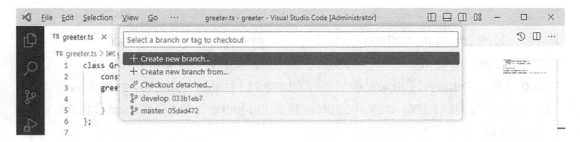

Figure 7-16. *Selecting a different branch*

Click the desired branch, and VS Code checks it out and sets it as the active branch.

Merging from a Branch

Suppose you have completed and tested some work on the development branch and you want this work to be published to production. Because the production code is on the master branch, you must bring all the work from the development branch to the master branch. This is a merge operation (which normally happens via pull requests, described later in this chapter). You can merge from a branch into another one via the Command Palette, using the Git: Merge Branch command. VS Code shows the list of branches, and you need to select the branch you want to merge from into the current branch (see Figure 7-17).

Note   Remember that the branch that receives the merge is the active branch, so make sure you have switched to the proper branch before starting a merge operation.

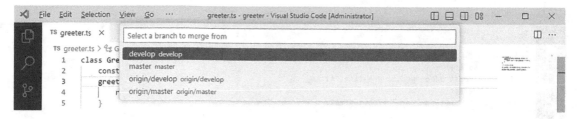

Figure 7-17. *Merging from a branch*

In the example, some changes were made and pushed to the development branch, then the master branch has been selected as the active one and changes from development will be merged into master.

Once the merge operation is completed, remember to push your changes to the remote repository.

Resolving Merge Conflicts

When you merge branches in which the same code files were modified, Visual Studio Code leverages the Git tooling to combine the different edits into one code inside the target files. However, sometimes VS Code cannot automatically combine the edits, in which case it raises a *merge conflict*. If this happens, VS Code shows an editor where it highlights the code on which a conflict exists, displaying the current version and the incoming version with different colors, as you can see in Figure 7-18, which shows an example of one conflict due to edits on the same line of code in different branches.

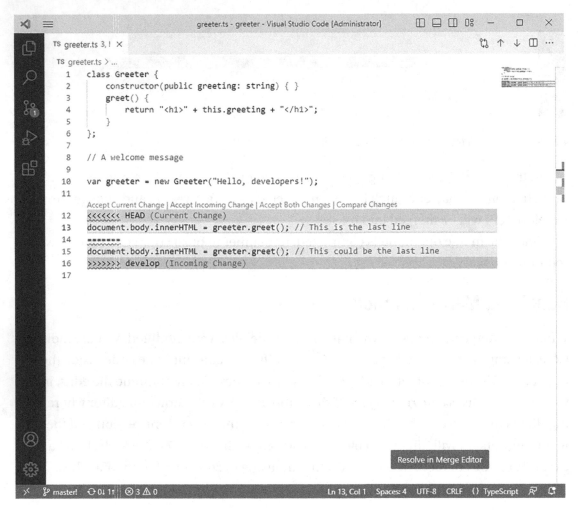

Figure 7-18. *Resolving merge conflicts*

Click the Resolve in Merge Editor button. At this point, Visual Studio Code compares changes at the top of the view and it allows for previewing the merged code at the bottom. Figure 7-19 shows how the Merge Editor appears at this point.

Figure 7-19. *Resolving merge conflicts*

You can resolve conflicts by clicking one of the available choices placed at the top of the line of code:

- *Accept Incoming*: You resolve the conflict by using changes in the incoming branch.

- *Accept Current*: You resolve the conflict by keeping changes done in the current branch.

- *Accept Combination*: You resolve the conflict by combining both changes.

When ready, click the Complete Merge button. As you can see, Visual Studio Code gives you an integrated and user-friendly way to resolve conflicts without the need to deal with complex Git command lines.

Hints About Rebasing Branches

Among the available commands for Git in Visual Studio Code, you will find one called Rebase. In Git, rebasing still allows you to include the changes made by a branch in another branch, but rebasing and merging accomplish this task differently.

More specifically, rebasing does not create overlaps between branches but rather appends code changes to the end of the target branch, which means that the history of the code is easier to understand, even if there is a need to frequently incorporate the commits of one branch into the other.

Rebasing therefore offers the possibility of accessing a more linear history, because, unlike merging, it allows you to not incorporate unnecessary commits into the target branch.

However, rebasing should be used with care. For example, if another team member is working on the same branch, it is preferable to avoid rebasing because this might lead to the duplication of the branch instead of merging changes.

Deleting Branches

Sometimes you might have branches that have been created only for testing some code and that are not really necessary in the application lifecycle management. In this case, in the Command Palette, you can use the Git: Delete Branch command.

With a user interface like what you see in Figure 7-17, VS Code shows the list of branches. Select the branch you want to delete and press Enter. Remember that the active branch cannot be deleted, and you first need to switch to a different branch. Also, remember that you can delete remote branches only if you created them.

Adding Power to the Git Tooling with Extensions

The integrated tools for Git cover all the needs that you, as a developer, may have when working with local and remote repositories to manage your source code, but there are extensions that provide additional power to the integrated tools.

This section describes the most useful free extensions that will improve your collaboration experience in Visual Studio Code.

Git History

Git History is a free extension that enables you to view the history of your source code, such as information and author about each commit and that can display how a file has gone through branches; plus it adds commands that make it easier to manage your code against Git. After you have installed the extension, you can right-click a file inside the folder view of Explorer Bar and select Git: View File History.

Figure 7-20 shows an example based on a file that has three commits. If available, the view shows the branches where the file has been included, comments and author for the commit, and the commit ID. The view also allows for searching and filtering contents by branch and author. Local branches are highlighted in green and remote branches in red.

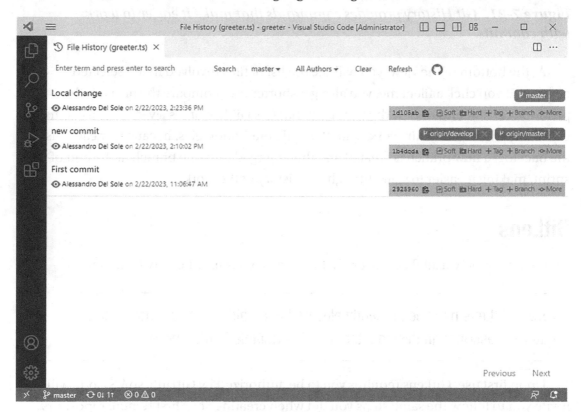

Figure 7-20. *Viewing the history of commits with Git History*

Note   If the commit author has associated a picture to the Git credentials, Git History shows the picture near the author name.

If you click the More shortcut at the right of each commit, a menu appears showing a number of very useful commands that make it easier to work with commits (see Figure 7-21).

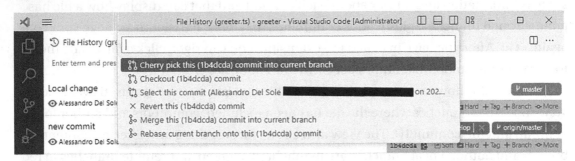

Figure 7-21. *Git History provides commands that make it easier to work with commits*

At the bottom of the view, you will see the list of files involved in the selected commit. If you click a filename, you also get shortcuts to compare the file with the previous version and to view the history of that file. Git History is a very useful extension, especially when your team works with the Agile methodologies, because for each task in the backlog, a new branch is created and then merged into one branch at the end of the sprint, making it easier to walk through the history of the work.

GitLens

Another extremely useful extension that will boost your productivity is GitLens.

Note   GitLens has been recently elevated to a paid extension; however, the features described in this chapter are still available in trial mode.

Upon first use, GitLens requires you to be authorized by GitHub, so VS Code will invite you to follow the same steps you did when creating your first remote repository. GitLens adds to VS Code many features and commands related to Git. For example, GitLens extends the Source Control Bar (see Figure 7-22) with a number of useful Git groups.

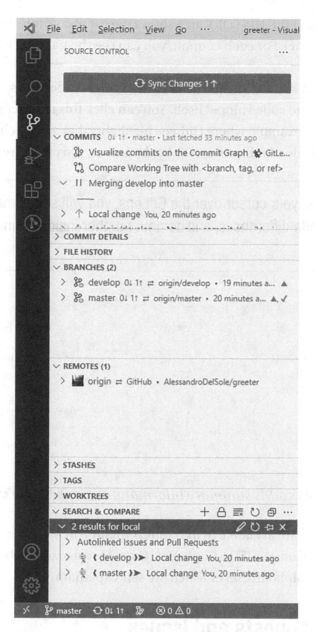

Figure 7-22. *The Source Control Bar extended by GitLens*

The GitLens extension adds several areas to the Source Control Bar. The BRANCHES and REMOTES areas show the list of local and remote branches, respectively, and, for each branch, GitLens displays the list of commits. Each commit can be expanded to see the commit message, the list of files involved in the commit, and an icon that represents the operation made on the file. The STASHES area shows stashed changes with a similar structure (if any). The FILE HISTORY area shows the list of commits for a file (this requires an open editor). For each commit, you can see the name, the author, and the time of last edit.

GitLens also adds summary information about edits made on a specific code snippet, right above the code snippet itself. You can click this to get commit details. Figure 7-23 shows an example where GitLens highlights that a code change to the Greeter class was made four hours earlier by the author, plus the commit details.

Note   If you hover your cursor over the GitLens, you will see some information such as author, code differences, and commit number inside an interactive popup box.

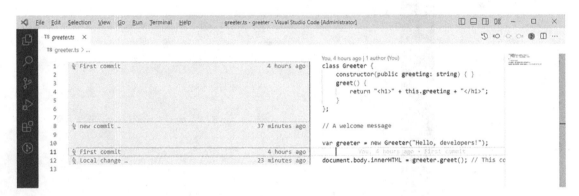

Figure 7-23. *GitLens adds summary information about a code snippet*

Other commands are available in the context menu when you right-click the code editor, such as Copy Commit ID to Clipboard, Copy Message to Clipboard, and Copy Remote File URL to Clipboard, all of which are self-explanatory.

GitHub Pull Requests and Issues

Pull requests in Git make it easier to perform code reviews, while issues enable you to keep track of feedback from other developers. With pull requests, your code is not automatically merged into a branch until someone else on the team reviews the code and accepts it. If you use GitHub for your repositories, an extension called GitHub Pull Requests and Issues is available to introduce support for pull requests in Visual Studio Code. When you first install the extension (and reload the environment), you are asked to sign in to GitHub. To accomplish this, you can either click **Settings** in the Side Bar and then click Sign In To Use GitHub Pull Requests and Issues, or click the Sign In button in the GitHub Bar. Simply follow the same steps you did to authorize GitLens.

After you provide your GitHub credentials and open a folder that is associated to a remote repository hosted on GitHub, you can leverage the GitHub Bar, which you enable by clicking the GitHub icon on the Side Bar. An example of the GITHUB view is provided in Figure 7-24, which refers to an existing pull request detected by the extension and that was opened (checked-out) previously in the repository.

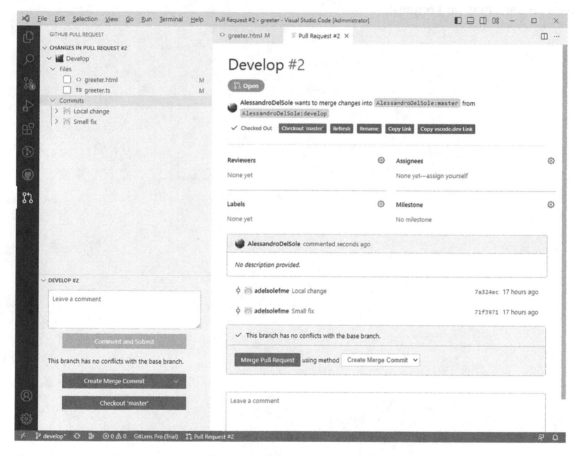

Figure 7-24. *The GitHub Pull Requests view*

When a pull request is detected, a new shortcut called GITHUB PULL REQUEST is added to the Explorer Bar to quickly move to the pull request information. The extension supports both viewing and submitting pull requests, regardless of their source, which can be VS Code, GitHub, or another development environment connected to the same repository. When pull requests are available, you see them listed in the view. If you select a pull request, a new editor window appears showing all the pull request details, and you have the option of adding comments and then closing, rejecting, or approving the pull request (see Figure 7-24).

You can also work on the pull request locally by clicking the Checkout button, which displays it under the Local Pull Request Branches node in the tree view.

New pull requests can be directly created from within Visual Studio Code via the Create Pull Request button available on the toolbar of the GITHUB view. This requires changes on the current branch. Figure 7-25 shows how the user interface appears when you create a new pull request.

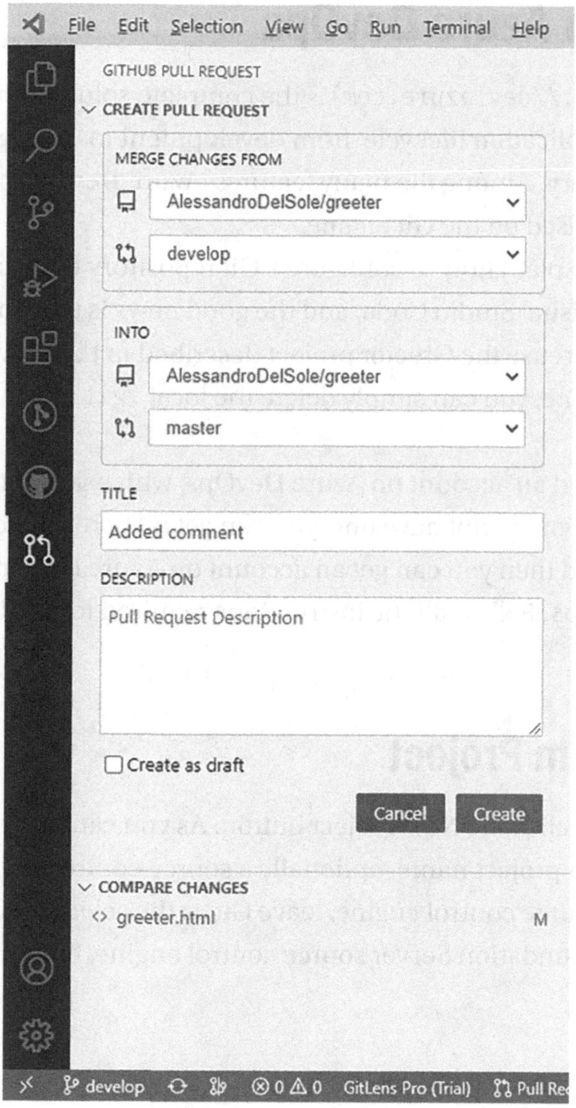

Figure 7-25. *Creating a pull request*

In addition to pull requests, you can create issues from within Visual Studio Code by using the + button located near the ISSUES view at the bottom of the bar, after which you can edit and then save them so that they are associated to the remote repository. Viewing issues happens inside the browser, so when you click the globe icon at the right side of an issue, the default web browser opens the GitHub page for the issue.

This is a very useful extension, especially if you work within Agile teams, but remember it only supports GitHub as the host.

Working with Azure DevOps

Azure DevOps (`https://dev.azure.com`) is the complete solution from Microsoft to manage the entire application lifecycle, from development to testing to continuous integration and delivery. Among the many features, Azure DevOps provides source control capabilities based on the Git engine.

In this section, I explain how to configure a Git repository that you can use for source control with Visual Studio Code, and the good news is that you do not need any extensions. I also reuse the Greeter project described in the previous sections. If you want to do the same, you can simply delete the local `.git` folder located under the project folder.

You obviously need an account on Azure DevOps, which you can create by using a Microsoft account. If you do not have one, you can get a Microsoft account at `https://www.outlook.com`, and then you can get an account on Azure DevOps at `https://aka.ms/SignupAzureDevOps`. Follow all the instructions required to configure your account for the first time.

Creating a Team Project

From the home page, click the New Project button. As you can see in Figure 7-26, you need to supply a team project name, optionally a source control engine, and a work item process. About the source control engine, leave Git as the selection. Azure DevOps also supports the Team Foundation Server source control engine, but this is out of scope.

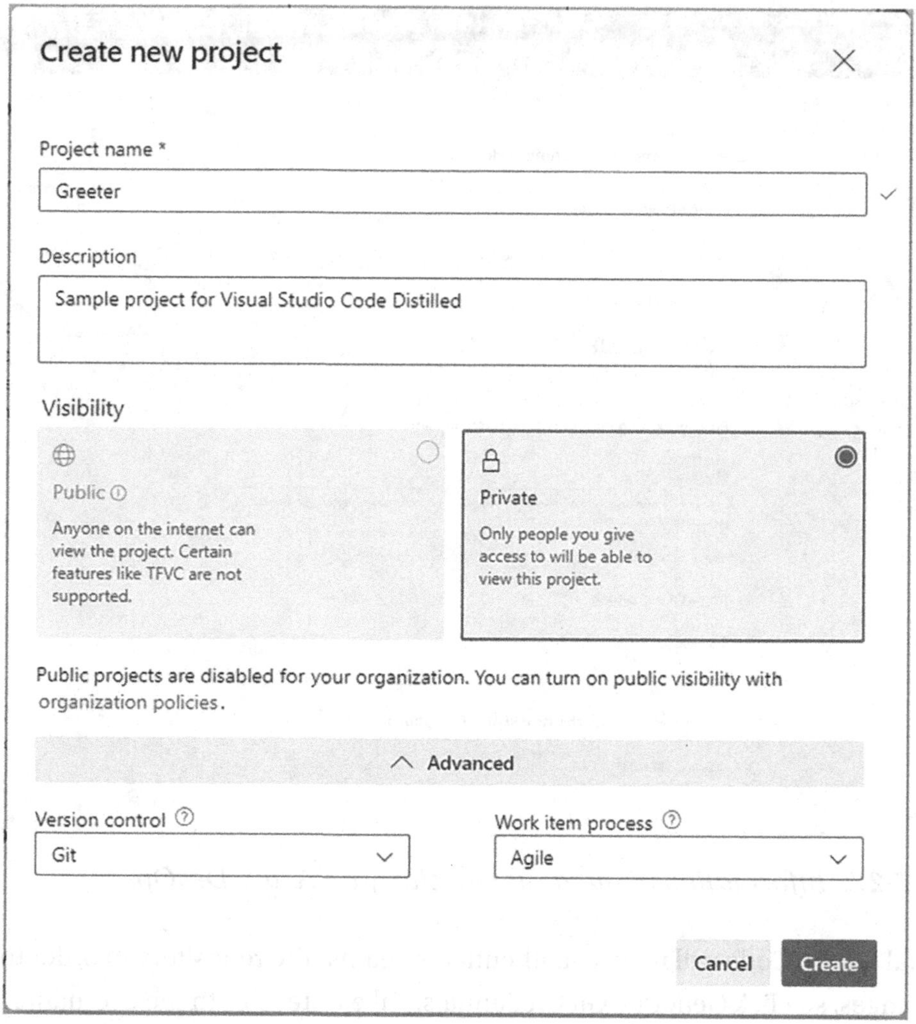

Figure 7-26. *Creating a team project in Azure DevOps*

Enter a project name and click Create. After a few seconds, your new team project will be ready. At this point, the Azure DevOps site shows a page with all the information about your new team project. Now click Repos on the left side of the screen so that you can see all the information about the new Git repository (see Figure 7-27). Notice that the new repository is created with the same name as the new project. Copy the repository URL into the clipboard, as it will be necessary very shortly.

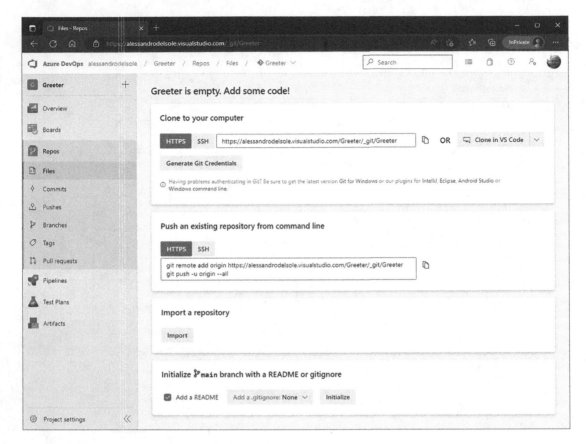

Figure 7-27. *Information about a Git repository on Azure DevOps*

Visual Studio Code will need to authenticate against the repository in order to push changes, so click Generate Git Credentials. Take note of both the username and password that is generated because they will be used shortly, and keep in mind that this is the only option you have to see and store the password.

Now that a remote repository is set up, you have several options to associate it to Visual Studio Code. You could clone the repository to the local machine, or you could even use the Git CLI. However, the simplest yet most effective option is to use the VS Code tools you learned about in the first part of this chapter, as described next.

Connecting Visual Studio Code to a Remote Repository

Go back to Visual Studio Code. The first thing to do is initialize a local Git repository (see the "Initializing a Local Git Repository" section earlier in the chapter for a refresher). Once you have a local repository set up, you can connect it to the remote Azure DevOps repository with little effort.

In the Source Control Bar, click the **...** button, then choose Remote ➤ Add Remote. You first need to specify the name of the remote repository (which is the one you specified in Azure), then you will have the option to enter the URL of the remote repository you created, so paste in the URL and press Enter (see Figure 7-28).

Figure 7-28. *Specifying an Azure DevOps remote repository*

You are also asked to provide a name, which is used as a project identifier. Enter a name of your choice, with no blank spaces, then press Enter. At this point, Visual Studio Code will first ask for your username and then for the password that was generated previously as Git credentials in the DevOps portal. This should no longer be necessary the next time you connect to Azure DevOps. After entering your credentials, Visual Studio Code links the local repository to the remote one, but note that you do not get a confirmation message of the operation completion, only indicators running on the Status Bar.

The very last step is to push the branch to the remote repository, using any of the options described in the first part of this chapter; however, you need to take care about the main branch. As previously mentioned, due to recent changes in Azure DevOps that reflect what GitHub also does, when you create a repository on Azure DevOps, the main branch is now named `main` rather than `master`. The problem is that VS Code still creates a `master` branch. So basically you need to push the `master` branch from VS Code and then create a pull request to merge `master` into `main` so that you can work with the new branch.

Note All these steps are necessary if you connect existing code to a remote repository. If you start from creating a remote repository for a new project, you can clone the repository in VS Code so that you start with the main branch directly.

Once the changes are pushed, they are visible in the Repos view of the Azure DevOps project (see Figure 7-29).

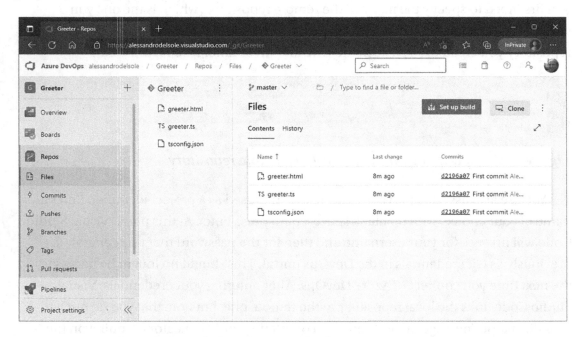

Figure 7-29.   *The source code has been pushed to Azure DevOps*

Now that your code has been pushed remotely, other developers can collaborate on the project. The key point is how easy it has been to set up a connection between a local Git repository and a remote Azure DevOps one, all from within Visual Studio Code.

Summary

Writing software involves collaboration, whether you are part of a development team, involved in open-source projects, or are an individual developer who has interactions with customers. In this chapter, you have explored how Visual Studio Code provides integrated tools to work with Git, the popular open-source and cross-platform source control provider.

You learned how to create a local repository with the Git Bar and how to associate it to a remote repository with a couple of commands from the integrated terminal. You have also learned how to handle file changes, including commits, and how to create and manage branches directly from within the environment. In addition, you were introduced to some useful extensions, such as Git History, Git Lens, and GitHub Pull Requests and Issues, that will boost your productivity by adding important features that every developer needs when it comes to team collaboration. Finally, you learned how easy it is to link a local repository to a remote Git repository hosted on Azure DevOps, the premiere cloud solution from Microsoft to manage the whole application lifecycle. Behind the scenes, Visual Studio Code invokes the Git commands to execute operations over your source code, and it is preconfigured to work with this external tool.

However, Visual Studio Code is not limited to work with a small set of predefined tools; rather, it can be configured to work with basically any external program. This is what you learn about in the next chapter.

CHAPTER 8

Automating Tasks

As described in previous chapter, Visual Studio Code is more than a simple code editor because it enables you to execute operations such as compiling and testing code by running external tools. In this chapter, you learn how VS Code can execute external programs via tasks, by both existing tasks and customized tasks. To run the examples provided in this chapter, you need the following software:

- Node.js, a free and open source JavaScript runtime based on Chrome's JavaScript engine, which you can download from `https://nodejs.org`

- The TypeScript compiler (tsc), which you install via the Node.js command line with the following command:

```
> npm install -g typescript
```

Using Node.js and TypeScript helps you avoid dependencies on the operating system and proprietary development environments. Obviously, all the topics discussed in this chapter apply to other languages and platforms as well.

Understanding Tasks

At its core, Visual Studio Code is a code-centric tool, so it often requires executing external programs to complete operations that are part of the application lifecycle, such as compilation, debugging, and testing.

In Visual Studio Code terminology, integrating with an external program within the flow of the application lifecycle is a *task*. Running a task means not only executing an external program but also getting the output of the external program and displaying it in the most convenient way inside the user interface, such as the integrated Terminal.

© Alessandro Del Sole 2023
A. Del Sole, *Visual Studio Code Distilled*, https://doi.org/10.1007/978-1-4842-9484-0_8

A task is basically a set of instructions and properties represented with the JSON notation, stored in a special file called `tasks.json`. If VS Code can detect the type of project or source code inside the folder, a `tasks.json` file is not always necessary, and VS Code does all the work for you. If VS Code cannot detect the type of project or source code, or if you are not satisfied with the default settings of a task, under the current folder, it generates a hidden subfolder called `.vscode` and, inside this folder, generates a `tasks.json` file. If VS Code can detect the type of project or source code inside the folder, it also prefills the `tasks.json` content with the proper information; otherwise, you need to configure `tasks.json` manually. For a better understanding, I explain tasks that VS Code can detect and that it configures on your behalf, and then I discuss how to create and configure tasks manually.

Tasks Types

There is no limit to how many types of tasks can be available for a source code folder, but the most common are the following:

- *Build task*: A build task is configured to compile the source code, assets, metadata, and resources into a binary or executable file, such as libraries or programs.

- *Test task*: A test task is configured to run unit tests in the source code.

- *Watch task*: A watch task starts a compiler in the so-called watch mode. In this mode, a compiler always watches for changes to any unresolved files after the latest build and recompiles them at every save.

Visual Studio Code provides built-in shortcuts to execute a build task. When new tasks are added, VS Code updates itself to provide shortcuts for the new tasks. Additionally, you can differentiate tasks of the same type. For example, you can have a default build task and other custom build tasks that can be executed only in specific situations.

Running and Managing Tasks

The first approach to understanding tasks in practice is to run existing, preconfigured tasks. For the sake of simplicity, start Visual Studio Code and open the project folder called `simple` from the collection of examples you downloaded previously from the TypeScript Samples repository on GitHub (`https://github.com/Microsoft/TypeScriptSamples`).

Visual Studio Code detects it as a TypeScript project, and therefore it preconfigures some tasks (in the next section, I provide more details about task auto-detection). Now open the Terminal menu. As you can see in Figure 8-1, there are several commands related to tasks.

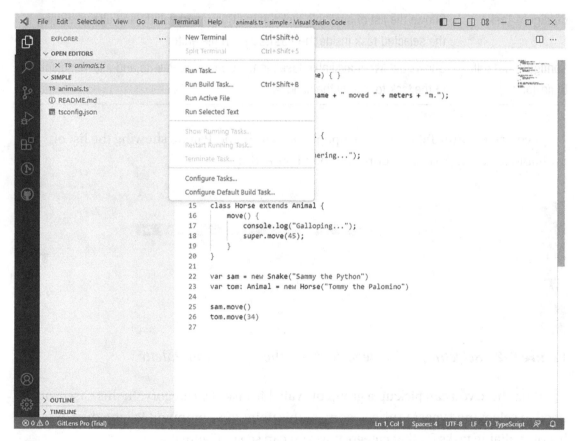

Figure 8-1. *Commands for running and managing tasks in the Terminal menu*

An explanation of each command is provided in Table 8-1.

Table 8-1. *Commands for Task Execution and Management*

Command	Description
Run Task	Shows the list of available tasks in the Command Palette and runs the selected task.
Run Build Task	Runs the default, preconfigured build task (if any).
Terminate Task	Forces a task to be stopped.
Restart Running Task	Restarts the currently running task.
Show Running Tasks	Shows the output of the currently running task in the Terminal panel.
Configure Tasks	Shows the list of available tasks in the Command Palette and allows editing the selected task inside the `tasks.json` file editor.
Configure Default Build Task	Shows the list of available tasks in the Command Palette and allows selection of the task to use as the build task.

If you select Run Task, VS Code opens the Command Palette showing the list of available task categories, as represented in Figure 8-2.

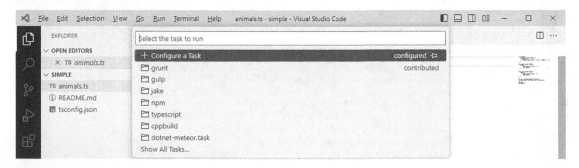

Figure 8-2. *Selecting task categories from the Command Palette*

From here you can pick up a group of available tasks by category. In this case, you need to select the `typescript` category. At this point the Command Palette displays the list of available tasks for that category, as you can see in Figure 8-3.

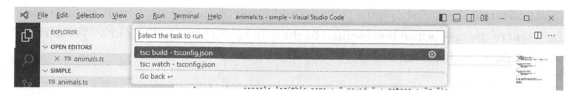

Figure 8-3. *Running a task from the Command Palette*

As you can see, there are two tasks, `tsc: build` and `tsc: watch`, both pointing to the `tsconfig.json` project file. This means that either task will run against the specified file. `tsc` is the name of the command-line TypeScript compiler, whereas `build` and `watch` are two preconfigured tasks whose descriptions were provided previously. If you select `tsc build`, Visual Studio Code launches the `tsc` compiler and compiles the TypeScript code into JavaScript code, as shown in Figure 8-4.

Note   In the case of TypeScript, the build task compiles TypeScript code into JavaScript code. In the case of other languages, the build task generates binaries from the source code. More generally, a build task produces the expected output from the compilation process depending on the language. Also, the list of available tasks varies depending on the type of project or folder you are working with. For example, for .NET projects, only a task called build is available.

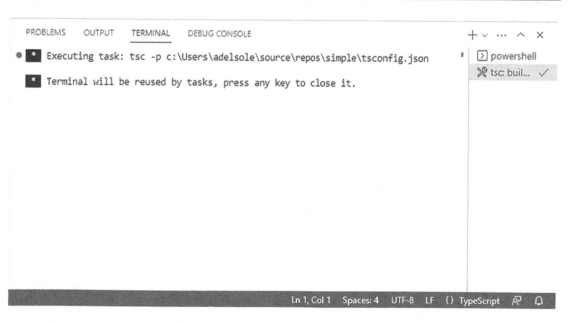

Figure 8-4. *Executing a build task*

The Terminal panel shows the progress and result of the task execution. In this case, the result of the task is also represented by the generation of a `.js` file and a `.js.map` file, now visible in the Explorer Bar.

Note   If the Terminal shows an error message saying that a `.ps1` file could not be loaded because running scripts is disabled on the systems, first try to restart VS Code as an administrator and to repeat the steps. If this does not solve the issue, you need to enable script execution on your machine. You can do this on your own if you are the computer administrator; otherwise, you need to ask the administrator of your network. You can find more detailed information on how to enable script execution depending on your environment and on how to enable specific privileges at `https://go.microsoft.com/fwlink/?LinkID=135170`.

You can stop and restart a task using the Terminate Task and Restart Running Task commands, respectively, both described in Table 8-1. Now suppose there is a critical error that prevents the build task from completing successfully. For demonstration purposes, remove a closing bracket from the code of the `animals.ts` file and run the build task again. At this point, Visual Studio Code will show the detailed log from the `tsc` tool in the Terminal panel, as shown in Figure 8-5, describing the error and the line of code that caused it.

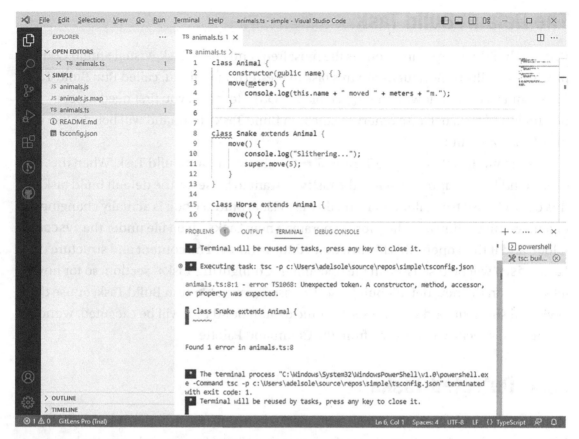

Figure 8-5. *Visual Studio Code shows the output of the external tool in a convenient way*

In the real world, this error probably would not happen because you have the Problems panel and red squiggles in the code editor that both highlight the error. But this is actually an example of how Visual Studio Code integrates with an external tool and shows its output directly in the Terminal panel, helping to solve the problem with the most detailed information possible. With tasks, the Terminal also shows specific annotations. For example, it highlights with red squiggles the root of the code that raised the error, and it shows icons close to each command in the task and that represent the status of the command. For example, invoking the `tsc` compiler raised an error and the corresponding line shows an error icon.

The Default Build Task

Because building the source code is the most frequently used task, Visual Studio Code provides a built-in shortcut to run this task in the Terminal menu, called Run Build Task (Ctrl+Shift+B on Windows and ⇧+⌘+B on macOS). However, you first need to set a default build task, because otherwise the Run Build Task command will behave like the Run Task command.

To accomplish this, choose Terminal ➤ Configure Default Build Task. When the Command Palette appears, select the task you want to be set as the default build task. In this case, choose tsc build. When you do this, Visual Studio Code is actually changing its default configuration and therefore generates a new `tasks.json` file under the `.vscode` folder, and it then opens this file in a new editor window. The content and structure of `tasks.json` will be discussed in the upcoming "Configuring Tasks" section, so for now let's focus on the new default build task. Choose Terminal ➤ Run Build Task, or use the keyboard shortcut, and you will see how the default build task will be executed, without the need to specify it every time from the Command Palette.

Auto-Detected Tasks

Visual Studio Code can auto-detect tasks for the following environments: Grunt, Gulp, Jake, and Node.js. Auto-detecting tasks means that Visual Studio Code can analyze a project built for one of the aforementioned platforms and generate the appropriate tasks without needing to create custom ones. Figure 8-6 shows an example based on the Node debugger extension for Visual Studio Code, whose source code is available at `https://github.com/Microsoft/vscode-node-debug`.

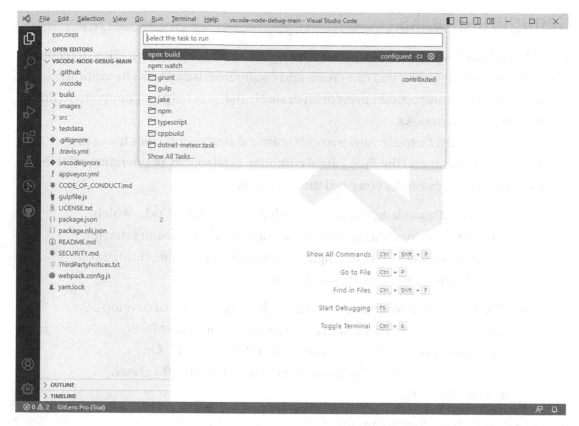

Figure 8-6. *Auto-detected tasks*

The source code of this extension is made of JavaScript and TypeScript files and is built on the Node.js runtime. So Visual Studio Code has been able to detect a number of tasks that work well with this kind of project, such as the npm build and npm watch tasks. You can then open the npm category to view the full list of preconfigured tasks that can run against npm.

Auto-detected tasks are very useful because they allow you to save a lot of time in terms of task automation. However, more often than not, you will have needs that are not satisfied by existing tasks, so you need to make your own customizations.

Note   In order to auto-detect tasks, behind the scenes VS Code requires that specific environments are installed. For example, VS Code can auto-detect tasks based on Node.js only if Node.js is installed; similarly, it can auto-detect tasks based on Gulp only if Gulp is installed, and so on.

Configuring Tasks

When Visual Studio Code cannot auto-detect tasks for a folder, or when auto-detection does not satisfy your needs, you can create and configure custom tasks by editing the tasks.json file. In this section I present an example that will help you understand how to configure your own tasks.

More specifically, I explain how to compile Pascal source code files using the OmniPascal extension and the Free Pascal compiler, available to all operating systems.

To complete the example, you need the following:

- The OmniPascal language extension for Visual Studio Code, which you can download via the Extensions panel. This extension is useful to enable Pascal syntax highlighting and code navigation, though you can still compile source files without it.

- The Free Pascal compiler, which includes all you need to develop applications using Pascal and provides a free command-line compiler. Free Pascal is available for Windows, macOS, Linux, and other systems, and you can download it from https://www. freepascal.org.

Let's start with the Pascal example.

Task Example: Compiling Pascal Source Code

In this section, I explain how to create a custom task that allows you to compile Pascal source code files by invoking the Free Pascal command-line compiler from VS Code. Assuming you have downloaded and installed the required software as listed in the preceding text, locate the Free Pascal folder installation on disk (usually C:\FPC\ VersionNumber on Windows and /FPC/VersionNumber on macOS and Linux), then open the examples folder. In Visual Studio Code, open any folder containing some Pascal source code. I use one called fcl-json.

Figure 8-7 shows how Visual Studio Code appears with Pascal source files currently opened.

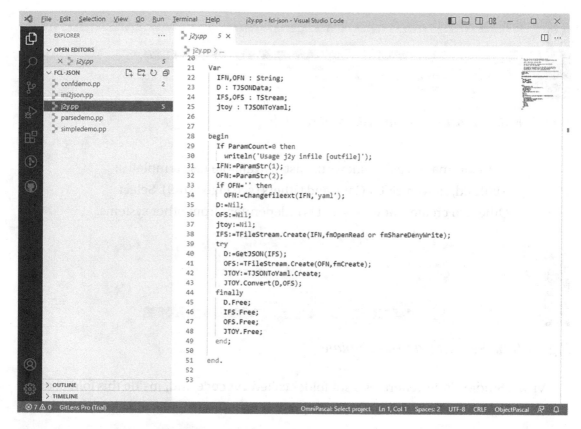

Figure 8-7. *Editing Pascal source code*

The OmniPascal extension installed previously enables syntax colorization and the other common editing features. Now imagine you want to compile the source code into an executable binary by invoking the Free Pascal command-line compiler. You can accomplish this by creating a custom task. Follow these steps to create a new `tasks.json` file and set up the custom task:

1. Choose Terminal ➤ Configure Tasks. When the Command Palette appears asking for a task to configure, select Create tasks.json file From Template (see Figure 8-8). There is no existing task to configure at this particular point, so the only thing you can do is create a new `tasks.json` file.

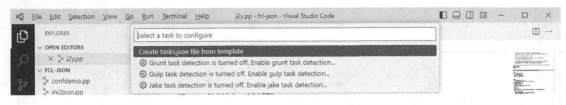

Figure 8-8. *Creating a new task from scratch*

2. The Command Palette shows the list of available task templates: MSBuild, maven, .NET Core, and Others (see Figure 8-9). Select Others to create a new task that is independent from other systems.

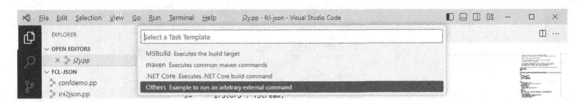

Figure 8-9. *Selecting a task template*

Visual Studio Code generates a subfolder called .vscode and, inside this folder, a new tasks.json file whose content at this point is the following:

```
{
    // See https://go.microsoft.com/fwlink/?LinkId=733558
    // for the documentation about the tasks.json format
    "version": "2.0.0",
    "tasks": [
        {
            "label": "echo",
            "type": "shell",
            "command": "echo Hello"
        }
    ]
}
```

The core node of this JSON file is an array called tasks. It contains a list of tasks, and for each task, you can specify the text that VS Code will use to display it in the Command Palette (label), the type of task (type), and the external program that will be executed (command). An additional JSON property called args allows you to specify command-line arguments for the program you invoke. The list of supported JSON properties is available in Table 8-2 in the upcoming "Understanding tasks.json Properties" section, but if you are impatient, you can quickly look at the table and then return here.

Now suppose you want to create a build task, which, by convention, is the type of task you use to compile source code. You can accomplish this by modifying tasks.json as follows:

```json
{
    // See https://go.microsoft.com/fwlink/?LinkId=733558
    // for the documentation about the tasks.json format
    "version": "2.0.0",
    "tasks": [
        {
            "label": "build",
            "type": "shell",
            "command": "fpc",
            "args": ["${file}"]
        }
    ]
}
```

The key points are the following:

- The label property value is now build so that the task is clearly provided as the build task.

- The type property value is shell, meaning it will be executed by the operating system's shell.

- The command property value is fpc, which is the filename of the Free Pascal compiler.

- The args property value is an array of command-line arguments to be passed to the external program; in this case there is only one argument, which is the active source file, represented by the $(file) variable.

Note   As a general rule, an external program can be invoked without specifying its full path only if such a path has been registered in the operating system's environment variables, such as PATH on Windows. In the case of Free Pascal, the installer claims to take care of registering the program's path, but remember to look at the environment variables for other programs.

You could certainly specify the name of the file you want to compile, but using a variable is more flexible so that you can simply compile any file that is currently active in the code editor. Variables are discussed in the section "Understanding Substitution Variables" and summarized in Table 8-3 later in this chapter. Notice how IntelliSense helps you find the appropriate properties in tasks.json, as shown in Figure 8-10.

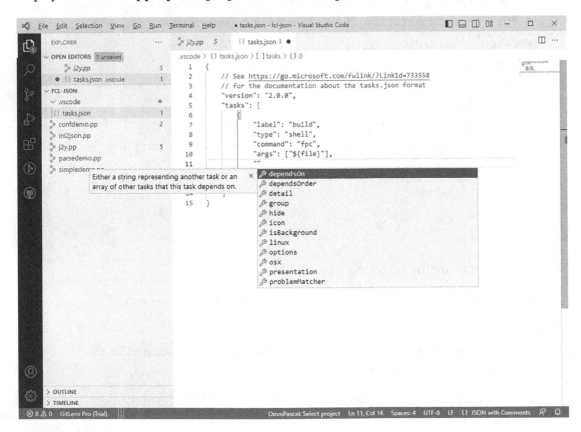

Figure 8-10. *IntelliSense helps in defining task properties*

Save and close `tasks.json`, then open one of the Pascal source files. Now you can run the newly created build task. Choose Terminal ➤ Run Task and, from the Command Palette, select the build task (see Figure 8-11).

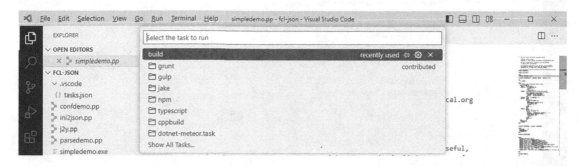

Figure 8-11. *Selecting the new task*

At this point, VS Code asks what would you like to do to detect any problems encountered during the execution of the external program so that it can display them in the Problems panel. Detecting problems in the program's output is the job of a so-called *problem matcher*. This is a more complex topic and is discussed in the section "Understanding Problem Matchers" later in this chapter. For now, select Continue Without Scanning the Task Output (see Figure 8-12).

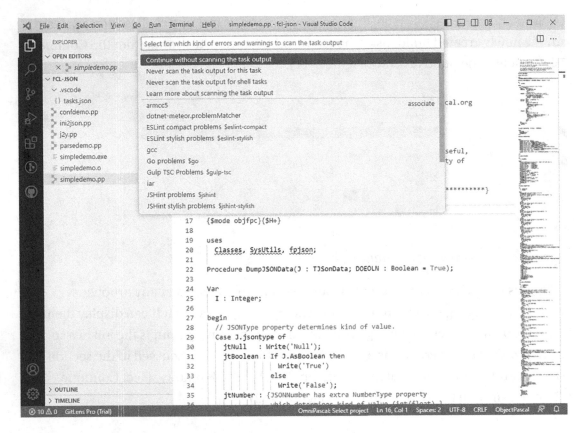

Figure 8-12.   *Selecting a problem matcher*

The Free Pascal compiler is executed in the Terminal panel, where you also see the program output, as demonstrated in Figure 8-13.

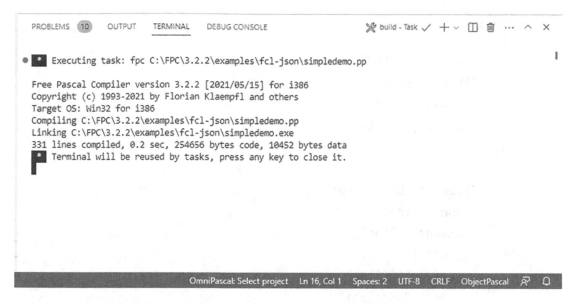

Figure 8-13. *Executing the Free Pascal compiler*

If the execution succeeds, you will find a new binary file in the source code's folder. If it fails, the compiler's output displayed in the Terminal panel will help you understand what the problem was. I now explain more about default tasks, task templates, JSON properties in tasks.json, and variables.

Multiple Tasks and Default Build Tasks

The tasks.json file can define multiple tasks. As introduced earlier in this chapter, among others, common tasks are build and test, but you might want to implement multiple tasks that are specific to your scenario. For example, suppose you want to use the Free Pascal compiler to build Delphi source code files.

The Free Pascal command-line compiler provides the -Mdelphi option, which enables compilation based on the Delphi compatibility mode. You can therefore modify tasks.json as follows:

```
{
    // See https://go.microsoft.com/fwlink/?LinkId=733558
    // for the documentation about the tasks.json format
    "version": "2.0.0",
```

```
    "tasks": [
        {
            "label": "build",
            "type": "shell",
            "command": "fpc",
            "args": ["${file}"]
        },
        {
            "label": "Delphi build",
            "type": "shell",
            "command": "fpc",
            "args": [
                    "${file}",
                    "-Mdelphi"
                ]
        }
    ]
}
```

As you can see, there is a new custom task called Delphi build in the tasks array, which still invokes the Free Pascal compiler on the active file, but with the -Mdelphi option being passed as a command-line argument. Now if you choose Terminal ➤ Run Task again, you see both tasks in the Command Palette, as demonstrated in Figure 8-14.

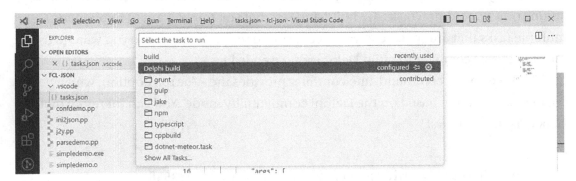

Figure 8-14. *All defined tasks are displayed in the Command Palette*

It is common to have multiple build tasks, and even multiple tasks of the same type, but in most cases, you will usually run the same task and keep other tasks for very specific situations. Related to the current example, you will usually build Pascal source files and sometimes build Delphi source files, so a convenient choice is to configure a default build task for Pascal files. As you learned in the "The Default Build Task" section previously, you can easily accomplish this with the following steps:

1. Choose Terminal ➤ Configure Default Build Task.

2. In the Command Palette, select the build task defined previously by adding an `isDefault` parameter (as you will see shortly in code).

3. With a Pascal source file active, choose Terminal ➤ Run Build Task or press the keyboard shortcut for your system.

This command automatically starts the default build task, without having to manually select a task every time.

Understanding tasks.json Properties

There are a number of properties available to customize a task. Table 8-2 provides a summary of common properties that you can use with custom tasks.

Table 8-2. Available Properties for Task Customization

Property Name	Description
`label`	A string used to identify the task (e.g., in the Command Palette).
`type`	Represents the task type. For custom tasks, supported values are `shell` and `process`. With `shell`, the command is interpreted as a shell command (such as bash, cmd, or PowerShell). With `process`, the command is interpreted as a process to be executed.
`command`	The command or external program to be executed.
`args`	An array of command-line arguments to be passed to the command.
`windows`	Allows specifying task properties that are specific to the Windows operating system.

(continued)

Table 8-2. (*continued*)

Property Name	Description
osx	Allows specifying task properties that are specific to macOS.
linux	Allows specifying task properties that are specific to Linux and its distributions.
group	Allows for defining task groups and for specifying to which group a task belongs.
presentation	Defines how Visual Studio Code handles the task output in the user interface (see the following example).
options	Allows for providing custom values about the cwd (current working directory), env (environment variables), and shell (default shell) options.

The windows, osx, and linux properties are discussed separately in a later section. The group property allows you to group tasks by category. For instance, if you consider the two multiple tasks created previously, they are both related to building code, so they might be grouped into a category called build. This is accomplished by modifying tasks.json as follows:

```
{
    // See https://go.microsoft.com/fwlink/?LinkId=733558
    // for the documentation about the tasks.json format
    "version": "2.0.0",
    "tasks": [
        {
            "label": "build",
            "type": "shell",
            "command": "fpc",
            "args": ["${file}"],
            "group": {
                "kind": "build",
                "isDefault": true
            },
        },
```

```
    {
        "label": "Delphi build",
        "type": "shell",
        "command": "fpc",
        "args": ["${file}", "-Mdelphi"],
        "group": "build"
    }
    ]
}
```

Notice how IntelliSense shows the built-in supported values for the group property (see Figure 8-15).

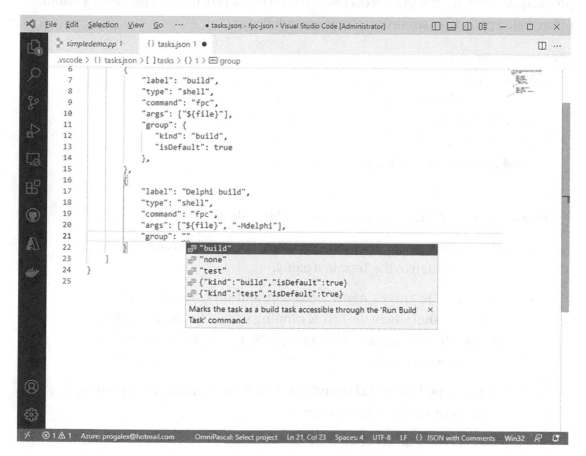

Figure 8-15. *IntelliSense helping with groups*

You can also specify additional values for individual tasks in a group. For example, if you want to set a task as the default one in the group, you might change the JSON as follows:

```
"group": {
    "kind": "build",
    "isDefault": true
  }
}
```

The kind property represents the group name and isDefault is self-explanatory. You can also customize the way VS Code handles the task output via the presentation property. When you type **presentation** and then press Tab, IntelliSense adds a number of key/value pairs with some default values, as follows:

```
"presentation": {
    "echo": true,
    "reveal": "always",
    "focus": false,
    "panel": "shared",
    "showReuseMessage": true
}
```

Following is the description of each key and its values:

- echo can be true or false and specifies whether the task output is actually written to the Terminal panel.

- reveal can be always, never, or silent and specifies whether the Terminal panel where the task is running should be always visible, never visible, or visible only when a problem matcher is not specified and some errors occur.

- focus can be true or false and specifies if the Terminal panel should get focus when the task is running.

- panel can be shared, dedicated, or new and specifies if the Terminal instance is shared across tasks, or if an instance must be dedicated to the current task, or if a new instance should be created at every task run.

- showReuseMessage can be true or false and specifies whether a message should be displayed to inform that the Terminal panel will be reused by a task and that therefore it is possible to close it.

The values you see in the preceding snippet are the default values. In case of default values, a key can be omitted. For example, the following markup demonstrates how to create a new Terminal panel at every run without showing a reuse message:

```
"presentation": {
    "panel": "new",
    "showReuseMessage": false
}
```

Other values can be omitted because the default values seen in the preceding text are acceptable for this example.

Note   The list of supported properties is much longer, but most of them are not of common use. If you want to get deeper knowledge about the full list of available properties, you can look at the tasks.json schema, which provides detailed comments about each property; the schema is available at https://code. visualstudio.com/docs/editor/tasks-appendix.

Understanding Substitution Variables

Visual Studio Code also offers several predefined variables that you can use instead of regular strings and that are useful to represent file and folder names when passing these to a command. Table 8-3 provides a summary of supported variables.

Table 8-3. *Supported Substitution Variables*

Variable	Description
${workspaceFolder}	Represents the path of the currently opened folder.
${workspaceFolder Basename}	Represents the name of the currently opened folder without any slashes.
${file}	The path to the active code file.
${relativeFile}	The active code file relative to ${workspaceFolder}.
${fileBasename}	The active code file's base name, without path and leading slash.
${fileBasenameNo Extension}	The active code file's base name without the extension.
${fileDirname}	The path of the directory that contains the active code file.
${fileExtname}	The file extension of the active code file.
${cwd}	The current working directory of the task.
${lineNumber}	The currently selected line number in the active file.
${selectedText}	The currently selected text in the active file.
${env.VARIABLENAME}	References an environment variable, such as {$env.PATH}.
${userHome}	Platform-independent variable that represents the root folder for user contents.
${relativeFileDirname}	The name of the directory for the current opened file, relative to workspaceFolder.

Using variables is very common when you run a task that works at the project/folder level or against filenames that you either cannot predict or do not want to hardcode. You can check the variables documentation for further details at https://code. visualstudio.com/docs/editor/variables-reference.

Operating System–Specific Properties

Sometimes you might need to provide task property values that are different based on the operating system. In Visual Studio Code, you can use the windows, osx, and linux properties to specify different values of a property, depending on the target.

For example, the following `tasks.json` implementation shows how to explicitly specify the path of an external tool for Windows and Linux (the directory names might not be the same on your machine):

```json
{
    // See https://go.microsoft.com/fwlink/?LinkId=733558
    // for the documentation about the tasks.json format
    "version": "2.0.0",
    "tasks": [
        {
            "label": "build",
            "type": "shell",
            "args": ["${file}"],
            "windows": {
                "command": "C:\\Program Files\\FPC\\fpc.exe"
            },
            "linux": {
                "command": "/usr/bin/fpc"
            }
        }
    ]
}
```

More specifically, you need to move the property of your interest under the operating system property and provide the desired value. In the preceding code, the `command` property has been moved from the higher level down to the `windows` and `linux` property nodes.

Reusing Existing Task Templates

In the previous example about compiling Pascal source code, you saw how to create a custom task from scratch. However, for some particular scenarios, you can leverage existing task templates, which consists of `tasks.json` files already preconfigured to work with specific commands and settings.

The list of task templates may vary depending on the extensions you have installed, but assuming you have installed only the C# extension, your list should look like that shown in Figure 8-9. For .NET development, you can use the template called .NET Core: Execute .NET Core Build Command (see Figure 8-9 for a reference). This generates the following tasks.json file:

```json
{
    // See https://go.microsoft.com/fwlink/?LinkId=733558
    // for the documentation about the tasks.json format
    "version": "2.0.0",
    "tasks": [
        {
            "label": "build",
            "command": "dotnet",
            "type": "shell",
            "args": [
                "build",
                // Ask dotnet build to generate full paths for filenames.
                "/property:GenerateFullPaths=true",
                // Do not generate summary otherwise it leads to duplicate
                errors in Problems panel
                "/consoleloggerparameters:NoSummary"
            ],
            "group": "build",
            "presentation": {
                "reveal": "silent"
            },
            "problemMatcher": "$msCompile"
        }
    ]
}
```

This template is very useful if you want to work with Microsoft Visual Studio solutions inside VS Code or, more generally, with C# projects. It is worth mentioning that this template has been included for solutions created with .NET 5 and higher, but the dotnet tool can build any kind of solution so it can be reused for different purposes.

The second template is called Maven and is tailored to support the same-named build automation tool for Java. Such a template generates the following `tasks.json` file:

```json
{
    // See https://go.microsoft.com/fwlink/?LinkId=733558
    // for the documentation about the tasks.json format
    "version": "2.0.0",
    "tasks": [
        {
            "label": "verify",
            "type": "shell",
            "command": "mvn -B verify",
            "group": "build"
        },
        {
            "label": "test",
            "type": "shell",
            "command": "mvn -B test",
            "group": "test"
        }
    ]
}
```

Obviously, Maven must be installed on your machine (you can find it at `https://maven.apache.org`). The template called MSBuild works with legacy Visual Studio solutions that target the .NET Framework, which goes beyond the cross-platform development purposes of Visual Studio Code, so it is not discussed here.

In general, these templates are useful for at least two reasons:

- They provide ready-to-use configurations for projects of the targeted type, where you might need only a few adjustments.

- They provide a complete task structure, where you only need to replace the command and target and optionally the presentation and the problem matcher.

Among the others, tasks can detect problems in your code and present them in the Problems panel. This is possible because of problem matchers, discussed in the next section.

Understanding Problem Matchers

Problem matchers scan the task output text for known warning or error strings and report these inline in the editor and in the Problems panel. Visual Studio Code ships with a number of built-in problem matchers for TypeScript, JSHint, ESLint, Go, C# and Visual Basic, Lessc, and Node Sass (see https://code.visualstudio.com/docs/editor/tasks#_processing-task-output-with-problem-matchers).

Built-in problem matchers are extremely useful, because for the aforementioned environments, VS Code can present problems that occurred at build time in the Problems panel, but it can also highlight the line of code in the code editor that caused the problem.

You can also define custom problem matchers to scan the output of an external program. For instance, a problem matcher for scanning the Free Pascal compiler could look like the following:

```
        "problemMatcher": {
            "owner": "external",
            "fileLocation": ["relative", "${workspaceRoot}"],
            "pattern": {
"regexp": "((([A-Za-z]):\\\\(?:[^\\/:*?\\\"
<>|\\r\\n]+\\\\)*)?[^\\/\\s\\(:*?\\\"<>|\\r\\n]*)\\((\\d+)\\):
\\s.*(fatal|error|warning|hint)\\s(.*):\\s(.*)",
// The first match group matches the filename which is relative.
        "file": 1,
// The second match group matches the line on which the problem occurred.
        "line": 2,
// The third match group matches the column at which the problem occurred.
        "column": 3,
// The fourth match group matches the problem's severity. Can be ignored.
Then all problems are captured as errors.
        "severity": 4,
        // The fifth match group matches the message.
        "message": 5
            }
```

The owner property represents the language service, whose value is external in this case, but it could be, for example, cpp in the case of a C++ project. But the most important property is pattern, where you specify a regular expression (regexp) to match error strings sent by the external program. Also notice, with the help of comments, how matches are grouped by target. Building problem matchers can be tricky and it is out of the scope of this book, so I recommend that you read the official documentation available at https://code.visualstudio.com/docs/editor/tasks#_defining-a-problem-matcher.

Running Files with a Default Program

If you are editing a file whose type is associated with the operating system, you do not need to create custom tasks to run it in VS Code. For example, you can run a batch program (.bat) in Windows or a shell script file (.sh) on macOS by simply clicking Terminal ➤ Run Active File.

The filename is passed to the current Terminal program on your system (PowerShell on Windows or the bash shell on Linux and macOS) so that the operating system tries to open the file with the program that is registered with the file extension, if any. In the case of a batch or shell script file, the operating system executes the file. The output is displayed in the Terminal panel.

Note   Only the output of the operating system or of command-line tools will be redirected to the Terminal panel. For instance, if you try to edit a .txt file and then choose Terminal ➤ Run Active File, such a file will be opened inside the default text editor on your system, and there will be no additional interactions with the Terminal panel.

Summary

There are many features in Visual Studio Code that make it different from a simple code editor. Tasks are among these features. With tasks you can attach external programs to the application lifecycle and run tools like compilers. VS Code ships with task auto-detection for some environments, but it allows you to create custom tasks when you need to associate specific tools to a project or folder.

By working on the `tasks.json` file and with the help of IntelliSense, you can include the execution of any external program in your folders. The execution of external programs like compilers is certainly useful, but it would not be so important if VS Code could not make a step forward: debugging code, which is discussed in the next two chapters, first with .NET and then with Python.

CHAPTER 9

Building and Debugging Applications

Being an end-to-end development environment, Visual Studio Code offers opportunities that you will not find in other code editors. In fact, in Visual Studio Code, you can work with many project types and debug your code in several languages. This chapter first provides a general overview of application development, and then it explains how to build .NET projects supported in Visual Studio Code and how to use all the built-in, powerful debugging features. Even if you do not plan to use C# with Visual Studio Code, I recommend that you read this chapter because most of the concepts are applicable to other languages, especially TypeScript, JavaScript, and Python.

Creating Applications

Visual Studio Code is independent from proprietary project systems and platforms and, consequently, it does not offer any built-in options to create projects. This means that you need to rely on the tools offered by each platform. This section explains how to build projects based on .NET, but you can similarly create projects with the command-line interface offered by other platforms.

I also recommend that you create a dedicated folder on disk for the following examples. With the help of the file manager tool on your system (Windows Explorer on Windows, Finder on macOS, and Nautilus on Linux distributions such as Ubuntu), create a folder called VSCode under the root folder, such as C:\VSCode or ~/Library/VSCode. In this folder, you will shortly create new applications.

© Alessandro Del Sole 2023
A. Del Sole, *Visual Studio Code Distilled*, https://doi.org/10.1007/978-1-4842-9484-0_9

Note   The following topics are discussed in the context of .NET 7, but Visual Studio Code also supports .NET 5 and 6, as well as .NET Core versions up to 3.1. All explanations and examples therefore apply to .NET Core as well.

The Status of Microsoft .NET

After releasing .NET Core a few years ago, Microsoft has had in mind the vision of a complete unification between .NET Framework and .NET Core, working on a single, cross-platform API that could bring the great power of .NET to any developer on any system.

As you might know, .NET Core is a cross-platform, open-source, modular runtime to build applications using C#, F#, and Visual Basic that run on Windows, macOS, and Linux distributions. With .NET Core, you can create different kinds of applications such as web applications, Web API REST services, Console applications, and class libraries. Its bigger brother, the .NET Framework, also includes the ability to create desktop applications, such as Windows Forms and Windows Presentation Foundation, but the .NET Framework's biggest limitation is that it only runs on Windows. After passing through .NET 5, an update for both .NET Core and .NET Framework with which Microsoft brought together the two technologies and offers a unified development platform, they have released .NET 6, which completed the transition to one .NET API. At this writing, .NET 7 is the latest release, with many improvements and additional API unification. For example, with .NET 7 you can use the latest version of .NET MAUI, the new cross-platform development technology that allows you to create applications for Android, iOS, Tizen, Windows and Mac Catalyst from one, shared codebase.

Note   From now on, I show examples based on the .NET 7 runtime because it is the latest available, but I refer to .NET without any version numbers. The reason is that such examples will also work on .NET 6 (and the development approach is the same).

Setting Up .NET for VS Code Development

There are several options to get .NET. The first option is to download the .NET Coding Pack (`https://code.visualstudio.com/docs/languages/dotnet#_net-coding-pack`).

This includes Visual Studio Code, the .NET Software Development Kit, and essential extensions.

The second option, which is good for existing Visual Studio Code users, is to download the .NET Software Development Kit (`https://code.visualstudio.com/docs/languages/dotnet#_installing-the-net-software-development-kit`) and then the .NET Extension Pack (`https://marketplace.visualstudio.com/items?itemName=ms-dotnettools.vscode-dotnet-pack`). The Software Development Kit includes all the necessary tools, such as the command-line interface, compilers, and debuggers, whereas the Extension Pack includes recommended extensions such as the C# extension.

For the following explanations and examples, I'm assuming you have downloaded and installed .NET and the C# extension on your machine.

Creating .NET Projects

.NET ships with a rich command-line interface that provides many options to create different kinds of projects and individual files. You can create projects and files from the command line by using the `dotnet` tool, more specifically by invoking the `dotnet new` command. For example, if you want to create a Console application with C#, you enter the following command:

```
> dotnet new console
```

By default, the `dotnet` tool assumes you want to use C# unless you explicitly specify a different language. For example, the following command enables you to create a Console application with Visual Basic:

```
> dotnet new console -lang VB
```

Table 9-1 provides a comprehensive list and description of all the available templates.

Table 9-1. *Available .NET Project and File Templates*

Template Name	Short Name	Language
Console Application	Console	C#, F#, VB
Class Library	Classlib	C#, F#, VB
WPF Application	Wpf	C#, VB
WPF Class Library	Wpflib	C#, VB
WPF Custom Control Library	wpfcustomcontrollib	C#, VB
WPF User Control Library	wpfusercontrollib	C#, VB
Windows Forms (WinForms) Application	Winforms	C#, VB
Windows Forms Class Library	winformslib	C#, VB
Windows Forms Control Library	winformscontrollib	C#, VB
Worker Service	Worker	C#
Unit Test Project	Mstest	C#, F#, VB
NUnit 3 Test Project	Nunit	C#, F#, VB
NUnit 3 Test Item	nunit-test	C#, F#, VB
xUnit Test Project	Xunit	C#, F#, VB
Razor Component	razorcomponent	C#
Razor Page	Page	C#
MVC ViewImports	viewimports	C#
MVC ViewStart	viewstart	C#
Blazor Server App	blazorserver	C#
Blazor WebAssembly App	blazorwasm	C#
ASP.NET Core Empty	Web	C#, F#
ASP.NET Core Web App (Model-View-Controller)	Mvc	C#, F#
ASP.NET Core Web App	webapp, razor	C#
ASP.NET Core with Angular	Angular	C#

(*continued*)

Table 9-1. (*continued*)

Template Name	Short Name	Language
ASP.NET Core with React.js	React	C#
ASP.NET Core with React.js and Redux	Reactredux	C#
Razor Class Library	razorclasslib	C#
ASP.NET Core Web API	Webapi	C#, F#
ASP.NET Core gRPC Service	Grpc	C#
dotnet gitignore file	Gitignore	
global.json file	Globaljson	
NuGet Config	Nugetconfig	
Dotnet local tool manifest file	tool-manifest	
Web Config	Webconfig	
Solution File	Sln	
Protocol Buffer File	Proto	
EditorConfig File	editorconfig	
.NET MAUI App	Maui	C#
.NET MAUI Blazor App	maui-blazor	C#
.NET MAUI Class Library	mauilib	C#
.NET MAUI ContentPage	maui-page-xaml	XAML
.NET MAUI ContentPage	maui-page-csharp	C#
.NET MAUI ContentView	maui-view-xaml	XAML
.NET MAUI ContentView	maui-page-csharp	C#
.NET MAUI Resource Dictionary	maui-dict-xaml	XAML
Android Activity	android-activity	C#
Android Application	Android	C#
Android Class Library	Androidlib	C#

(*continued*)

Table 9-1. (*continued*)

Template Name	Short Name	Language
Android Java Library	android-bindinglib	C#
Android Layout template	android-layout	C#
Android Wear Application	androidwear	C#
iOS Application	ios	C#
iOS Binding Library	iosbinding	C#
iOS Class Library	ioslib	C#
iOS Controller	ios-controller	C#
iOS Storyboard	ios-storyboard	C#
iOS Tabbed Application	ios-tabbed	C#
iOS View	ios-view	C#
iOS View Controller	ios-viewcontroller	C#
Mac Catalyst Application	maccatalyst	C#
Mac Catalyst Binding Library	maccatalystbinding	C#
Mac Catalyst Class Library	maccatalystlib	C#
Mac Catalyst Controller	maccatalyst-controller	C#
Mac Catalyst Storyboard	maccatalyst-storyboard	C#
Mac Catalyst View	maccatalyst-view	C#
Mac Catalyst View Controller	maccatalyst-viewcontroller	C#

Note   You can get the full list of templates by typing `dotnet new list` in a command prompt. This can be useful with new .NET releases that introduce new templates.

In this section, I show an example based on C# and an ASP.NET web application built on the Model-View-Controller (MVC) pattern. Open a command prompt or a Terminal instance on the VSCode folder created previously, depending on your system.

Type the following command to create a new empty folder called HelloWeb:

```
> mkdir HelloWeb
```

Then, move into the new directory. On Windows and Linux, you can type

```
> chdir HelloWeb
```

On macOS, the command is instead cd, which is also commonly used on Windows as a shortcut for chdir.

Next, type the following command to build a new .NET web application using C#:

```
> dotnet new mvc
```

The mvc command-line switch specifies that the new web application is based on the MVC pattern and the .NET SDK will generate all the plumbing code for some controllers and views. You can also use the web switch and create an empty web application, but having some autogenerated pages will help with describing the debugging features. Once the project has been created, .NET will automatically restore NuGet packages for the project. You can also do this manually by typing the following command:

```
> dotnet restore
```

If you were to type dotnet run, the development server would start running and then you would need to open your browser and launch the application manually. However, the goal is understanding how to run and debug the application in Visual Studio Code. So, open the project folder with VS Code. You can also type code . to open Visual Studio Code from the command line. Thanks to the C# extension, VS Code recognizes the presence of the .csproj project file, organizing files and folders and enabling all the powerful code editing features you learned previously.

The next step is to run the application. As a general rule, in Visual Studio Code you have two options:

- Running the application with an instance of the debugger attached, where a debugger is available for the current project type. In the case of .NET, this ships with its own debugger that integrates with VS Code.

- Running the application without an instance of the debugger attached.

Let's start with the second option, and then the debugging features are described in detail in the next section. You can choose Run ➤ Run Without Debugging. Visual Studio Code first asks you to specify an environment, so select .NET Core. VS Code then starts the default build task. For Web applications, VS Code starts an instance of the development server. The application should automatically start in the browser. If this does not happen, you need to manually open the browser and enter the web address you see in the Terminal panel.

Note   The first time you run some code, VS Code might show a popup message saying that required assets are needed to enable building and debugging. Accept the offer and VS Code will do the rest.

Figure 9-1 shows the web application built previously.

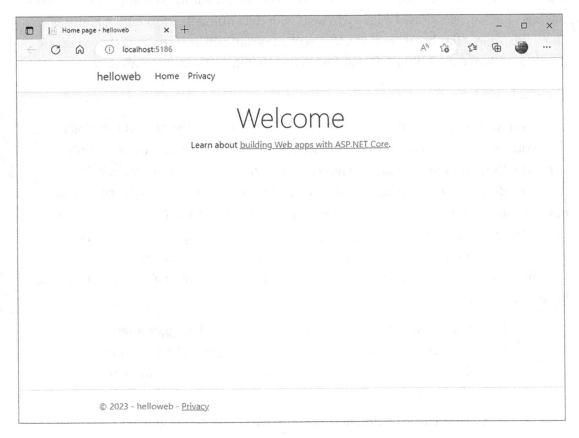

Figure 9-1. *The .NET web application running*

Note   Your browser might show a warning saying that the website is not secure. Because the local development environment is currently being used, you can ignore the warning and proceed to display the web page. Also, some browsers might ask to add a security exception for the current site, which you might want to accept to avoid the warning every time.

ASP.NET web applications use an open-source development server called Kestrel (`https://github.com/aspnet/AspNetCore`), which provides independence from proprietary systems. By default, Kestrel listens for the application on a random port between 5000 and 5300 for HTTP and between 7000 and 7300 for HTTPS. This means your application can be reached at `http://localhost:5000 or different port number`. You can change the default port setting in a file called `launch.json`, which is discussed more thoroughly in the later section "Configuring the Debugger."

With the preceding simple steps, you have been able to create and run a .NET project in VS Code that you can certainly edit as you need with the powerful C# code editing features.

Creating Projects on Other Platforms

Obviously, .NET is not the only platform you will use with VS Code. Depending on the platform, you will use specific command-line tools to build new projects. In the next chapter, you learn how to work with Python projects, but providing some context in this chapter is worthwhile as well. For example, with Node.js you can quickly create JavaScript projects based on the Express.js framework (`https://expressjs.com`).

Express is a minimal and flexible Node.js web application framework that provides a robust set of features to develop web and mobile applications. It facilitates the rapid development of Node-based web applications and includes features such as setting up middleware to respond to HTTP requests, defining a routing table used to perform different actions based on HTTP methods and URL, and dynamically rendering HTML pages based on passing arguments to templates. An easy way to start creating apps with Express is to use the Express application generator (`https://expressjs.com/en/starter/generator.html`), which you install with the following command:

```
> npm install -g express-generator
```

Next, you can generate a JavaScript project with the following command:

```
> express expressexample
```

Note that npm requires using all lowercase letters. You can then type **code** . to open the new project in Visual Studio Code. Figure 9-2 shows a JavaScript project created with the Express JavaScript framework inside Visual Studio Code.

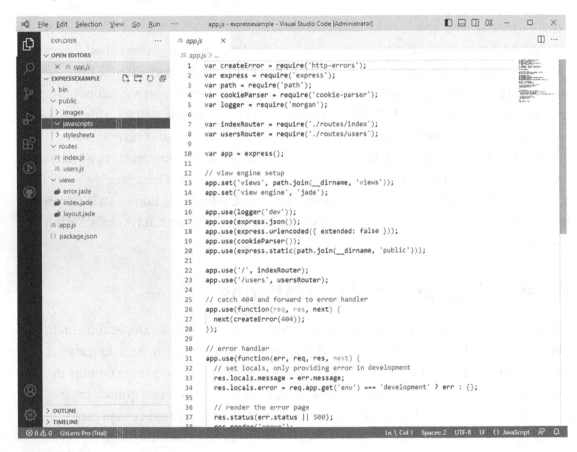

Figure 9-2. *A JavaScript project created with the Express JavaScript framework in VS Code*

You follow a similar process with other command-line tools that allow you to generate projects, such as the Yeoman generator (https://yeoman.io/), still available for Node.js, and that also allow you to generate ASP.NET Core projects and VS Code extensions. For example, you can create mobile apps with the Apache Cordova framework (https://cordova.apache.org). Cordova is a JavaScript-based framework, and it works very well with Node.js. Apps you build with Cordova are based on JavaScript, HTML, and Cascading Style Sheets (CSS). First, install Cordova with the following command:

```
> npm install -g cordova
```

Then you can easily build a Cordova project with the following command:

```
> cordova create mycordovaproject
```

where `mycordovaproject` is the name of the new project. Once you have a new or existing Cordova project, you can install the Cordova Tools extension for Visual Studio Code (`https://marketplace.visualstudio.com/items?itemName=vsmobile.cordova-tools`). This extension adds support for Cordova projects to the integrated debugger for Node.js, providing specific configurations to target Android and iOS devices, as well as simulators.

Note   You also need some additional specific tools for Cordova, depending on which system you intend to target. For iOS, you need to install the tools described in the iOS Platform Guide from Apache Cordova (`https://cordova.apache.org/docs/en/latest/guide/platforms/ios/index.html`). For Android, you need to install the tools described in the Android Platform Guide from Apache Cordova (`https://cordova.apache.org/docs/en/latest/guide/platforms/android/index.html`).

Debugging Your Code

The code-debugging capability of Visual Studio Code is one of its most powerful features and probably the one that makes it a notch above other code editors. Visual Studio Code ships with an integrated debugger for Node.js applications and can be extended with third-party debuggers. For instance, if you have .NET installed, the C# extension for Visual Studio Code detects the availability of a compatible debugger and takes care of attaching it to VS Code.

This section considers the scenario of using C# and .NET as the example of how debugging works, so reopen the `HelloWeb` folder that you created previously.

Note All the features discussed in this chapter apply to all the supported debuggers (both built-in and via extensibility), so they are not specific to C# and .NET.

The Run view provides a way to interact with the debugger. Figure 9-3 shows how it appears at this point.

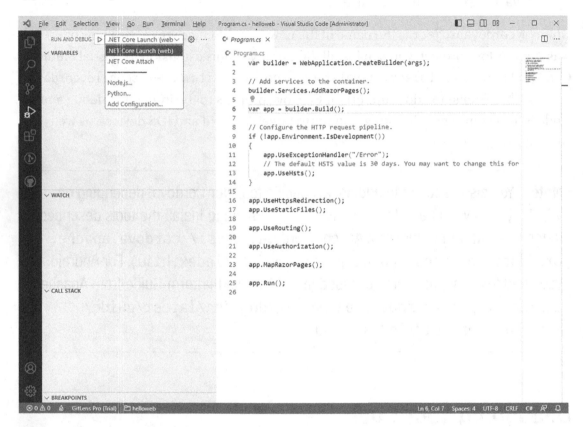

Figure 9-3. *Run view*

At the top of the view, you can see the RUN toolbar, which provides the following items:

- The Start Debugging button, represented with the play icon (the white and green arrow). Clicking this button starts the application with an instance of the debugger attached.

- The configuration drop-down box. Here you can select a debugger configuration for running the application.

- The settings button, represented with the gear icon and whose tooltip says Open launch.json (details coming shortly).

- A submenu represented by the ... button that contains the list of available and selected views, plus the Debug Console command, which opens the Debug Console panel where you see the output messages from the debugger.

After this quick overview, you are ready to learn about debugger configurations, and then you will walk through the debugging tools available in VS Code.

Configuring the Debugger

Before a debugger can inspect an application, it must be configured. For Node.js and for platforms like .NET, where an extension takes care of everything, default configurations are provided. Figure 9-3 shows the two predefined configurations, .NET Core Launch (Web) and .NET Core Attach.

The first configuration is used to run the application within the proper host, with an instance of the debugger attached. For an ASP.NET web application like in the current example, the host is the web browser. In the case of a Console application, the host would be the Windows Console or the Terminal in macOS and Linux. The second configuration can be used to attach the debugger to another running .NET application.

Note Actually, there is a .NET Core Launch configuration that is different for each kind of application you create with .NET. For example, the configuration for Console applications is called .NET Core Launch (console). The concept to keep in mind is that a Launch configuration is provided to attach an instance of the debugger to the current project.

Debugger configurations are stored in a special file called launch.json. Visual Studio Code stores this file in the .vscode subfolder (along with tasks.json). This special JSON file contains the markup that instructs Visual Studio Code about the output binary that must be debugged and about the application host. The contents of launch.json for the current .NET Core sample look like the following:

```
{
    "version": "0.2.0",
    "configurations": [
        {
            // Use IntelliSense to find out which attributes exist for C#
            debugging
            // Use hover for the description of the existing attributes
            // For further information visit https://github.com/OmniSharp/
            omnisharp-vscode/blob/master/debugger-launchjson.md
            "name": ".NET Core Launch (web)",
            "type": "coreclr",
            "request": "launch",
            "preLaunchTask": "build",
            // If you have changed target frameworks, make sure to update
            the program path.
            "program": "${workspaceFolder}/bin/Debug/net7.0/helloweb.dll",
            "args": [],
            "cwd": "${workspaceFolder}",
            "stopAtEntry": false,
            // Enable launching a web browser when ASP.NET Core starts.
            For more information: https://aka.ms/VSCode-CS-LaunchJson-
            WebBrowser
            "serverReadyAction": {
                "action": "openExternally",
                "pattern": "\\bNow listening on:\\s+(https?://\\S+)"
            },
            "env": {
                "ASPNETCORE_ENVIRONMENT": "Development"
            },
            "sourceFileMap": {
                "/Views": "${workspaceFolder}/Views"
            }
        },
        {
            "name": ".NET Core Attach",
            "type": "coreclr",
```

```
        "request": "attach"
    }
  ]
}
```

As you can see, the syntax of this file is similar to the syntax of `tasks.json`. In this case you have an array called `configurations`. For each configuration in the array, the most important properties are

- `name`, which represents the configuration-friendly name.

- `type`, which represents the type of runtime the debugger is running on.

- `request` (`launch` or `attach`), which determines whether the debugger is attached to the current project or to an external application.

- `preLaunchTask`, which contains any task to be executed before the debugging session starts. Usually, this property is assigned with the default build task.

- `program`, which represents the binary that will be the subject of the debugging session.

- `env`, which represents the environment. In the case of .NET, a value of `Development` instructs VS Code to run the Kestrel development server.

If you wanted to implement custom configurations, `launch.json` is the place where you would add them. Because these two configurations, and more generally default configurations, are enough for most of the common needs, custom configurations are not covered in this book. The documentation provides additional details about this topic (`https://code.visualstudio.com/docs/editor/debugging#_add-a-new-configuration`).

Note   If you click the Add Configuration button located at the bottom-right corner of the code editor when `launch.json` is the active file, you can select from a built-in list of configurations that you can add to `launch.json`. This can be useful especially in those cases where VS Code should detect a project type and its configuration but doesn't.

Managing Breakpoints

Before starting a debugging session, it is useful to place one or more breakpoints to discover the full debugging capabilities in VS Code. You place breakpoints by clicking the whitespace near the line number or by pressing F9 on the line of your interest. For instance, you can place a breakpoint on line 9 of the `Startup.cs` file, as shown in Figure 9-4.

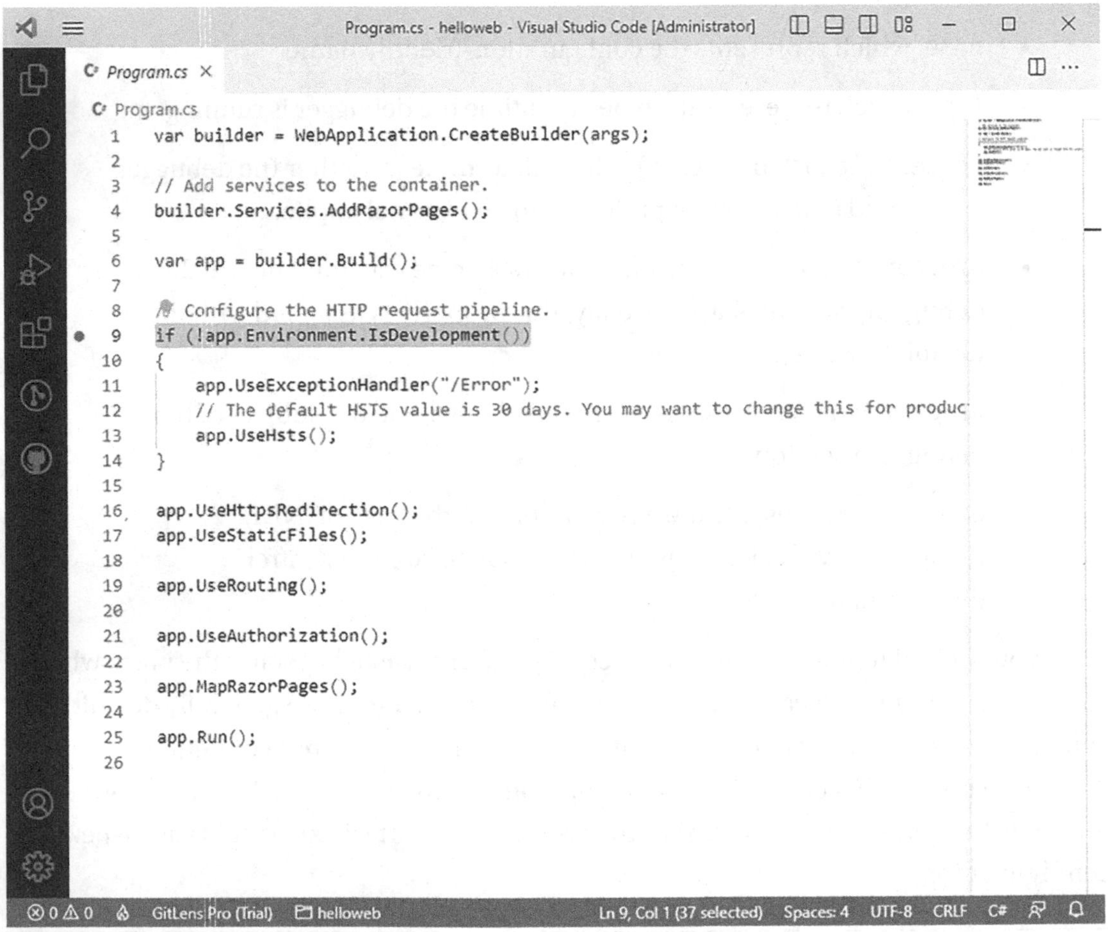

Figure 9-4. Adding breakpoints

You can remove a breakpoint by simply clicking it again, or you can manage breakpoints in the Breakpoints area of the Run view (see Figure 9-5). You can also temporarily disable a breakpoint by pressing Shift+Click.

Figure 9-5. *Managing breakpoints*

Here you can see the list of files that contain breakpoints and the line numbers. You can also cause the debugger to break on user-unhandled exceptions (default) and on all exceptions. You can click the Add Function Breakpoint (+) button. Instead of placing breakpoints directly in source code, a debugger can support creating breakpoints by specifying a function name. This is useful in situations where source is not available but a function name is known.

Debugging an Application

Now it is time to start a debugging session so that you can see in action all the debugging tools and make decisions when breakpoints are hit. In the Run view, make sure the .NET Core Launch (Web) configuration is selected, then click the Start button or press F5. Visual Studio Code launches the debugger, and it will display the output of the debugger in the Debug Console panel. It will also break when it encounters an exception or a breakpoint, like in the current example.

Figure 9-6 shows VS Code hitting a breakpoint and all the debugging instrumentation. The line of code highlighted in yellow is the line that will be executed as the next one.

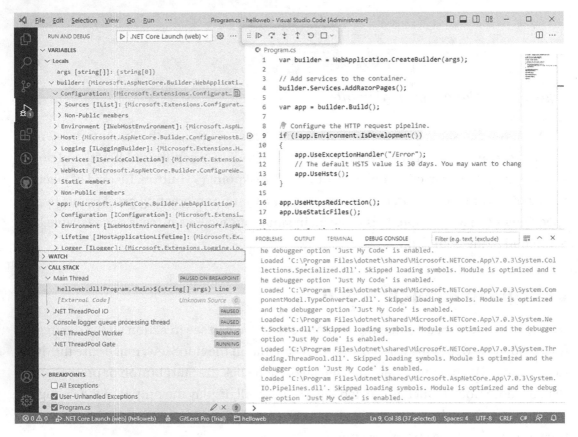

Figure 9-6. *The debugging tools available when a breakpoint is hit*

Notice that the status bar becomes orange while debugging and the Debug Console window shows information about the debugging process. On the left side, the Debug view shows a number of tools:

- **VARIABLES**, which shows the list of variables that are currently under the debugger control and that you can investigate by expanding each variable. This panel includes a sublist called Locals, which displays the list of the variables that are currently in scope. Each can be further expanded to see their details.

- **WATCH**, a place where you can evaluate expressions.

- **CALL STACK**, where you can see the stack of method calls. If you click a method call, the code editor takes you to the code that is making that call.

- **BREAKPOINTS**, where you can manage breakpoints.

At the top of the window, also notice the debugging toolbar (see Figure 9-6) called the Debug action pane, which is composed of the following commands (from left to right):

- **Continue**, which allows you to continue the application execution after breaking on a breakpoint or an exception.

- **Step Over**, which executes one statement at a time, except for method calls, which are invoked without stepping into.

- **Step Into**, which executes one statement at a time. Statements within method bodies are also executed one at a time.

- **Step Out**, which executes the remaining lines of a function starting from the current breakpoint.

- **Restart**, which you select to restart the application execution.

- **Stop**, which you invoke to stop debugging.

These commands are also available in the Run menu, together with their keyboard shortcuts. For example, if you click the Step Over button, the highlighted line runs and the execution advances one line (see Figure 9-7). If you hover your cursor over a variable name in the code editor, a convenient popup box enables you to easily investigate values and property values (depending on the type of the variable), as demonstrated in Figure 9-7, which shows a popup box that includes information about the `builder` variable. You can expand properties and see their values, and you can also investigate properties in the VARIABLES area of the Run and Debug Bar.

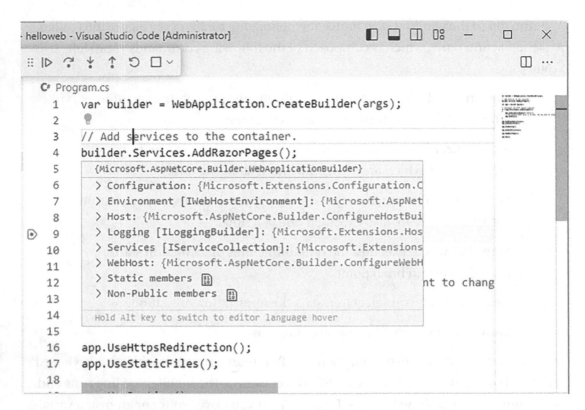

Figure 9-7. *Investigating property values at debugging time*

Note   Sometimes it is necessary to execute some code before a variable's value is available for investigation. In Visual Studio Code, this is known as *lazy variables*. When debugging JavaScript code, the value of a lazy variable is not available by default, to avoid expensive code execution, but it will show an expander icon that you can click in order to evaluate the necessary code. You can force lazy variables to be automatically expanded (and evaluated) in the debugger settings (see Figure 9-11).

Evaluating Expressions

You have an option to use the Watch tool to evaluate expressions. While debugging, click the Add Expression (+) button in the Watch box, then type the expression you want to evaluate. For instance, if you type **builder != null**, the Watch tool returns true or false depending on whether the object has an instance. Figure 9-8 shows an example.

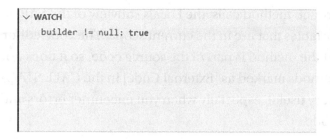

Figure 9-8. *Evaluating expressions*

The Call Stack

The debugger also offers the Call Stack feature, which allows you to step through the hierarchy of method calls. When you click a method call in the stack, the code editor opens the containing file, highlighting the method call (see Figure 9-9).

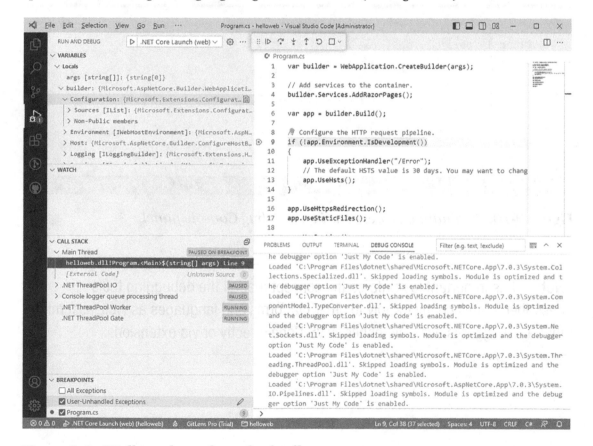

Figure 9-9. *Walking through method calls*

As you walk through method calls, the Locals subview of the VARIABLES panel also updates to show variables that are in the current scope. The code editor can highlight method calls only if the method is part of the source code, so it does not allow further control over the methods marked as [External Code] in the CALL STACK (see Figure 9-9), but this feature is very useful, especially when you encounter errors and you need to step back through the code.

The Debug Console Panel

The Debug Console is certainly the place where VS Code shows the debugger output, but, as the name implies, it is also an interactive panel where you can evaluate expressions. You can type the expression near the > symbol and then press Enter.

Figure 9-10 shows an example that evaluates whether the builder variable is null.

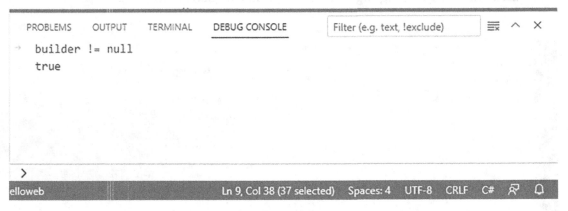

Figure 9-10. *Evaluating expressions in the Debug Console panel*

Note   It is important to reinforce the concept that all the debugging tools described in this chapter apply to other platforms and languages as well, assuming that a debugger is available either by VS Code directly or via extensions.

Configuring Debug Options

Settings in Visual Studio Code allow you to customize the general debugging experience. Figure 9-11 shows the Debug settings, located under the Features node.

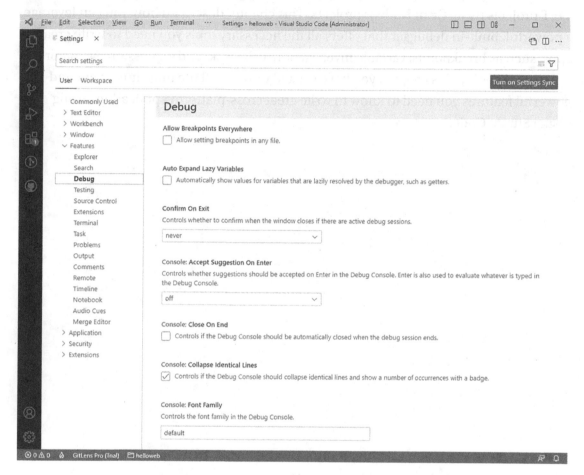

Figure 9-11. *Configuring the debugging settings*

Settings are self-explanatory and, as with any other VS Code settings, they can also be manually edited in the `settings.json` file. Notice how it is also possible to auto-expand lazy variables, mentioned previously. In this settings area, you find options that are related to the general debugging experience. For specific debugger options, such as debugging for C# or C++, you need to open the Extensions node and then walk through the debugging settings for each specific extension.

Summary

The power of Visual Studio Code as a development environment comes out when you work with real applications. With the help of specific generators, you can easily generate .NET projects using C# or Node.js projects. This chapter described how you can leverage a powerful, built-in debugger that offers all the necessary tools you need to write great apps, such as breakpoints, variable investigation, call stack, and expression evaluators.

By completing this chapter, you have walked through all the most important and powerful features you need to know to write great cross-platform applications using Visual Studio Code.

CHAPTER 10

Building Applications with Python

Python is a very popular and powerful programming language that can be used to develop applications of any kind, and it is especially useful to build data science and data analysis applications.

Python is an interpreted, object-oriented programming language that can be learned by developers of any background. This chapter describes how Visual Studio Code supports building and debugging Python code, including specific code-editing features. Obviously, the chapter's focus is not the Python language but rather how Python can be used with VS Code.

Chapter Prerequisites

In this chapter, I provide examples of running and debugging Python code. Following along with these examples requires that you install the following components before you continue reading:

- The Python interpreter with its tools, which you can download from the Python official site (`https://www.python.org/downloads`). The download page automatically detects your operating system and offers the appropriate download package for Windows, macOS, and Linux distributions. On Windows 10 and higher, Python can also be installed from the Microsoft Store.

- The Python extension for Visual Studio Code provided by Microsoft, which you can install via the Extensions panel. There are several extensions for Python in the Marketplace, but I recommend that you download the official one, shown in Figure 10-1, because it dramatically improves the development experience with a debugger and additional coding tools.

239

© Alessandro Del Sole 2023
A. Del Sole, *Visual Studio Code Distilled*, https://doi.org/10.1007/978-1-4842-9484-0_10

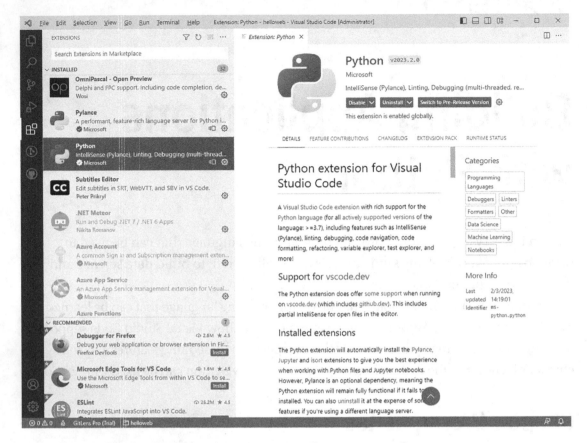

Figure 10-1. *The official Python extension from Microsoft*

Note   This chapter walks through a simple code example, but in the real world you might want to build more complex applications, in which case you need additional components. For instance, building data science applications requires Anaconda (`https://www.anaconda.com`), a distribution that includes Python and the R programming languages, plus a set of libraries specific for data science. If you instead need to do web development, you might want to consider Django (`https://www.djangoproject.com`), a web framework built with Python.

If you haven't already created a dedicated folder on disk for the code examples (mine is called VSCode), as suggested in the previous chapters, I recommend doing so for this chapter.

Now that you have all the minimum required tools installed, you are ready to start coding and debugging with Python in Visual Studio Code.

Creating Python Applications

Previously in the book you learned that Visual Studio Code is independent from proprietary project systems and platforms and, consequently, does not offer any built-in options to create projects, and this is also true for the Python programming language.

What you can do with Visual Studio Code is open existing Python files and projects or create new code files from within the development environment. As an example, let's consider a simple battleships game available in one code file at pythonfiddle.com/battleships-game-in-python/.

In Visual Studio Code, create a new file and then select Python as the language from the well-known drop-down menu located in the bottom-right corner. The source code in its current state will not work with the latest versions of the Python interpreter, because it is missing parentheses that enclose parameters of the print function and some string-to-integer conversions. The modified and working code for Python is listed here for your convenience:

```python
import random
board = []
for x in range(0,5):
  board.append(["O"] * 5)
def print_board(board):
  for row in board:
    print (" ".join(row))
print ("Let's play Battleship!")
print_board(board)
def random_row(board):
  return random.randint(0,len(board)-1)
def random_col(board):
  return random.randint(0,len(board[0])-1)
ship_row = random_row(board)
ship_col = random_col(board)
print (ship_row)
print (ship_col)
```

```python
for turn in range(4):
      guess_row =  int(input("Guess Row:"))
      guess_col = int(input("Guess Col:"))
      if guess_row == ship_row and guess_col == ship_col:
        print ("Congratulations! You sunk my battleship!")
        break
      else:
          if turn == 3:
                board[guess_row][guess_col] = "X"
                print_board(board)
                print ("Game Over")
                print ("My ship was here:
                [" + str(ship_row) + "][" + str(ship_col)
                + "]")
          else:
                if (guess_row < 0 or guess_row > 4) or
                   (guess_col < 0 or guess_col > 4):
                    print ("Oops, that's not even in the ocean.")
                elif(board[guess_row][guess_col] == "X"):
                    print
                            ("You guessed that one already.")
                else:
                    print ("You missed my battleship!")
                    board[guess_row][guess_col] = "X"
                print (turn + 1)
                print_board(board)
```

Save the file as BattleshipsGame.py. This is a simplified implementation of the
battleships game and is mostly for learning purposes, but it is enough to understand
how Visual Studio Code can support Python development. You will immediately notice
powerful editing features as you type the source code, such as (but not limited to)
IntelliSense and parameter hinting, but before highlighting Python-specific editing
features, I walk you through running and debugging Python code.

Running Python Code

Visual Studio Code automatically attempts to retrieve an appropriate Python interpreter on your machine when you assign this language to a code file or open an existing file. Sometimes VS Code might not be able to do this even if you previously installed a Python interpreter successfully, in which case you receive a warning similar to the one shown in Figure 10-2.

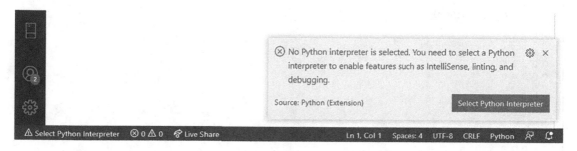

Figure 10-2. *Visual Studio Code could not find a Python interpreter*

Clicking the Select Python Interpreter button in the warning card or the same-named item at the bottom-left corner of the Status Bar enables you to pick your favorite version of the Python interpreter (see Figure 10-3).

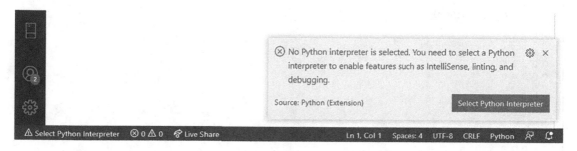

Figure 10-3. *Selecting a version of the Python interpreter*

This is a very nice option in case you need to select a specific version and not necessarily the most recent one. Once you have selected a Python interpreter, the name appears on the Status Bar, replacing the Select Python Interpreter button with the name of the selected interpreter, and you can either run or debug your code. Let's start with running code, which you can do by choosing Run ➤ Run Without Debugging. The Python runtime builds the code file and, if no error is found, the output of the code is displayed in an instance of the Terminal panel. Figure 10-4 shows an example based on the sample game provided previously.

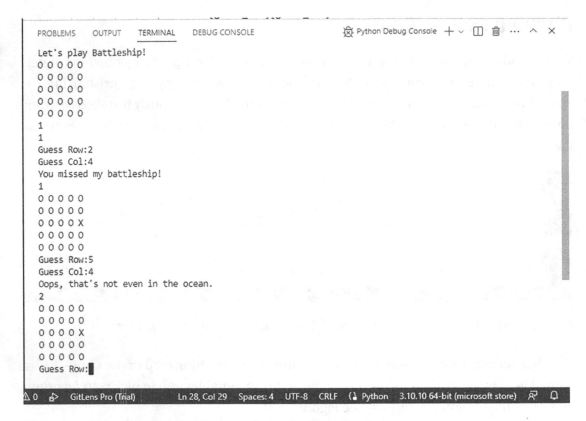

Figure 10-4. *Output of Python code in the Terminal*

The Terminal allows user input, so you can enter the values for the battleships. Behind the scenes, Visual Studio Code invokes a tool called Launcher, which is installed together with the Python interpreter and makes it possible to run Python code from the command line.

Note   In more specific development scenarios based on the Anaconda libraries, such as data science, Visual Studio Code can display additional tool windows and show charts and calculation results inside the development environment. More details are available from the official Data Science Tutorial (`code.visualstudio.com/docs/python/data-science-tutorial`).

For the next example, make sure you add a breakpoint at the following line (as described in Chapter 9):

```
if guess_row == ship_row and guess_col == ship_col:
```

This is to demonstrate how debugging tools for Python work. You start debugging Python code by pressing F5, by clicking the Run and Debug button in the Run panel, or by choosing Run ➤ Start Debugging. At this point Visual Studio Code asks you what file or program you want to debug, as shown in Figure 10-5.

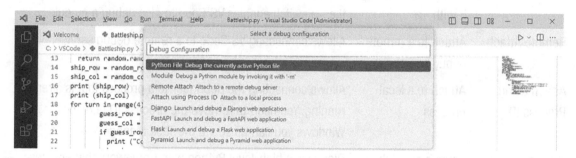

Figure 10-5. *Selecting the debugging target*

You can select any one of the configurations, which are provided by the Python extension for VS Code, described in Table 10-1.

Table 10-1. *Debug Configurations for Python*

Configuration Name	VS Code Description	Description
Python File	Debug the currently active Python file	Starts debugging the currently active Python file, where "active" means the file in the active editor.
Module	Debug a Python module by invoking it with -m	A Python module can be considered a code library, comparable to namespaces in a C# library. Debugging with the -m switch enables VS Code to also debug a module.
Remote Attach	Attach to a remote debug server	Allows connecting VS Code to a remote debug service.
Attach using Process ID	Attach to a local process	Allows connecting the debugger to a process that is already running. You need to retrieve the process ID (e.g., on Windows you can do so via the Task Manager).
Django	Launch and debug a Django web application	Django is a high-level Python web framework that enables rapid development of secure and maintainable websites. With this option, you can debug a Django project in VS Code.
FastAPI	Launch and debug a FastAPI web application	FastAPI is a modern web framework for building APIs with Python (requires version 3.6 or higher). With this configuration, you can use VS Code to debug a FastAPI project.
Flask	Launch and debug a Flask web application	Flask is another framework that allows building web applications with Python. With this configuration, VS Code makes it possible to debug Flask projects.
Pyramid	Launch and debug a Pyramid web application	Pyramid is a framework for Python that allows you to create web applications based on the Model-View-Controller (MVC) pattern. With this configuration, you can debug a Pyramid project in VS Code.

For the current example, select the first option, Python File, which allows you to debug the current code file. The application starts in the integrated Terminal and VS Code's Status Bar becomes orange, which indicates that the application is in debug mode. In the Terminal, you can enter the values for the battleships game, and then, because you previously set a breakpoint, the execution will break at the line where you placed the debugger. This will enable all the toolboxes in the Run panel as well as data tips in the code editor (see Figure 10-6).

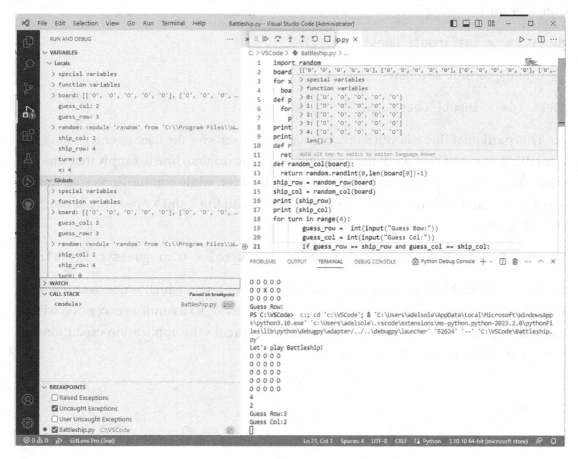

Figure 10-6. *The application in debug mode and debugging tools enabled*

If you hover your cursor over a variable name in the code editor, you can see its current value. For instance, if you hover over the guess_col variable, you will see that it contains the integer value you entered during the execution. However, Python debugging tools offer more: if you hover over a complex type like the board variable, which is a list of arrays, you will see how a sophisticated data tip shows values for each array in the list. You can expand the Special Variables and Function Variables groups to get more information about runtime functions.

The values you see through data tips are also visible in the Locals group of the VARIABLES tool in the Run panel. Debugging tools for Python can catch runtime exceptions and display appropriate information to solve them. To understand how this works, you can intentionally introduce a runtime exception in the current sample file. Consider the following line:

```
guess_row = int(input("Guess Row:"))
```

Change the line as follows:

```
guess_row = input("Guess Row:")
```

This particular line will still work, because it still waits for the user to enter something from the keyboard; the difference from the original line is simply that the input, of type str, is not converted into an int. However, while comparisons with the equality operator will succeed, comparisons made with the < and > operators at the following line:

```
if (guess_row < 0 or guess_row > 4) or (guess_col < 0 or guess_col > 4):
```

will fail, because this line attempts to compare the user input, which is now a string, with an integer value, and such a comparison is not supported, so a runtime exception will happen. Figure 10-7 shows how Visual Studio Code breaks the application execution when it encounters a runtime exception.

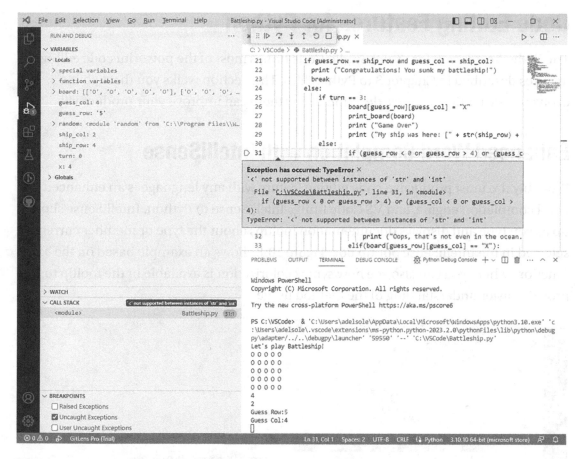

Figure 10-7. *Debugging runtime exceptions in Python*

More specifically, the exception information is displayed in a different-colored tooltip that is displayed right below the line of code that caused the error. In this tooltip, you can see the exception type (TypeError in this case), the number and contents of the line of code, and the full error message. Actually, the tooltip also displays the name of the file that caused the exception in the form of a hyperlink. This is very useful when the exception was raised by a different file in the execution hierarchy, enabling you to quickly go to the problem by clicking the filename.

As you have seen, debugging Python code in Visual Studio Code is a rich experience, but the Python extension offers even more functionality, such as a dedicated language service and additional features, discussed in the next section.

Code Editing Features for Python

The Python extension for Visual Studio Code brings most of the powerful code editing features described in Chapter 3 to Python files. This section walks you through the evolved code editing features, describing how these can improve your productivity.

Enhanced Word Completion with IntelliSense

Probably the most productive code editing feature with any language is an enhanced word completion engine, and VS Code brings IntelliSense to Python. IntelliSense shows up as you type and displays documentation tooltips about the type or member currently selected in the IntelliSense popup box. Figure 10-8 shows an example based on the bin function, where you can also see how syntax colorization is available in the tooltip to provide easier understanding of the method usage.

Figure 10-8. *IntelliSense in action with Python*

Understanding Function Parameters with Parameter Hints

Connected to IntelliSense is Parameter Hints. When you type the name of a function, you get suggestions on how to provide parameters, as demonstrated in Figure 10-9, which is based on the pow function.

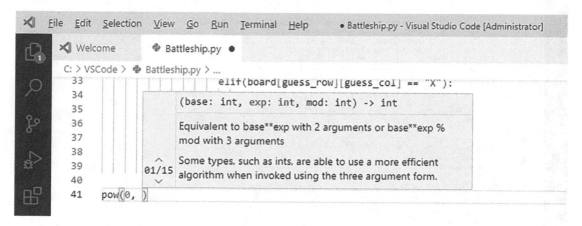

Figure 10-9. *Parameter Hints explains how to provide function parameters*

As you can see, the parameter you are currently supplying is highlighted in bold, while a description of the parameter itself is provided as the text content of the tooltip.

Quickly Retrieving Type Definitions

Among the code editor productivity features, Go to Definition and Peek Definition (see Chapter 3) are certainly very useful and popular, and these are also available to Python code files. To understand how they work in Python, right-click the board parameter of the print_board statement in the last line of the code file.

If you click Go to Definition, the cursor moves to the place where the board variable is declared. If you instead select Peek and then Peek Definition, the definition is shown inside an interactive popup box, where you can make your edits directly (see Figure 10-10).

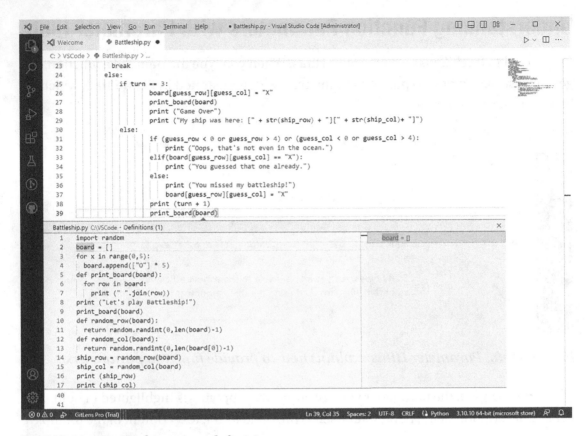

Figure 10-10. *Peeking type definitions*

Finding References

As explained in Chapter 3 and exactly like for other languages such as C#, you can quickly search for all references of a given type, member, or variable in Python. Simply right-click the object of your choice in the code editor and select Find All References. For instance, you can do this with the board variable in the sample code file and you will see where it was used across the code via the already well-known interactive editor, which highlights occurrences and shows a list of references on the left. Figure 10-11 demonstrates this.

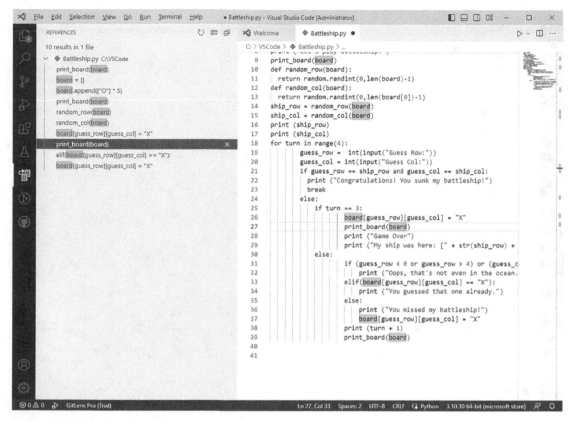

Figure 10-11. *Finding object references*

Renaming Symbols

With the Python extension, renaming symbols is an easy task. You can just right-click
a symbol, select Rename Symbol (or press F2), and provide the new name, and all the
occurrences in the source code will be renamed accordingly. When typing the new
name, you can also press Shift+Enter and see a preview of all the occurrences that will be
renamed.

Figure 10-12 shows an example based on the board variable, with the preview
enabled.

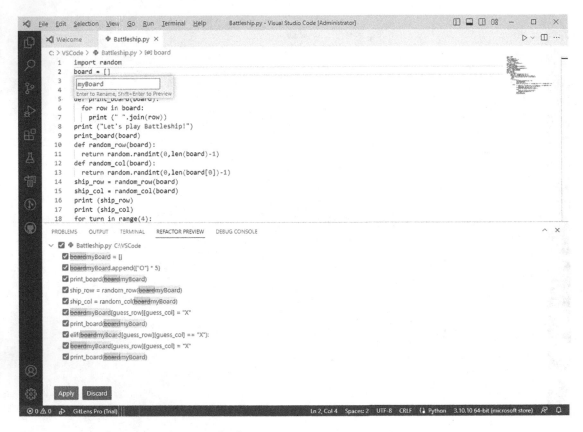

Figure 10-12. *Renaming symbols*

If you enabled the Refactor Preview panel, you need to click the tick icon in order to accept your changes. If you instead entered a new name without looking at the preview, simply press Enter and all the occurrences of (including references to) the symbol will be renamed.

Finding Code Issues with Linters

Linters highlight syntactical and stylistic problems in your code. Just as an example, linters highlight missing brackets or parentheses in a code block or highlight the usage of an undefined variable, underlining the code with squiggles. Linting is not enabled by default, but you can quickly do this via the Command Palette. You can type **Python Select Linter** directly, or just **Python** and then pick the appropriate command. Figure 10-13 shows how to enable linting with the list of commands filtered as I was typing.

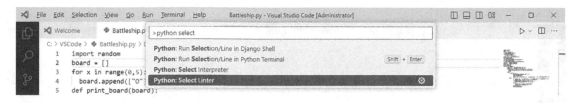

Figure 10-13. *Enabling Python linters*

When you select this command, the Command Palette also displays a list of available linters for Python. This is actually up to your choice, but I suggest using *pylint*, which is the official Microsoft linter provided via the Python extension. When the linter is enabled, the code editor displays squiggles under code that has issues, and these code issues are also detailed in the Problems panel, as shown in Figure 10-14.

Note   If you have experience with C# in Visual Studio Code, you might expect the same behavior of live code analysis as you type, but, with Python, linters show squiggles under code that has issues only after saving a code file or by explicitly invoking the linter from the Command Palette. An enhancement to this is provided by the Pylance extension, described shortly.

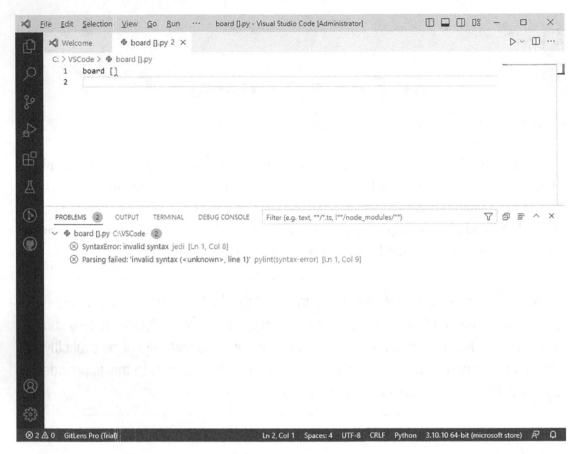

Figure 10-14. *Linters highlight code issues in the editor and in the Problems panel*

Note   Linters, as well as the other editing features, can be further customized with the Settings user interface and via the `settings.json` file. Because the goal of this book is to provide guidance on the most effective ways to get productive quickly, I am showing the fastest configuration options available with a few mouse clicks. If you want to dig deep into setting customizations, bookmark the related documentation at `https://code.visualstudio.com/docs/python/linting`, where you will also find more details about the pylint linter and summary information about the other linters listed in the Command Palette.

Advanced Code Editing with Pylance

Without a doubt, the Python extension for Visual Studio Code tremendously improves developer productivity and the coding experience, but Microsoft is doing even more. In fact, Microsoft is offering a new extension called Pylance, which introduces code refactorings, IntelliCode (an evolved code completion engine powered by artificial intelligence), and other improvements.

When you open (or create) a Python code file, Visual Studio Code shows a popup box that offers to install Pylance, as shown in Figure 10-15. As an alternative, you can download the Pylance extension from the Extensions tool directly (see Figure 10-16).

Figure 10-15. *Visual Studio Code offering to install the Pylance extension*

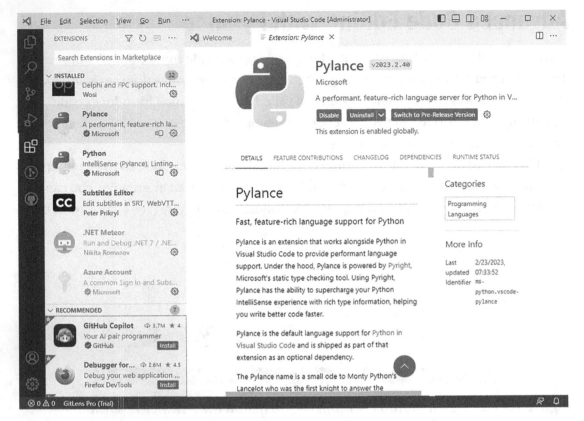

Figure 10-16. *The Pylance extension details*

Once Pylance has been installed, IntelliSense will be powered by IntelliCode. This tool learns from your code and from your patterns and offers an improved editing experience based on your coding styles, enabling IntelliSense to provide even better suggestions based on the coding context.

Pylance is not limited to offering an improved IntelliSense engine, but it makes it easier to write better code with new code refactorings and live code analysis. For instance, Pylance enables linters to show error squiggles as you type. As another example, whereas the Python extension, by default, only allows sorting `import` directives, Pylance introduces new refactorings: Extract Method, Extract Variable, and automatic addition of the required `import` directives when adding code via IntelliSense or code snippets. For a better understanding of how this all works, select the following code block of the sample file, as shown in Figure 10-17:

```
for x in range(0,5):
  board.append(["0"] * 5)
```

```
def print_board(board):
  for row in board:
    print (" ".join(row))
print ("Let's play Battleship!")
```

You will see a light bulb icon appear, which means that there are some suggestions to refactor the selected code block.

Figure 10-17. *Enabling suggestions for code fixes*

If you hover your cursor over the light bulb icon, you will see a tooltip saying Show Fixes. Click it to see available suggestions for the current context; in this case there is one suggestion, Extract Method. Click this suggestion and VS Code will extract a new method for the selected block, adding the related method call. This is demonstrated in Figure 10-18.

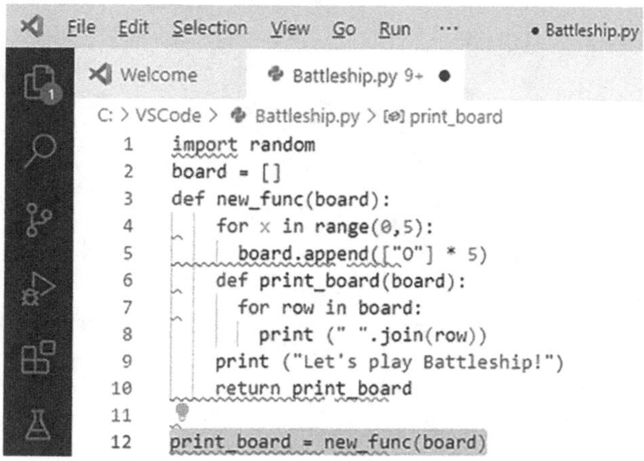

Figure 10-18. *Extracting a method*

The new method is created with a default name (`new_func`), but VS Code offers you the option to rename it via the Rename Symbol user interface. Similarly, the code fix called Extract Variable enables you to extract a variable from a code block, and it is available through the light bulb icon only if the context of the code allows you to extract variables. The light bulb icon is not the only shortcut to retrieve code fixes for a code block; you can also select a code block, right-click, and then select Refactor from the context menu.

Managing Pylance Settings

Like for other extensions, you can manage Pylance options under Visual Studio Code settings. Figure 10-19 shows how the Pylance settings appear and how they can be located under the Extensions node.

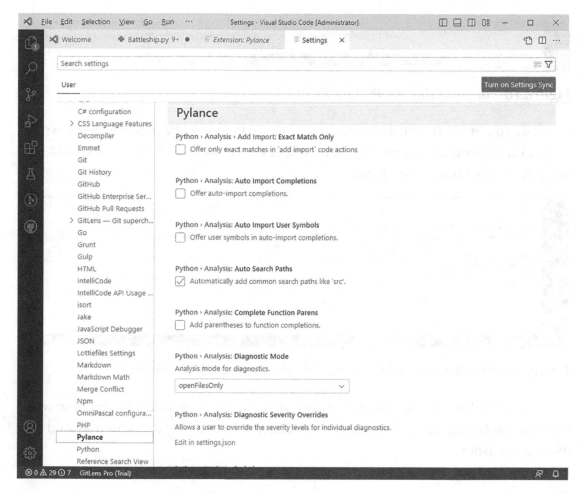

Figure 10-19. *Changing Pylance settings*

You can further customize the coding experience by changing options whose name are self-explanatory and that Visual Studio Code describes appropriately.

Running Python Scripts

Python is also an interpreted language, so it allows you to run arbitrary code without the need of a backing build process. Visual Studio Code supports Python as an interpreter, providing an option to write and run code via an REPL (read-eval-print-loop) interactive console, available within the Terminal.

You enable the Python REPL in the Command Palette by selecting the Python: Start REPL command·(see Figure 10-20).

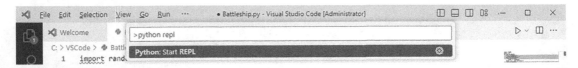

Figure 10-20. *Enabling the Python REPL console*

At this point the Terminal appears and loads the Python REPL, where you can write and run arbitrary code. Figure 10-21 shows an example based on declaring a variable and printing its contents onscreen.

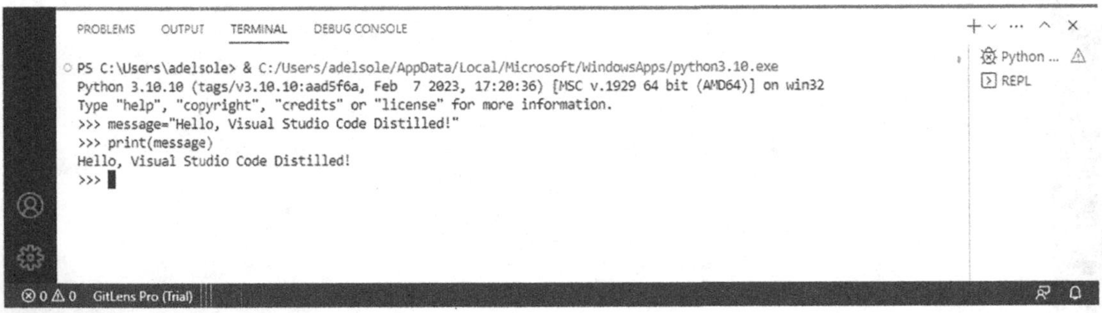

Figure 10-21. *Running arbitrary code in the Python REPL console*

This is another important tool for Python developers, because it is a very common way to use this language and certainly a way that leverages one of the most powerful of its characteristics.

Summary

Python is a very popular and powerful programming language and it is fully supported by Visual Studio Code. It offers full support for evolved code editing, debugging, and even for advanced development with data science tools and libraries.

Visual Studio Code enhances support for Python with the official Python extension, which makes working with Python very similar to working with other languages and platforms. That means you can apply existing skills and knowledge if you are approaching Python for the first time but have experience with C# or Node.js.

Microsoft also offers the Pylance extension, which provides an improved IntelliSense experience with IntelliCode and additional code refactorings. An interactive REPL for interpreted code completes the integrated tooling for Python.

Once again, Visual Studio Code demonstrates how versatile it is, providing a perfect environment for Python and its most popular flavors.

CHAPTER 11

Deploying Applications to Azure

Azure is Microsoft's premiere cloud solution that offers many services, from hosting web applications and SQL databases to remote virtual machines, artificial intelligence services, and many more.

With Visual Studio Code, it is easy to deploy your code to Azure through a number of extensions that support multiple environments, such as Node.js and .NET, and that offer an integrated experience so that you can work directly within your development environment. Many extensions for Azure development are available, each targeting different scenarios, but it would require an entire book to describe them all, so in this chapter, I cover two of the most popular extensions: Azure App Service, which supports publishing web applications, and Azure Functions, which enables you to work with serverless apps directly from Visual Studio Code.

Note This chapter requires an active Microsoft Azure subscription to complete the examples. If you do not have one, you can get a free trial at `https://azure.microsoft.com/en-us/free`.

Introducing Azure Extensions

Visual Studio Code supports developing with the most popular and powerful Azure services. Support is integrated in the development environment with specific extensions available in the Visual Studio Marketplace. Table 11-1 lists and describes common extensions for Azure development.

© Alessandro Del Sole 2023
A. Del Sole, *Visual Studio Code Distilled*, https://doi.org/10.1007/978-1-4842-9484-0_11

Table 11-1. *Common Extensions for Azure Development*

Extension	Description
Azure Account	Allows you to sign into one or more Azure subscriptions.
Azure App Service	Provides integrated support to deploy web applications to the cloud.
Azure CLI Tools	Installs all the command-line tools required to work with all the Azure services.
Azure Databases	Allows you to create, browse, and manage SQL Azure, MongoDB, Cosmos DB, PostgreSQL, and DocumentDb databases directly within VS Code via an integrated browser.
Azure Functions	Provides integrated support for writing, testing, and deploying Azure Functions.
Azure Machine Learning	Formerly called Visual Studio Code for AI Tools, allows you to create, build, train, and deploy machine learning models based on your Azure subscriptions.
Azure Resource Manager	Allows you to manage Azure resource groups in VS Code.
Azure Storage	Allows you to connect to blobs, tables, files, and queue storage in your Azure subscriptions. It also allows you to upload folders directly from within VS Code.
Docker	Allows you to publish containerized applications from Visual Studio Code, with improved code editing features for Docker and YAML files.
Kubernetes	Provides integrated support to deploy Docker containers to Kubernetes, an open-source system for automating deployment, scaling, and management of containerized applications, supported by Azure.

I recommend that you bookmark the official documentation, available at
`https://code.visualstudio.com/docs/azure/extensions`, for further details and
examples. Noteworthy is that Visual Studio Code can support Docker and Kubernetes for
containerized applications, which is something very important for many developers.

Deploying Web Applications

Deploying web applications to Azure with Visual Studio Code is very easy. You can retake the HelloWeb sample applications created with C# and .NET in Chapter 9, but it's worth remembering that publishing to Azure is not limited to these technologies, but is also possible for Node.js.

Note   Visual Studio Code, the Microsoft Azure platform, and Azure extensions for VS code continuously evolve. New releases might introduce changes to what is described in this chapter.

Installing Extensions

The first thing you need to do is install the Azure App Service extension from the Marketplace. This extension also needs the Azure Account and the Azure Resources extensions, but these are installed together with the App Service, so you do not need to take any additional steps.

The Azure Account extension is required to enable developers to log in to their Azure account from within Visual Studio Code and to select which subscription to use. The Azure Resources extension is used to manage resources groups, which are the places where your cloud services are organized. Figure 11-1 shows the Azure App Service extension in the Extensions panel.

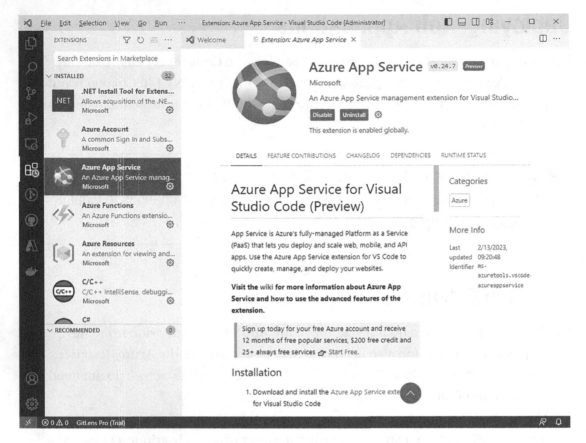

Figure 11-1. *The Azure App Service extension from Microsoft*

Signing In to Azure Subscriptions

Once the Azure App Service extension has been installed, along with the Azure Account and Azure Resource Groups extensions, you need to sign in before you can use any service.

To accomplish this, you can use the Azure: Sign In command from the Command Palette or the Sign in to Azure shortcut in the App Service node of the Azure Side Bar. Either action opens an instance of your default browser pointing to the Microsoft Account login service. Simply enter your credentials, sign in, and close the browser window once you are logged in. Now in Visual Studio Code you can open the Azure extension and see the list of services associated with your subscription.

Note   If you don't see the list of subscriptions, you can read the official troubleshooting guide (`https://github.com/microsoft/vscode-azure-account/wiki/Troubleshooting`). For example, a very common way to solve this problem is by typing the `Azure Select Tenant` command in the Palette and selecting the subscription.

Figure 11-2 shows an example based on my subscription.

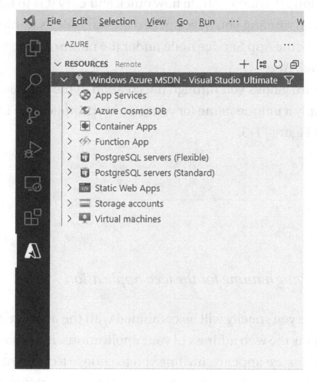

Figure 11-2. *The Azure services view*

Note   The Microsoft Azure offering is very extensive and spans a plethora of services, so I recommend that you look at the official website (`https://azure.microsoft.com/en-us/free`) for detailed information. In addition, do not forget to enter the management portal (`https://portal.azure.com`), which gives you access to the full tools and options to create and manage your services and resources.

The hierarchical view displays resources and the services they contain, and it also supports multiple subscriptions.

You can quickly interact with each service by expanding its node and accessing the available options by right-clicking its name.

Publishing Web Applications

Visual Studio Code makes the process of publishing web apps to Azure very easy. The goal of this section is to demonstrate how quick and easy it is to publish a web application to Azure. Assuming you have opened the HelloWeb sample project, in the Azure view, right-click the App Service node under the name of your subscription and select Create New Web App.

A three-step wizard guides you through the creation of the application. The first step asks you to supply a unique name for your new web application in the Command Palette, as shown in Figure 11-3.

Figure 11-3. *Specifying a name for the web application*

Because the name you specify will be combined with the azurewebsites.net domain and represents the web address of your applications, if the name is already taken, a validation message appears, inviting you to choose a different name. You might want to specify a name that is different from vscodedistilled, which is the name I use for the examples in this chapter.

The next step is to specify the target environment for your web application; this is necessary because the Azure extension cannot detect which technology your app is based on. Figure 11-4 shows the list of available options.

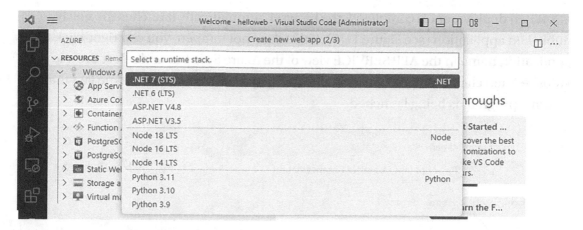

Figure 11-4. *Specifying a target platform*

Because the sample application was written on .NET 7, select this as the target platform. The last step of the wizard asks you to specify a pricing tier. I suggest using the Free (F1) tier, as shown in Figure 11-5.

Figure 11-5. *Specifying a pricing tier*

After you complete these three easy steps, Visual Studio Code first builds the project in Release mode (and the result will be visible in the Terminal) and then starts creating the necessary resources inside your Azure subscription, and you will be able to see the progress in a popup box that appears in the bottom-right corner of the environment. When everything is ready, a popup message asks if you want to deploy or cancel. Click Deploy. VS Code might tell you that some configuration is still missing, but this will be added if you click the Add Config button on the warning dialog. As a final step, another popup message asks if you want to enable automatic deployment. Click Yes so that the application will be published.

When deployment is completed, the browser automatically launches the newly published application (see Figure 11-6). If this does not happen, you can right-click the application name in the APP SERVICE view of the Azure Side Bar and select Browse Website, then click the Open button in the dialog that informs you about the fact that an external program is being launched.

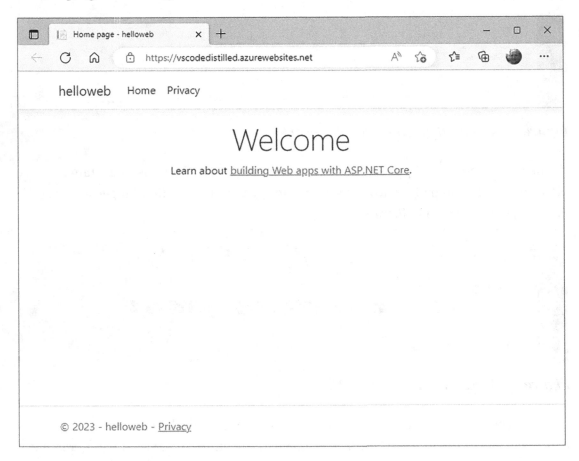

Figure 11-6. *The web application running in the cloud*

You need no additional steps. Your application is up and running in the browser, hosted in your Azure subscription. You can further manage your Azure services and resources, both within Visual Studio Code and in the Azure portal (`https://portal.azure.com`). Though managing resources in the Azure portal is a bigger topic and is out of the scope of this chapter, Figure 11-7 shows the management page for the sample web application, where you can see the full list of available settings on the left side and information on the deployment, the data center, and statistics in the main view.

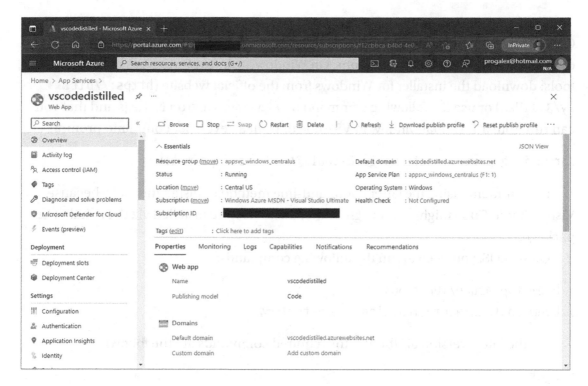

Figure 11-7. *Managing App Services in the Azure portal*

Creating and Deploying Azure Functions

Put succinctly, Azure Functions (`https://docs.microsoft.com/en-us/azure/azure-functions`) is a service that allows you to run code on-demand in the cloud, and it is considered part of the growing trend of *serverless computing*. The biggest benefit of using Azure Functions is that functions are triggered only when invoked, which not only reduces the use of cloud resources but also reduces maintenance and infrastructure needs, thereby providing more cost savings.

Configuring Visual Studio Code

Azure supports writing functions in several languages, such as C#, Python, Java, JavaScript, and Rust. Usually, tools are available for different development environments to write Azure Functions, such as Visual Studio 2022, and Visual Studio Code is no exception.

271

The first thing you need to develop Azure Functions with VS Code is Azure Functions Core Tools. This set of command-line tools is required to run the tasks necessary to develop, debug, and publish functions. On Windows, you have two ways to install these tools: download the installer for Windows from the official website (`https://bit.ly/3f1lHxR`) or use the following command that leverages `npm` on Node.js and that you can run from a Terminal window in VS Code or from a developer command prompt:

```
> npm i -g azure-functions-core-tools@4 --unsafe-perm true
```

I recommend using the latter command-line method to install the tools, because Visual Studio Code might not recognize that the tools were installed via the installer package.

On macOS, you need to run the following commands:

```
> brew tap azure/functions
> brew install azure-functions-core-tools@4
```

On the latest version of Ubuntu, the required commands are the following:

```
> wget
-q https://packages.microsoft.com/config/ubuntu/20.04/packages-microsoft-prod.deb
> sudo dpkg -i packages-microsoft-prod.deb
```

The installation commands vary depending on the Linux distribution, so you can locate the appropriate commands at `https://github.com/Azure/azure-functions-core-tools#linux`.

Once you have installed Azure Functions Core Tools, you need to install the Azure Functions extension for Visual Studio Code (see Figure 11-8).

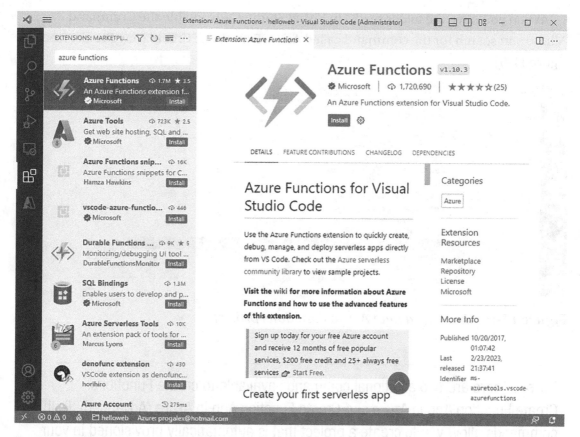

Figure 11-8. *The Azure Functions extension for VS Code*

The Azure Functions extension also needs the Azure Account one, which you already installed previously.

Creating Azure Functions

With the Azure Functions extension installed, VS Code simplifies the way you can create Azure Functions projects. For the current example about deploying Azure Functions, I show how to create a function stub using the built-in templates, but you can certainly use existing Azure Functions projects created with other environments or sample projects.

If you are starting with new code, you first need to have (or create) a new folder on disk where the new projects will be created. For the next example, I created a folder on disk called C:\VSCode\AzureFunctionsDistilled.

When you have the folder ready, in Visual Studio Code enable the Command Palette and search for the command called Azure Functions: Create New Project (see Figure 11-9).

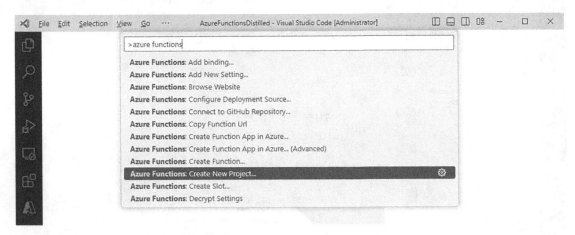

Figure 11-9. *Creating a new Azure Functions project*

Note   There are two additional commands available to create Functions: Create Function App in Azure and Create Function App in Azure (Advanced). Both commands allow you to create a project that is automatically provisioned in your Azure subscription, together with a local project for development and debugging. In this book, I'm not using these commands in order to better highlight the different phases of development and debugging, and then deployment.

When you click this command, an eight-step wizard starts. First, you are asked to select a target folder on disk, so pick the one you created previously. Then you are asked to select a language. For the sake of consistency with the previous examples, I selected C#, but you are free to use a different one. In the third step, you are asked to specify a runtime platform. If you selected C#, the wizard shows .NET versions and you can select the latest.

Note   The wizard identifies .NET 7 as .NET 7 (Isolated). Understanding what this means requires taking a step back into the previous versions of Azure Functions. Previously (and before .NET 5), Azure Functions only supported a tightly integrated mode for .NET functions, which run as a class library in the same process as the host. Though this mode provides deep integration between the host process and the functions, this integration also requires a tighter coupling between the host process and the .NET function. For example, .NET functions running in-process are required to run on the same version of .NET as the Functions runtime. To run outside these constraints, you can now choose to run in an isolated process. .NET 7 (Isolated) then means that support for running functions out-of-process is allowed.

If you selected another language, the list of target platforms will change depending on your language of choice.

In the fourth step, you have the option to select a project template (see Figure 11-10).

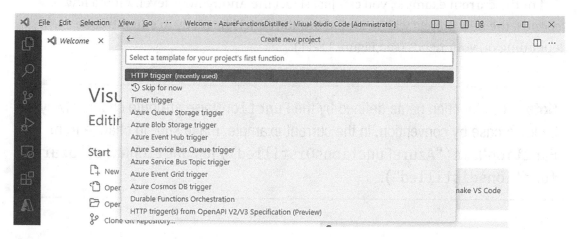

Figure 11-10. *Selecting an Azure Functions project template*

The project template you select here is not really relevant to the current example, whose goal is not to go into the details of Azure Functions development but rather to show how quick and easy building and deploying functions is. I selected the HttpTrigger template, which generates simple code that defines a function that is triggered on Azure when an HTTP/HTTPS request is intercepted, sending a response back.

In the fifth and sixth steps, you first enter a name for the new project (or leave the default project name, like `AzureFunctionsDistilled` in the current example) and then enter a namespace that will be used in the code. The namespace should be in the form `CompanyName.Function`; for example, my namespace is `AlessandroDelSole. AzureFunctionsDistilled`.

In the seventh step of the wizard, you specify a security access level: Anonymous, Function, or Admin. Table 11-2 provides a short description of each authorization level.

Table 11-2. *Azure Functions Authorization Levels*

Level	Description
Anonymous	No authorization required; all HTTP requests pass.
Function	Function authorization level is based on security keys generated in the Azure portal. Host keys (at the application level) and function keys (at the function level) can work as security keys in the Function level.
Admin	Similar to the Function level, but only works with host keys (at the app level).

For the current example, you can just select the Anonymous level. After a few seconds, the new project will be available and you will be ready to edit the code depending on your needs (see Figure 11-11).

Note   The function name defined by the `FunctionName` attribute should always be lowercase by convention. In the current example, make sure to change from `FunctionName("AzureFunctionsDistilled")` to `FunctionName("azure functionsdistilled")`.

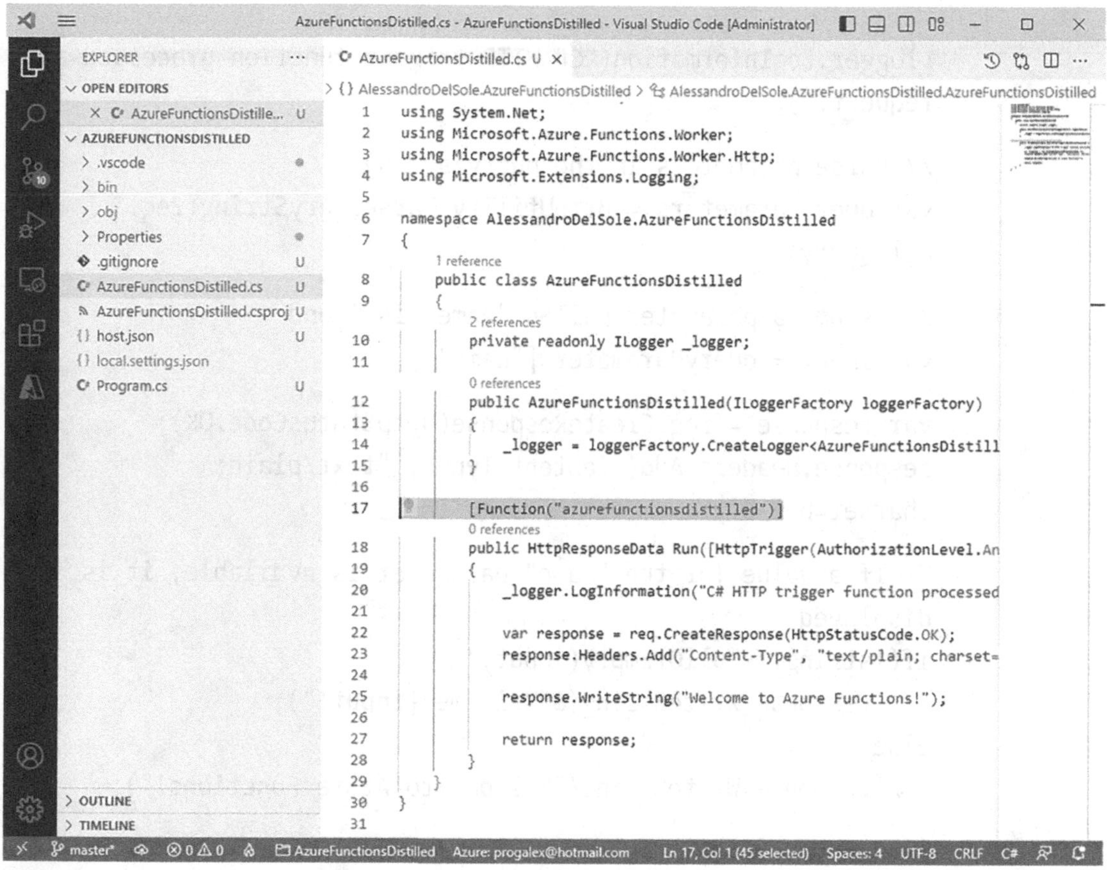

Figure 11-11. *Editing the Azure Functions project in VS Code*

Note   When you create an Azure Functions project, a local Git repository is also automatically initialized. At this writing, the extension settings do not allow for changing this behavior.

You are now working fully locally, which is a good opportunity to debug your code on a development environment before promoting the code to the Azure remote environment. Before debugging, extend the Run method as follows:

```
[Function("azurefunctionsdistilled")]
public HttpResponseData Run([HttpTrigger(AuthorizationLevel.
Anonymous, "get", "post")] HttpRequestData req)
```

```csharp
    {
        _logger.LogInformation("C# HTTP trigger function processed a
        request.");

        // Parse parameters in the query string
        var queryParameters = HttpUtility.ParseQueryString(req.
        Url.Query);

        // Assume a parameter called "name" is found
        var input = queryParameters["name"];

        var response = req.CreateResponse(HttpStatusCode.OK);
        response.Headers.Add("Content-Type", "text/plain;
        charset=utf-8");

        // If a value for the "name" parameter is available, it is
        displayed
        if(!string.IsNullOrEmpty(input))
            response.WriteString($"Welcome {input}");
        else
            response.WriteString("Welcome to Azure Functions!");

        return response;
    }
```

As you can see from the comments, the code parses the URL of the function to detect if any parameters where added in the form of a query string. If a parameter called name is found, the value is retrieved and displayed. Otherwise, a standard message is displayed.

At this point, press F5 to start debugging, exactly as you would do with any C# project, and after a few seconds the Terminal will show not only the compiler output but also a local URL that you can use to test the code (see Figure 11-12).

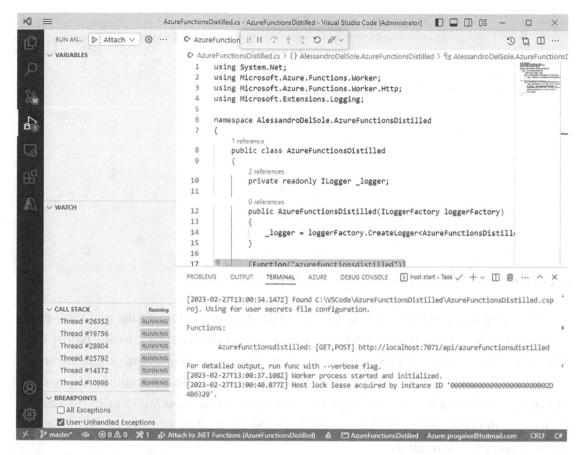

Figure 11-12. *Debugging an Azure function*

The URL shown in the Terminal is the following: `http://localhost:7071/api/`
`azurefunctionsdistilled`. 7071 is the port of the local development server, while
`azurefunctionsdistilled` is the name (all lowercase) of the function defined in
the code, and both will vary depending on the projects you create. You can paste the
aforementioned URL into the address bar of your browser plus a query string. In the
following example, my first name is passed to the `name` parameter:

`http://localhost:7071/api/azurefunctionsdistilled?name=Alessandro`

At this point, press Enter. Figure 11-13 shows the function running in the browser
and listening for `HTTP GET` and `POST` calls.

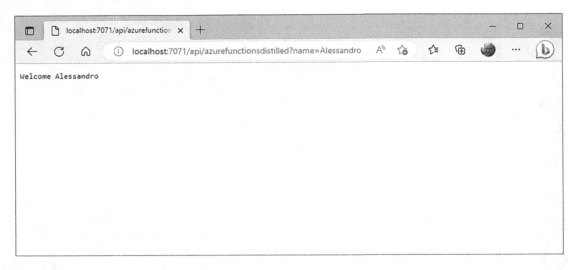

Figure 11-13. *Running an Azure function locally*

Assuming that you have done all your local development, debugging, and testing, you can publish the Azure function to the cloud, as described next. However, before the function is deployed to Azure you need to edit the web request timeout, otherwise any HTTP or HTTPS call will result in an Error 502 (Bad request). To accomplish this, open Visual Studio Code's Settings, and type `request timeout` in the search bar. In the Azure Functions: Request Timeout setting, enter **60** as the timeout in seconds. Finally, save the settings and you are ready to go.

Deploying Azure Functions

Deploying Azure Functions to your subscription in Visual Studio Code is an easy task. You can right-click the Function App node, under the subscription name in the RESOURCES, view and then select the Create Function App in Azure command (see Figure 11-14).

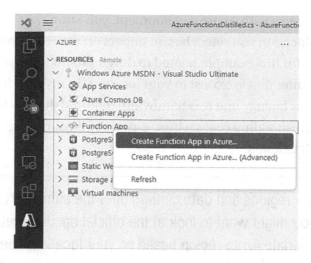

Figure 11-14. *Initiating the deploy process*

The Create Function App in Azure (Advanced) option is not discussed here because it relates to creating a function app with custom settings and resources. Once you click the highlighted shortcut, the Command Palette shows a quick wizard consisting of three steps. In the first step, specify a unique name (for the current example it is `azurefunctionsdistilled`) and then you need specify the target platform; the available options depend on the technology you used to build the app. Select the same platform you selected when creating the project.

In the last step of the wizard, you need to specify a data center location (see Figure 11-15).

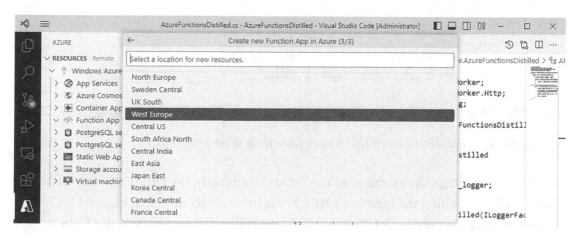

Figure 11-15. *Selecting a location for the data center*

If you have experience with Azure development, you know that this is a crucial choice, because the location you select has an impact on the costs charged to your subscription. At least for this example related to development purposes, make sure that you select the data center that is closest to your location (in my case it is West Europe), which translates to less latency and less bandwidth required during development and deployment, and corresponding cost savings, especially if your subscription does not have a spending limit enabled.

Note   Not all Azure regions and data centers offer the same services. For real-world scenarios, you might want to look at the official documentation about choosing the appropriate Azure region based on your location, needs, and requested services (`https://azure.microsoft.com/en-us/global-infrastructure/geographies`).

At this point, Visual Studio Code first builds the project in Release mode and then starts publishing the function to Azure. You can follow the progress in the Output panel and with the popup box that shows the name of the currently running task (see Figure 11-16).

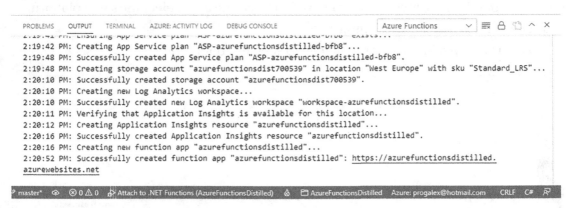

Figure 11-16. *Publication of the Azure function is in progress*

After the last step, the function will be up and running in the cloud, which you can easily verify by opening the function's URL in the browser, as shown in Figure 11-17. Remember that the function's URL is made by the unique name you supplied when creating the project, followed by the `azurewebsites.net` domain name and by the /

api/<functionname> part. In the case of an Azure Function, you can add the query string required to trigger the function itself. In Figure 11-18, you can see how the same query string used locally has also been supplied to the remote URL.

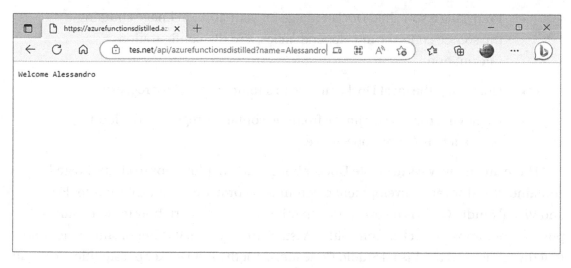

Figure 11-17. *The Azure function is running in the cloud*

As you have seen, Visual Studio Code makes it very simple not only to deploy an Azure Function, but also to create a project and interact with the Azure subscription directly from within the environment, which improves overall productivity.

Note   To avoid unexpected charges or consumption of your Azure credit, I recommend deleting all the resources that you no longer use, such as the sample applications created in this chapter. In VS Code you can quickly delete apps and functions by right-clicking on their name in the APP SERVICE and FUNCTIONS panels (respectively) of the Azure Side Bar and then selecting the appropriate Delete command. Additional resources can be deleted in the Azure portal.

Deploying Docker Images

Put succinctly, Docker (https://www.docker.com/) is a platform that allows you to publish an app and all of its dependencies through *containers*. This allows you to have applications that are independent from one another and that work autonomously.

Containers are deployed to a host such as Azure or another cloud service, and they are widely used with architectures based on microservices. In order to create a Docker container, you need to accomplish the following steps:

- Preparing a so-called Docker image for your app. An image contains the source code, the app dependencies, and the configuration information.

- Uploading the local Docker image to a remote container registry.

- Deploying the Docker image from the container registry to a cloud host, such as Azure App Service.

There are many ways to create Docker images and deploy apps to cloud-hosted containers, and several development environments provide integrated tools to do so, and Visual Studio Code is no exception. In this section you learn how to set up and publish your apps to Docker from within Visual Studio Code. It is important to mention that the focus is on the Visual Studio Code tools, not the full Docker possibilities. You will get the proper, necessary information but summarizing everything about Docker in this section is not possible. Do not forget to bookmark the official VS Code documentation (`https://code.visualstudio.com/docs/containers/app-service`) that you can check when you need to go to the next level.

Docker Prerequisites

Publishing apps to Docker containers requires the following prerequisites:

- The Docker Desktop software. A download link is automatically provided when you visit the Docker website (`https://www.docker.com`).

- The Docker extension for Visual Studio Code (see Figure 11-18).

- The Azure App Service extension for Visual Studio Code. You installed this previously if you followed the examples about publishing web applications to Azure.

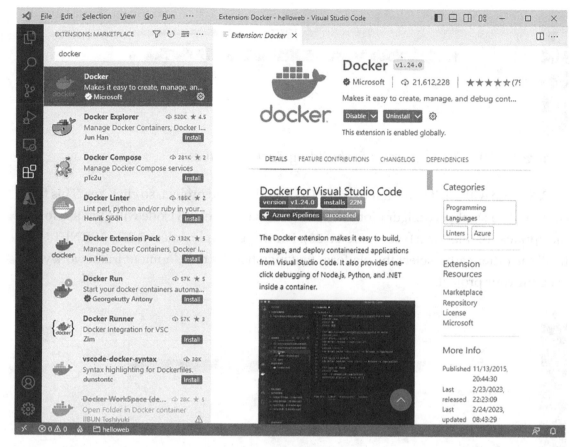

Figure 11-18. *The Docker extension for VS Code*

The next examples are built on the HelloWeb C# project created in Chapter 9, but remember that all the steps are platform- and language-agnostic. Having that said, open the HelloWeb project in VS Code.

Creating the Application Image

The application image contains the source code and the dependencies. You create the application image via the Docker Images: Build Image command, which is available in the Command Palette (see Figure 11-19).

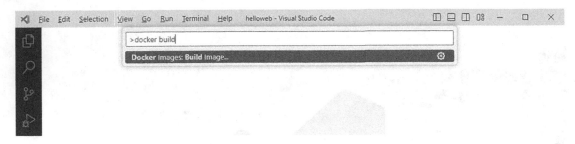

Figure 11-19. *The command for building docker images*

VS Code will ask if you want to add a Docker file to the project, so click Yes. This file contains the Docker configuration, so it is a necessary asset. VS Code will then ask for the application platform (see Figure 11-20). For this example, select .NET: ASP.NET Core. In all the other cases, select the platform that matches the development framework you used for your project.

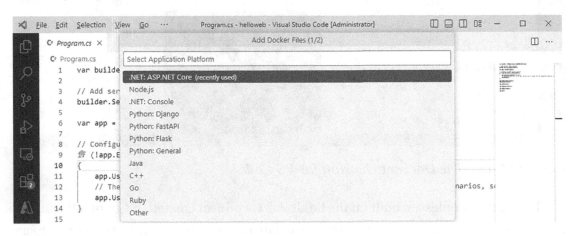

Figure 11-20. *Selecting the application platform*

At this point you are asked to choose between Windows and Linux as the host system. For the current example, select Windows. In the following steps, Visual Studio Code will ask you to specify:

- The port number that the application will use to listen to messages.

- If you want to include a Docker Compose file. This is optional and you can click No.

At this point, a Docker file is generated, and the application image is built. Figure 11-21 shows the Docker file in the active editor and the build results in the Terminal.

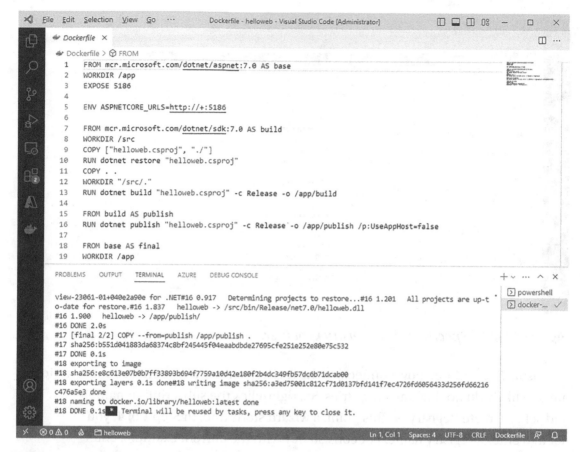

Figure 11-21. *The results of building the app image*

The application image has been created locally, and the next step is uploading the image to a remote container registry. It is worth mentioning that the Docker extension shows both the local and remote images. Keep this in mind, so you will not get confused.

Uploading the Application Image to a Container Registry

The application image built previously cannot be directly published to an App Service or Container app. It first needs to be published to a container registry. As the name implies, a container registry holds the list of application images.

To accomplish this, open the Docker panel and click the Connect Registry shortcut in the REGISTRIES view (see Figure 11-22). Also specify Azure as the registry provider.

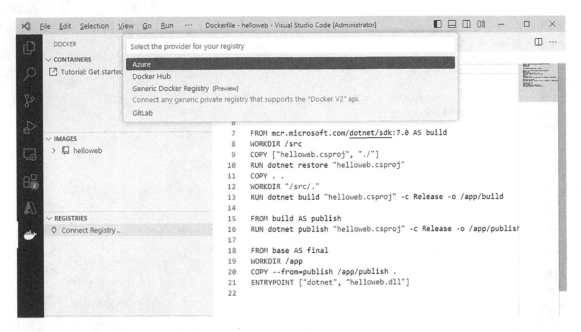

Figure 11-22. *Specifying the registry provider*

Visual Studio Code now connects to the registry service of your Azure subscription, but you likely do not have any registries. So, right-click the subscription name and select Create Registry. At this point, a wizard starts and, in Step 1 of 4, you need to enter a registry name. For consistency with the current example, enter `visualstudiocodedistilled` and then press Enter. In Step 2 of 4, you are then prompted with a list of stock-keeping units (SKUs). Available options are Basic, Standard, and Premium. Select Basic and press Enter. Step 3 of 4 requires you to select a resource group from a list of existing ones, or to create a new one. You can select one of the resource groups generated for the previous sections of this chapter. In the Step 4 of 4, you specify a registry location. Select the data center that is closest to your place of living. After a few seconds, the new registry will be visible in the REGISTRIES view and the application image will appear in the IMAGES view, as shown in Figure 11-23.

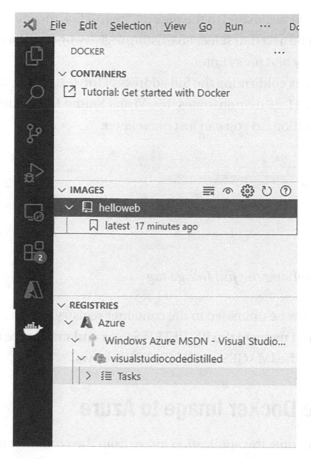

Figure 11-23. *The new registry has been created on Azure*

Uploading the image requires this to be tagged with the registry name. Right-click a build name (in Figure 11-23 the build name is identified as `latest 17 minutes ago`) and select Tag. A tag should have the following form: `registry/imagename:tag`. Visual Studio Code, via the Docker extension, automatically provides a valid tag, as demonstrated in Figure 11-24.

Figure 11-24. *Supplying the image tag*

Now the image can be pushed to the registry. Right-click the image name again and select Push. You will be asked to select an existing registry or create a new one. Select the one created previously and press Enter.

The very last step is confirming the full address of the target registry, which includes the image tag. Figure 11-25 demonstrates this. Visual Studio Code automatically provides the appropriate definition, so you can just press Enter.

Figure 11-25. *Supplying the full image tag*

The image will now be uploaded to the container registry. When ready, right-click the Azure subscription name in the REGISTRIES view and make sure the remote image is now visible in both the IMAGES and REGISTRIES views.

Deploying the Docker Image to Azure

The final step is uploading the application image from the container registry to an Azure App Service or Azure Container App. For the current example, the Azure App Service is used.

In the REGISTRIES view, right-click the build name and then select Deploy Image to Azure App Service (see Figure 11-26).

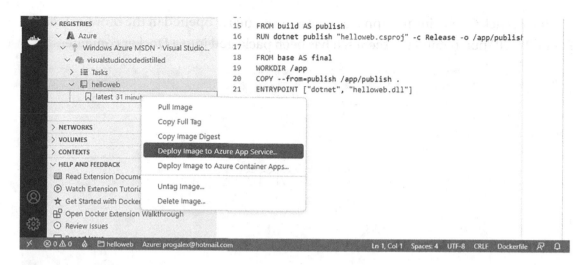

Figure 11-26. *Preparing to publish the image to Azure*

At this point, Visual Studio Code will open the Command Palette and start a wizard made of a few steps. The following are the most relevant:

1. Entering a globally unique name for the web application. Specify a name of your choice and press Enter.

2. Specifying a Linux service plan. This is required because your image will be hosted on a Linux server. If you do not have one, click the Create New App Service Plan command.

3. Specifying the pricing tier. Select Free (F1) and press Enter.

When the last step is completed, Visual Studio Code will start uploading the Docker image to the new web application service. When finished, Visual Studio Code shows the success message shown in Figure 11-27.

Figure 11-27. *The Docker image was successfully uploaded*

If you click Open Site, the application will be regularly opened in the browser (see Figure 11-28) but, behind the scenes, it has been packaged into a Docker container.

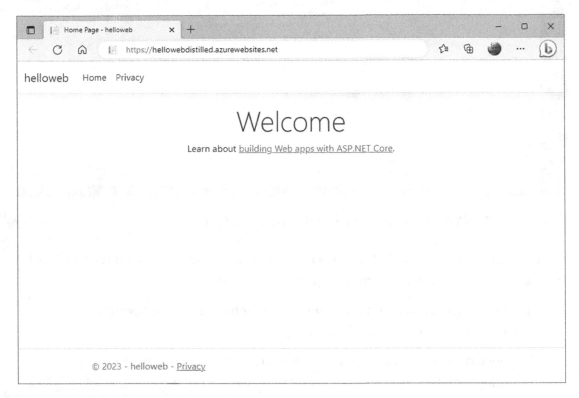

Figure 11-28. *The containerized app running in the browser*

There is obviously much more about Docker that cannot be included in this discussion, but you have seen how the Docker and Azure extensions provide an integrated experience to Visual Studio Code.

Summary

Once again, Visual Studio Code demonstrates its power and versatility even with cloud development based on Microsoft Azure. With the Azure extensions, you have access to your subscriptions directly from within the environment.

With specialized extensions, such as Azure App Service and Azure Functions, you can create, configure, and deploy your web applications and functions with limited effort and a few mouse clicks, reducing the need to manage resources in the Azure portal only to situations in which you need custom configurations. In addition, multiple languages and environments are supported, including .NET, Java, Python, and Node.js, extending the cloud development possibilities to a larger number of companies and developers.

In the last part of the chapter, you learned how to create Docker containers that can be managed and published directly from within Visual Studio Code. Continuing on your cloud journey, the next and last chapter of the book describes how to consume AI services from Visual Studio Code.

CHAPTER 12

Consuming AI Services

Without a doubt, artificial intelligence represents one of the most important topics for the present and future of application development.

All the biggest software vendors offer their own AI solutions and services, and many applications are already based on AI even if the user does not notice this.

As a developer, you need to have some knowledge of the possibilities offered by artificial intelligence and how you can implement solutions in your applications.

This chapter explains how you can consume AI services when developing apps from Visual Studio Code, taking advantage of coding and debugging tools when using client libraries. Obviously, the focus cannot be on explaining what artificial intelligence is, which branches of AI exist, and all the available offers. Instead, the focus of the chapter is explaining the steps you need to follow to consume most AI services from Visual Studio Code.

With regard to this, because you have created a Microsoft Azure account for the previous chapter, a few services from Azure are used. Due to the relevance of this topic, code examples are provided for C#, JavaScript, and Python. More specifically, you learn how to analyze an image and extract relevant information.

Note   Artificial intelligence services, usage, and implementations should always be done according to the so-called Responsible AI principles. This basically means that artificial intelligence should be offered with good intentions, to empower people and businesses to achieve positive results. You can read Microsoft's point of view on their AI blog (`https://blogs.microsoft.com/on-the-issues/2023/02/02/responsible-ai-chatgpt-artificial-intelligence/`)

© Alessandro Del Sole 2023
A. Del Sole, *Visual Studio Code Distilled*, https://doi.org/10.1007/978-1-4842-9484-0_12

Introducing Azure for AI

Microsoft Azure provides many artificial intelligence services, and most of them are available via API and Software Development Kits (SDKs).

Table 12-1 provides a summary of the available services. Note that this list might change in the future. You can periodically check the product page for updates (`https://azure.microsoft.com/en-us/products/`).

Table 12-1. *Most Important Azure Services for AI*

Service	Description
Azure Bot Service	Allows you to create conversational bots.
Azure Databricks	Provides support for working with Big Data.
Azure Cognitive Services	A group of AI services to analyze images, faces, videos, speech, and text.
Language Understanding (LUIS)	Allows you to analyze natural language.
Azure Machine Learning	Azure service to train AI models.
Personalizer	Allows you to generate personalized customer experiences.
Health Bot	A specialized bot aimed to create healthcare assistants.
Translator	Provides machine translations via API calls.
Azure OpenAI	Provides advanced language models for many use cases.
Azure Applied AI	Provides specialized services to help businesses solve common problems via AI.

The AI offer from Azure is really wide, so for this chapter, the choice is on the Azure Cognitive Services, more specifically on the Computer Vision service. This service allows you to analyze images and extract a lot of information. In the next section you learn how to set up your projects in Visual Studio Code and how to invoke such a service.

Note   If you work behind a proxy or company firewall, your code might not be able to reach the Azure services. If this is the case, contact your network administrator to open the necessary ports.

General Considerations

Generally speaking, AI services from Azure can be consumed via REST APIs. In this way, any platform and language can invoke the services. For some services, Microsoft also provides client libraries that allow you to work in a way that is specific to a given language or platform. For example, with C# and Python, these libraries make it possible to work in an object-oriented and strongly-typed way. The code examples in this chapter use the aforementioned client libraries, so that you can leverage all the code editor features in VS Code. On Azure, services can be enabled in the Management Portal. This certainly includes Cognitive Services with Computer Vision.

Introducing Computer Vision

Computer Vision is a group of AI services included in the Cognitive Services (`https://azure.microsoft.com/en-us/products/cognitive-services`). Table 12-2 provides a description of services included with Computer Vision.

Table 12-2. *Computer Vision Services*

Service	Description
Computer Vision	Allows you to extract rich information from images and videos, including image understanding and text extraction.
Custom Vision	Allows you to build custom image analysis services.
Face API	Allows you to analyze and identify faces. It includes the Celebrity API that recognize celebrities in images and videos.

Computer Vision services can be set up in the Azure Management Portal, as you will see shortly, and can be consumed both via REST APIs and client libraries.

Setting Up Computer Vision Services

The sample code of the next examples shows how to analyze an image and retrieve information from it. Before starting, you need to set up an endpoint in the Azure Management Portal (`https://portal.azure.com`).

Following the lesson learned in Chapter 11, log in to the Azure Management Portal.

Note   There is no extension for Visual Studio Code that allows you to create AI endpoints from within the development environment, so you need to set up the resource inside the browser.

Once you are in the Portal, click the Create Resource button at the top-left corner of the page. When the Create a Resource page appears (see Figure 12-1), click AI + Machine Learning on the left. Finally, click the Create hyperlink under the Computer Vision item on the right.

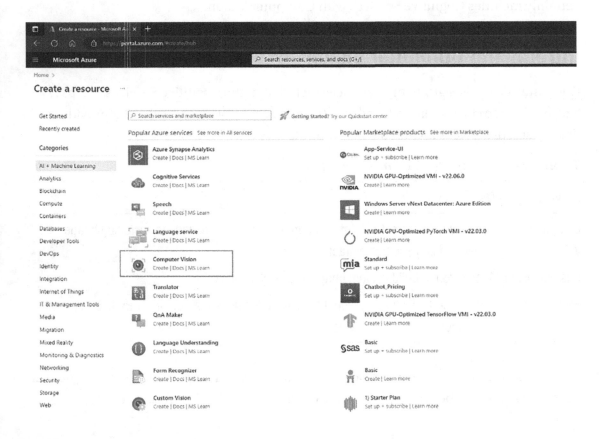

Figure 12-1. *Locating the Computer Vision service for creation*

When the Create Computer Vision page appears, you need to configure the basic information for your new service. In the Project Details group, you can select the subscription that will host the service and a new or existing resource group. In the Instance Details group, you need to specify a data center; make sure you select the one closest to your location. Then you need to specify a name, which is very important because it will be part of the service endpoint. The service name must be unique, so the sample `vscodedistilledcomputervision` name might not be available. The last setting is about the pricing tier. If you have no other AI services enabled, you can select the F0 Free tier, which is always recommended for development purposes.

Figure 12-2 summarizes all the aforementioned steps.

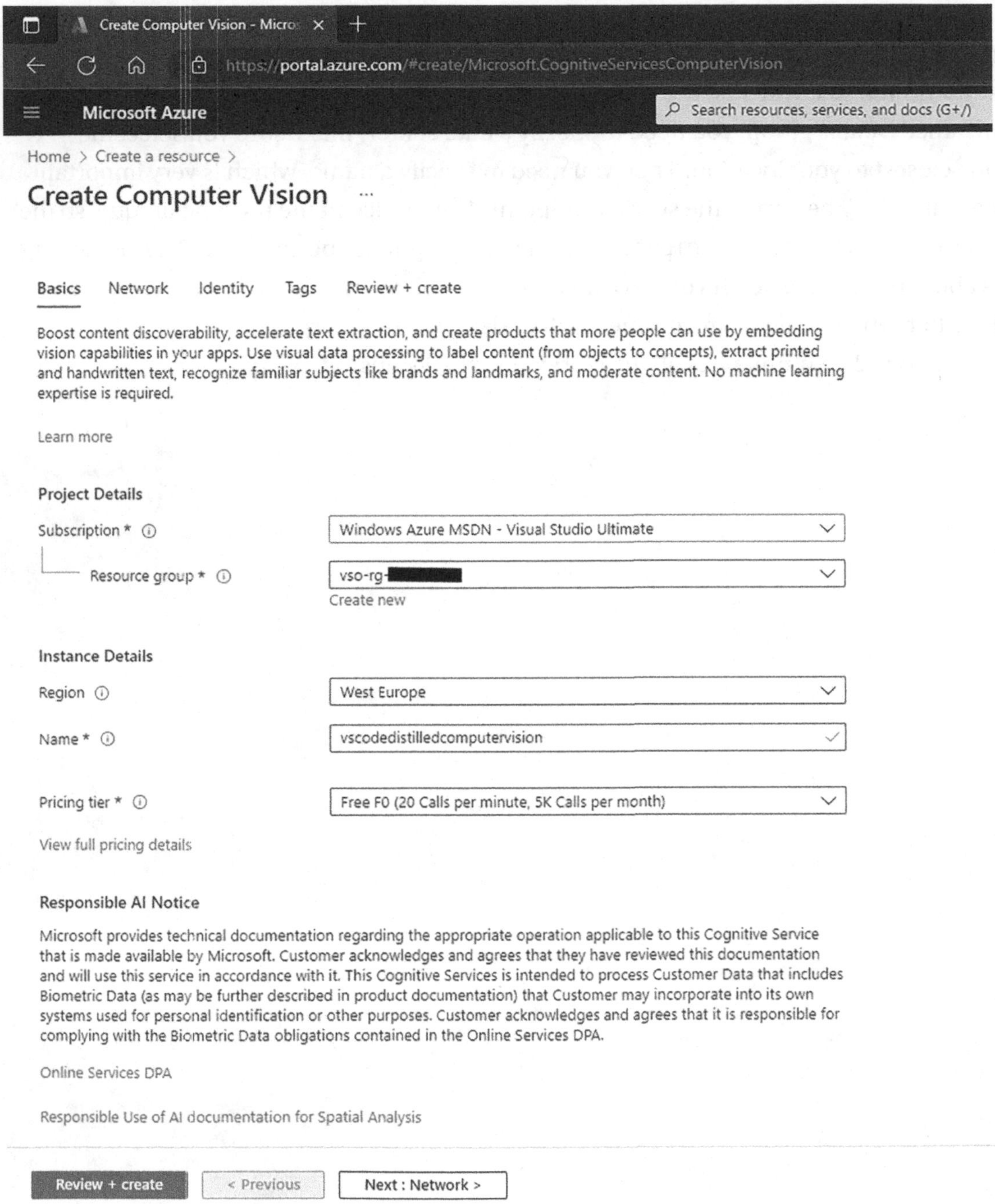

Figure 12-2. Configuring the basic service information

When ready, click the Next: Network ➤ button. In the next page, you can configure the network access. For the current example, the service will be reachable via all the networks, so make sure that the first option (All Networks) is selected (see Figure 12-3).

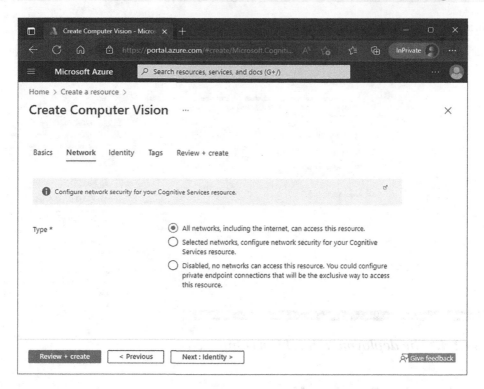

Figure 12-3. *Configuring network access*

You can then click the Next button. You can ignore the Identity and Tags pages that are not relevant for this example. You can further configure identities depending on your specific requirements. In the last page, you will see a Create button that you can click to generate a new Computer Vision service.

After a few seconds, the new resource will be deployed (see Figure 12-4). Click the Go to Resource button to access the service properties.

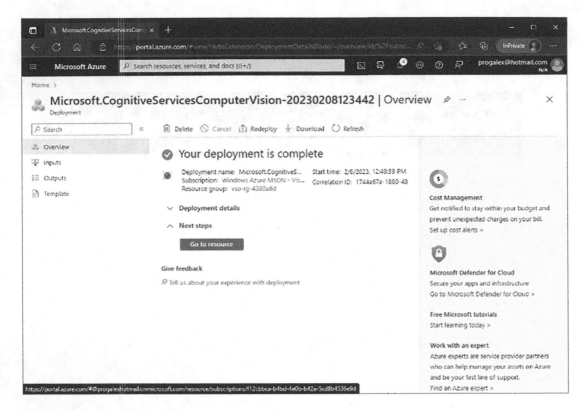

Figure 12-4.   *The deployment has been completed*

Retrieving the Service Keys

Whatever programming language or framework you use to consume Computer Vision APIs, you need to retrieve the service keys. These allow your code to authenticate against the service.

In the Keys and Endpoint page (see Figure 12-5), click the Keys and Endpoint item on the left.

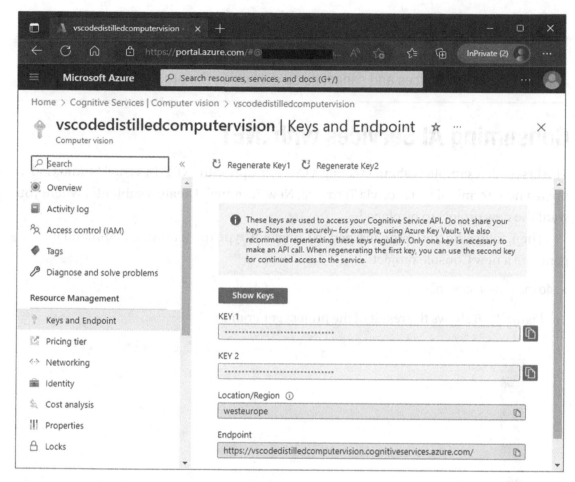

Figure 12-5. *Retrieving the service keys*

By default, keys are hidden so you have to click the Show Keys button. You do not need both keys. Key 1 is enough, but Key 2 is provided for security reasons. Take note of the Key 1 and Endpoint fields. These will be necessary in the next paragraphs when writing code. The service setup is now complete, so you can open Visual Studio Code to start developing an app that consumes the new AI service.

You will write code for three platforms: .NET, JavaScript, and Python. For this reason, in order to be consistent across all platforms, you will create a Console project that will display the image analysis results inside a Terminal instance. The code examples are independent from one another, so you can read them all or just look at the one that is closest to the development environment of your choice.

> **Note**   This chapter assumes you have the necessary knowledge of the programming languages used for the coming examples. In fact, the focus here is on the Cognitive Services and cannot be on explaining the programming languages.

Consuming AI Services with .NET

The first code example is about creating a Console app with .NET. In Visual Studio Code, open a new Terminal instance via Terminal, New Terminal. Create a subfolder where you want the new project to be placed.

Then, following the lesson learned in Chapter 9, type the following command to generate a new Console project:

```
> dotnet new console
```

Figure 12-6 shows the result of the project generation.

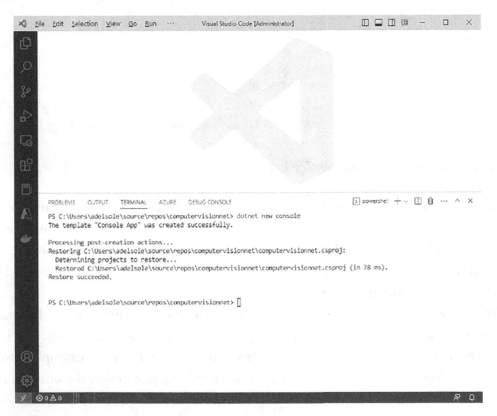

Figure 12-6. *Creating a new .NET Console project*

You can keep the Terminal open because you will need to type new commands shortly. In the meantime, open the new project in VS Code. Before writing any C# code, it is important to know that Microsoft provides a client library for .NET that simplifies the way you consume Computer Vision APIs in a strongly-typed and object-oriented approach. This means that you can use specific classes and methods instead of manually invoking REST APIs. It also means, with regard to VS Code, that you can leverage debugging and coding tools (such as IntelliSense) to use and investigate objects and their members. You will see more about this when you run the sample application.

The client library is provided via NuGet and it is called `Microsoft.Azure. CognitiveServices.Vision.ComputerVision`. You can quickly install the library to the project with the following command line:

```
> dotnet add package Microsoft.Azure.CognitiveServices.Vision.
ComputerVision
```

Figure 12-7 shows the results for this command.

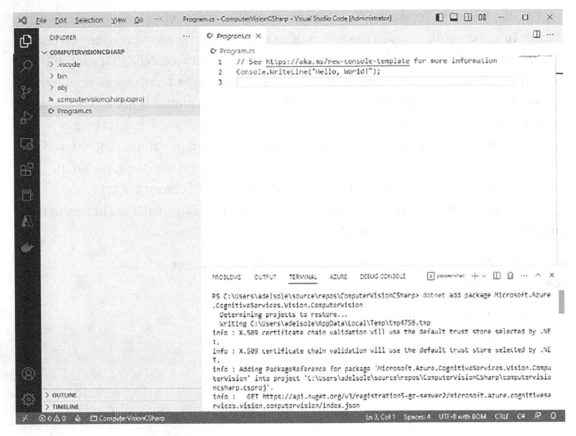

Figure 12-7. *Installing the Microsoft client library from NuGet*

Setting Up Variables and Constants

Open the Program.cs file and add the following code:

```
using Microsoft.Azure.CognitiveServices.Vision.ComputerVision;
using Microsoft.Azure.CognitiveServices.Vision.ComputerVision.Models;
namespace ComputerVisionNet
{
    class Program
    {
        static string serviceKey = "YOUR-KEY-GOES-HERE";
        static string endpoint =
            "https://YOUR-ENDPOINT.cognitiveservices.azure.com/";
```

```
private const string imageToAnalyze = "https://
moderatorsampleimages.blob.core.windows.net/samples/sample16.png";
```

Replace the serviceKey and endpoint variable contents with the key for your Computer Vision service and endpoint, respectively. The imageToAnalyze constant contains the URL of the image that will be analyzed. This image is provided for free by Microsoft as a sample image for the Computer Vision official samples, and it represents a puppy on a grass field. Figure 12-8 shows the sample image so you can understand what the analysis will be about.

Figure 12-8. *The sample image used for Computer Vision analysis (Courtesy: Microsoft Corp.)*

The Main method for the application looks like the following:

```
async static void Main(string[] args)
{
    // Create a client
    ComputerVisionClient client = Authenticate(endpoint,
    serviceKey);

    // Analyze an image to get features and other properties.
    await AnalyzeImageUrlAsync(client, imageToAnalyze);
}
```

The first line of code creates an instance of the `ComputerVisionClient` class, which allows you to access Computer Vision APIs in a managed way. Such an instance is created via the `Authenticate` method, implemented shortly, which takes the service key and endpoint as arguments and authenticates against the service. The second line of code performs the actual image analysis with a method called `AnalyzeImageUrlAsync`, also implemented shortly.

Creating Authenticated Service Clients

A service client is a class that exposes members for accessing the service APIs in an object-oriented way.

This is the biggest benefit of using a client library, rather than writing REST API calls manually. In .NET, the `Microsoft.Azure.CognitiveServices.Vision.ComputerVision` provides the `ComputerVisionClient` class.

Note   Microsoft provides .NET client libraries for most AI services included in the Azure offer, so the approach described in this chapter applies to other services as well.

An instance of this class must be created passing the authentication keys, which are the service key and the endpoint. The following method demonstrates how to accomplish this:

```
public static ComputerVisionClient Authenticate(string endpoint,
        string key)
{
    ComputerVisionClient client =
      new ComputerVisionClient(new ApiKeyServiceClientCredent
      ials(key))
      { Endpoint = endpoint };
    return client;
}
```

The argument for the constructor of the ComputerVisionClient class is an instance of the ApiKeyServiceClientCredentials class that receives and validates the service key. The Endpoint property of the ApiKeyServiceClientCredentials class is also assigned directly. The result of this method is an authenticated instance of the ComputerVisionClient class that callers use to perform image analysis.

Executing Image Analysis

Analyzing an image means understanding the contents of an image by detecting the presence of people, animals, objects, colors, and everything around.

The analysis result is collected into a list of tags, each representing an element detected in the image, with the related level of accuracy (confidence). In the current example, the image analysis is performed by the following AnalyzeImageUrlAsync:

```
public static async Task AnalyzeImageUrlAsync(ComputerVisionClient
client, string imageUrl)
{
    // A list that defines the features to be extracted from
    the image.
    List<VisualFeatureTypes?> features = new List<VisualFeature
    Types?>()
    {
        VisualFeatureTypes.Tags,
        VisualFeatureTypes.Color,
        VisualFeatureTypes.Description,
        VisualFeatureTypes.Objects,
        VisualFeatureTypes.Faces,
        VisualFeatureTypes.Adult
    };

    Console.WriteLine($"Analyzing the image
                {Path.GetFileName(imageUrl)}...");
    Console.WriteLine();
    // Analyze the URL image
    ImageAnalysis results = await client.
                AnalyzeImageAsync(imageUrl, visualFeatures:
                features);
```

The first part of the method declares a List<VisualFeatureTypes?> object, which contains a list of elements you want to detect. The type of elements is represented by the VisualFeatureTypes enumeration, whose most important values is Tags. This contains the tags and confidence level that the analysis engine will detect. Table 12-3 describes the possible values for the VisualFeatureTypes enumeration. The actual analysis is performed by the AnalyzeImageAsync method from the ComputerVisionClient class, which receives the source image and a list of VisualFeatureTypes object as arguments and returns an object of type ImageAnalysis. This exposes properties that return the results of the visual types described in Table 12-3.

Table 12-3. *VisualFeatureTypes Enumeration*

Value	Description
Adult	Detects if the image contains adult or racist contents.
Brands	Detects if the image contains brand names.
Categories	Categorizes the contents of an image.
Color	Detects the most relevant colors in the image.
Description	Generates one or more descriptions for the image.
Faces	Detects any faces in the image.
ImageType	Detects an image type.
Objects	Detects a list of objects in an image.
Tags	Creates a list of tags that represent the list of elements in an image.

As you type, you can realize the benefits of using a client library: Visual Studio Code enables IntelliSense, code refactoring, and all the most advanced editing tools against the types and members exposed by the library itself. Figure 12-9 shows how IntelliSense can help when invoking methods from the ComputerVisionClient class.

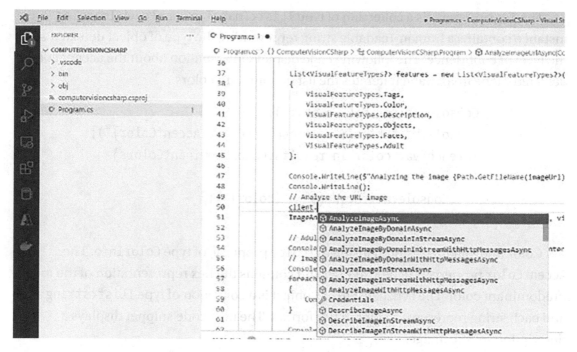

Figure 12-9. *IntelliSense enabled with the client library*

The next step is displaying the analysis result. The following code snippet shows information about adult classification:

```
// Adult content?
Console.WriteLine($"Is adult content?:
                    {results.Adult.IsAdultContent}");
```

Among the others, the Adult object, of type AdultInfo, exposes the IsAdultContent property, of type bool. It returns true if the image contains adult content. The following code snippet iterates through the list of detected tags, and it is probably the most relevant in the example:

```
// Image tags and their confidence score
Console.WriteLine("Tags:");
foreach (var tag in results.Tags)
{
    Console.WriteLine($"{tag.Name} {tag.Confidence}");
}
```

The `Tags` property is a collection of type `IList<ImageTag>`, and each `ImageTag` instance contains a human-readable string representing the type of object detected and the level of confidence. The following code displays information about the accent color detected in the image, and it iterates the list of dominant colors:

```
Console.WriteLine("Colors:");
Console.WriteLine($"    {results.Color.AccentColor}");
foreach(var color in results.Color.DominantColors)
{
    Console.WriteLine($"    {color}");
}
```

Color information is stored inside the `Color` property, of type `ColorInfo`. The `AccentColor` property is of type `string` and contains the hex representation of the most predominant color. The `DominantColors` object is a collection of type `IList<string>`, and each string represents a color in hex format. The next code snippet displays a description for the image:

```
Console.WriteLine("Description: ");
foreach(var text in results.Description.Captions)
{
    Console.WriteLine($"    {text.Text}");
}
```

The AI engine of Cognitive Services can generate meaningful phrases that describe the contents of the image. Each phrase is represented by an object of type `ImageCaption`, whose `Text` property is a string containing the phrase. All the generated phrases are stored inside the `Captions` collection, of type `IList<ImageCaption>`, provided by the `Description` property. There is usually at least one phrase. It is also possible to analyze the list of objects contained in the image, as follows:

```
Console.WriteLine("Objects:");
foreach(var obj in results.Objects)
{
    Console.WriteLine($"    {obj.ObjectProperty}");
}
```

The `ObjectProperty` property of each `Object` represents the name of a detected object. The last part of the sample application detects if there are any faces in the image:

```
Console.WriteLine($"Does it contain any faces?: {results.Faces.
Any()}");
Console.ReadLine();
        }
    }
}
```

The `Faces` collection, of type `IList<FaceDescription>`, contains information on faces detected in the image, but if you need to use AI to analyze faces, the recommendation is to look at the Face API.

Note   If you do not explicitly add values from the `VisualFeatureTypes` enumeration to the list of objects you want to retrieve, the code that walks through the result of the image analysis will be ignored.

Running the Application

Now that you have set up all the code required to perform image analysis based on artificial intelligence, you can see the result by running the application. You can press F5 or choose Run ➤ Start Debugging and you will see the analysis results in the integrated Terminal after a few seconds.

Figure 12-10 demonstrates this.

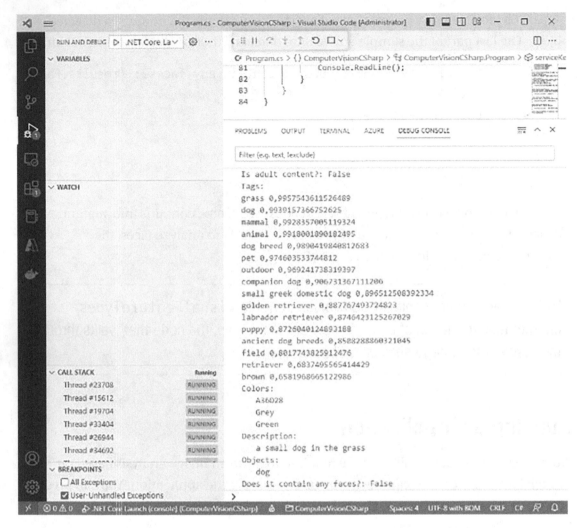

Figure 12-10. *The results of the image analysis via Cognitive Services*

Notice how the list of tags is automatically ordered by confidence (in descending order), and how the description is a complete, human-readable phrase. You can combine multiple AI services with Computer Vision to create great user experiences.

Using the Debugging Tools

There is another benefit in using a client library over regular code that sends HTTP REST requests, which is taking advantage of the full debugging experience.

You can certainly leverage debugging tools over the code that sends regular requests, but in specialized scenarios such as AI, having precise support is definitely a better option, especially if you do not have deep knowledge of the libraries you are using. Figure 12-11 shows how you can use the VS Code debugging tools for .NET when analyzing the image via the `ComputerVisionClient` class.

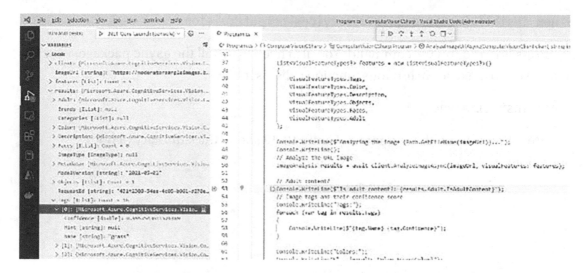

Figure 12-11. *Debugging tools in action on the ComputerVisionClient class*

As you can see, by placing a breakpoint in your code, you can investigate properties and their values also understand the backing .NET type.

Consuming AI Services with JavaScript

The second code example is about creating a JavaScript project that consumes the Azure Cognitive Services. You can open an instance of the integrated Terminal in Visual Studio Code to create a new folder that will contain the new project.

The name is up to you, although you can use `computervisionjs` for consistency with the companion code. Once the folder has been created, you need to type the following command line to initialize the project with a `package.json` file:

```
> npm init
```

Press Enter to run the command. Before writing any JavaScript code, it is important to know that Microsoft provides a client library that simplifies the way you consume Computer Vision APIs in an object-oriented approach. This means that you can use specific classes and functions instead of manually invoking REST APIs.

Such a library is provided via npm and it is called `cognitiveservices-computervision`. You can quickly install the library to the project with the following command line:

```
> npm install @azure/cognitiveservices-computervision
```

Press Enter to run the command. You also need to install the `async` package, which allows you to make asynchronous function calls, as follows:

```
> npm install async
```

Press Enter to run the command. Figure 12-12 shows the summary of both operations.

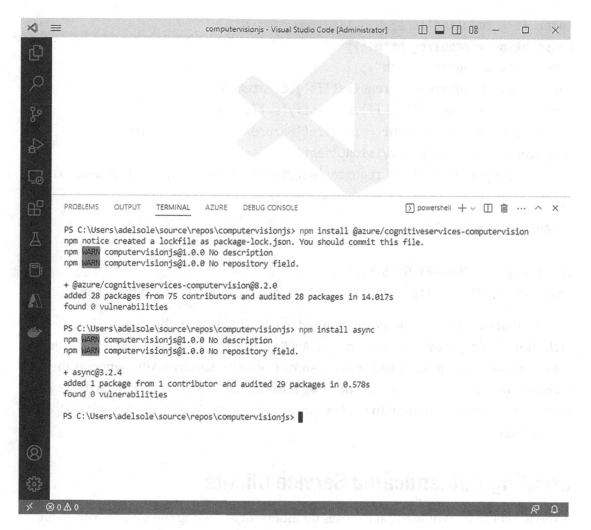

Figure 12-12.   Installing the Cognitive Services client library

When you're ready, add a file called index.js to the project folder. You will now learn the various parts required to execute artificial intelligence analysis over images.

Setting Up Variables and Constants

Open the index.js file and start by adding the following code:

```
'use strict';

const async = require('async');
```

```
const fs = require('fs');
const https = require('https');
const path = require("path");
const createReadStream = require('fs').createReadStream
const sleep = require('util').promisify(setTimeout);
const ComputerVisionClient = require('@azure/cognitiveservices-
computervision').ComputerVisionClient;
const ApiKeyCredentials = require('@azure/ms-rest-js').ApiKeyCredentials;

/**
 * Authenticated client instance
 */
const key = 'YOUR-KEY-GOES-HERE';
const endpoint = 'https://YOUR-ENDPOINT.cognitiveservices.azure.com/';
```

The first const declarations are required to use objects from the various libraries, including the ComputerVisionClient and ApiKeyCredentials objects. The first object is a client class that makes it easier to consume Cognitive Services APIs, whereas the second object allows you to authenticate against Cognitive Services. Replace the key and endpoint variable contents with the key for your Computer Vision service and endpoint, respectively.

Creating Authenticated Service Clients

A service client is an object that exposes members for accessing the service APIs in an object-oriented way.

This is the biggest benefit of using a client library, rather than writing REST API calls manually. In the Azure JavaScript SDK, the cognitiveservices-computervision library provides the ComputerVisionClient class.

Note   Microsoft provides client libraries for most AI services included in the Azure offer, so the approach described in this chapter applies to other services as well.

An instance of this class must be created by passing the authentication keys, which are the service key and the endpoint. The following code demonstrates how to accomplish this:

```
const computerVisionClient = new ComputerVisionClient(
        new ApiKeyCredentials({ inHeader:
        { 'Ocp-Apim-Subscription-Key': key } }), endpoint);
```

The parameter for the constructor of the `ComputerVisionClient` class is an instance of the `ApiKeyCredentials` object, and it receives and validates the service key. The result of this code is an authenticated instance of the `ComputerVisionClient` class that callers will use to perform image analysis.

Executing Image Analysis

Analyzing an image means understanding the contents of an image by detecting the presence of people, animals, objects, colors, and everything around.

The analysis result is collected into a list of tags, each representing an element detected in the image, with the related level of accuracy (confidence). In the current example, the image analysis is performed by the following code:

```
function computerVision() {
  async.series([
    async function () {

      // Image of different kind of dog.
      const imageUrl = 'https://moderatorsampleimages.blob.core.windows.
      net/samples/sample16.png';

      // Analyze URL image
      console.log('Analyzing the image...', imageUrl.split('/').pop());
      var results = await computerVisionClient.analyzeImage(imageUrl, {
      visualFeatures: ['Tags', 'Adult', 'Color', 'Description'] });
```

The first part of the method sets up the URL of the image to be analyzed, and then it invokes the `analyzeImage` method from the `ComputerVisionClient` class to analyze the image.

The second parameter for the method is an array called `visualFeatures` which contains a list of elements you want to detect. The most important type of element is `Tags`. This contains the tags and confidence level that the analysis engine will detect. Table 12-3 describes the possible values for the `visualFeatures` array. The `analyzeImage` method returns an object of type `AnalyzeImageResponse`. This exposes members that return the results of the visual types described in Table 12-3.

The next step is displaying the analysis result. The following code snippet shows information about adult classification:

```
console.log(`Is adult content?: ${results.adult.isAdultContent}`);
```

Among the others, the `adult` object, of type `AdultInfo`, exposes the `isAdultContent` property, of type `bool`. It returns `true` if the image contains adult content. The following code snippet iterates through the list of detected tags, and it is probably the most relevant in the example:

```
console.log('Image tags:');
console.log(`Tags: ${formatTags(results.tags)}`);
// Format tags for display
function formatTags(tags) {
                return tags.map(tag => (`${tag.name}
                (${tag.confidence.toFixed(2)})`)).join(', '); }
```

The `tags` property is an array of `ImageTag` objects, and each `ImageTag` instance contains a human-readable string representing the type of the object detected and the level of confidence. The following code displays information about the accent color, which is the most predominant color, detected in the image. It iterates the list of dominant colors:

```
console.log(`Accent color: ${results.color.accentColor}`);
console.log('Dominant colors:');
results.color.dominantColors.forEach(col=>console.log(col));
```

Color information is stored inside the `color` property, of type `ColorInfo`. The `accentColor` property is of type `string` and contains the hex representation of a color. The `dominantColors` object is an array of strings, and each string represents a color in hex format. The next code snippet displays a description for the image:

```
console.log('Description: ');
results.description.captions.forEach(dsc=>console.log(dsc.text));
```

The AI engine of Cognitive Services can generate meaningful phrases that describe the contents of the image. Each phrase is represented by an object of type `ImageCaption`, whose `text` property is a string containing the phrase. All the generated phrases are stored inside the captions collection, an array of ImageCaption, provided by the description property. There is usually at least one phrase. The code file is closed with a standard JavaScript promise and with the invocation to the computerVision method.

```
      console.log();
    },
    function () {
      return new Promise((resolve) => {
        resolve();
      })
    }
  ], (err) => {
    throw (err);
  });
}
computerVision();
```

Note   Put succinctly, in JavaScript a promise represents the eventual completion, or failure, of an asynchronous operation and its resulting value. If you want to learn more about promises, you can read the JavaScript documentation (https:// developer.mozilla.org/en-US/docs/Web/JavaScript/Reference/ Global_Objects/Promise).

Coding and Debugging Tools in Action

Like for .NET, one of the benefits of using a client library is that VS Code enables powerful editing tools, such as IntelliSense, plus the debugging tools you have seen previously.

For example, IntelliSense for JavaScript shows the list of members from the ComputerVisionClient class as you type, as it will do for all the other members. In addition, you can leverage the integrated debugging tools to investigate variables and, more generally, to control the execution flow. Figure 12-13 demonstrates this.

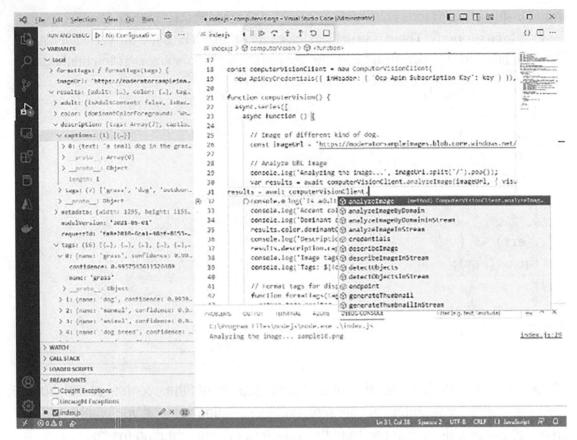

Figure 12-13. *Debugging tools and IntelliSense in action*

As you can see in Figure 12-13, Visual Studio Code enables IntelliSense for JavaScript when invoking types and members from the client library, and it allows you to investigate variable values at debugging time via the VARIABLES window.

Running the Application

Now that you have set up all the code required to perform image analysis based on artificial intelligence, you can see the result by running the application. You can press F5 or choose Run ➤ Start Debugging and then select the Node.js debugger. You will see the analysis results in the integrated Terminal after a few seconds.

Figure 12-14 demonstrates this.

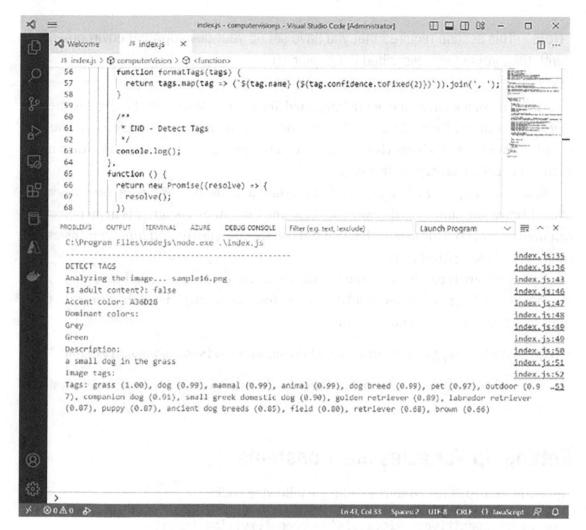

Figure 12-14. *The results of the image analysis via Cognitive Services*

Notice how the list of tags is automatically ordered by confidence (in descending order), and how the description is a complete, human-readable phrase. With a similar approach, you can even combine multiple Cognitive Services.

Consuming AI Services with Python

The third and last code example is about creating a Python application that consumes the Azure Cognitive Services.

Note   This section requires that you have set up your development environment with the Python tools described in Chapter 10.

You can open an instance of the integrated Terminal in Visual Studio Code to create a new folder that will contain a new Python code file. The name is up to you, but you could use `computervisionpython` for consistency with the companion code. Add a new Python file called `main.py` to this folder.

Before writing any Python code, it is important to know that Microsoft provides a client library that simplifies the way you consume Computer Vision APIs in an object-oriented approach. This means that you can use specific classes and functions instead of manually invoking REST APIs.

Such a library is provided via the `pip` library manager and it is called `azure-cognitiveservices-vision-computervision`. You can quickly install the library to the folder via the following command line:

```
> pip install --upgrade azure-cognitiveservices-vision-computervision
```

You now learn the various parts required to execute artificial intelligence analysis over images.

Setting Up Variables and Constants

Open the `main.py` file and start writing the following code:

```
from azure.cognitiveservices.vision.computervision import
ComputerVisionClient
from azure.cognitiveservices.vision.computervision.models import
OperationStatusCodes
from azure.cognitiveservices.vision.computervision.models import
VisualFeatureTypes
from msrest.authentication import CognitiveServicesCredentials

from array import array
import os
from PIL import Image
import sys
```

```
import time

subscription_key = "YOUR-KEY-GOES-HERE"
endpoint = "https://YOUR-ENDPOINT.cognitiveservices.azure.com/"
```

The `from` and `import` declarations are required to use objects from the various libraries, including the `ComputerVisionClient` and `CognitiveServiceCredentials` objects. The first object is a client class that makes it easier to consume Cognitive Services APIs, whereas the second object allows you to authenticate against Cognitive Services. Replace the key and `endpoint` variable contents with the key for your Computer Vision service and endpoint, respectively.

Creating Authenticated Service Clients

A service client is an object that exposes members for accessing the service APIs in an object-oriented way.

This is the biggest benefit of using a client library, rather than writing REST API calls manually. In the Azure Python SDK, the `azure-cognitiveservices-vision-computervision` library provides the `ComputerVisionClient` class.

Note   Microsoft provides client libraries for most AI services included in the Azure offer, so the approach described in this chapter applies to other services as well.

An instance of this class must be created passing the authentication keys, which are the service key and the endpoint. The following code demonstrates how to accomplish this:

```
computervision_client = ComputerVisionClient(endpoint, CognitiveServices
Credentials(subscription_key))
```

The parameter for the constructor of the `ComputerVisionClient` class is an instance of the `CognitiveServiceCredentials` object that receives and validates the service key. The result of this code is an authenticated instance of the `ComputerVisionClient` class that callers will use to perform image analysis.

Executing Image Analysis

Analyzing an image means understanding the contents of an image by detecting the presence of people, animals, objects, colors, and everything around.

The analysis result is collected into a list of tags, each representing an element detected in the image, with the related level of accuracy (confidence). In the current example, the image analysis is performed by the following code:

```
url = "https://moderatorsampleimages.blob.core.windows.net/samples/
sample16.png"

image_analysis = computervision_client.analyze_image(url,
                              visual_features=[VisualFeatureTypes.tags,
                              VisualFeatureTypes.description,
                              VisualFeatureTypes.adult,
                              VisualFeatureTypes.color,
                              VisualFeatureTypes.objects])
```

The first part of the code snippet sets up the URL of the image to be analyzed, and then it invokes the `analyze_image` method from the `ComputerVisionClient` class to analyze the image.

The second parameter for the method is an array called `visual_features` which contains a list of elements you want to detect from the `VisualFeatureTypes` enumeration. The most important type of element is `tags`. This contains the tags and confidence level that the analysis engine will detect. Table 12-3 describes the possible values for the `VisualFeatureTypes` enumeration. The `analyze_image` method returns an object of type `ClientRawResponse`. This exposes members that return the results of the visual types described in Table 12-3.

The next step is displaying the analysis result. The following code snippet shows information about adult classification:

```
print("Is adult content?")
print(image_analysis.adult.is_adult_content)
```

Among the others, the `adult` object, of type `AdultInfo`, exposes the `is_adult_content` property, of type `bool`. It returns `true` if the image contains adult content. The following code snippet iterates through the list of detected tags, and it is probably the most relevant in the example:

```
print("Tags:")
for tag in image_analysis.tags:
    print("'{}' with confidence {:.2f}%".format(tag.name, tag.
    confidence * 100))
```

The tags property is an array of ImageTag objects and each ImageTag instance contains a human-readable string representing the type of object detected and the level of confidence. The following code displays information about the accent color (that is, the predominant color) detected in the image, and it iterates the list of dominant colors:

```
print("Accent color:")
print(image_analysis.color.accent_color)
print("Dominant colors:")
for col in image_analysis.color.dominant_colors:
    print(col)
```

Color information is stored inside the color property, of type ColorInfo. The accent_color property is of type string and contains the hex representation of a color. The dominant_colors object is an array of strings, and each string represents a color in hex format. The next code snippet displays a description for the image:

```
print("Image description:")
for des in image_analysis.description.captions:
    print(des.text)
```

The AI engine of Cognitive Services can generate meaningful phrases that describe the contents of the image. Each phrase is represented by an object of type ImageCaption, whose text property is a string containing the phrase. All the generated phrases are stored inside the captions collection, an array of ImageCaption, provided by the description property. There is usually at least one phrase. It is also possible to analyze the list of objects contained in the image, as follows:

```
print("Objects:")
for obj in image_analysis.objects:
    print(obj.object_property)
```

The object_property property of each Object represents the name of a detected object.

Coding and Debugging Tools in Action

Like for .NET and JavaScript, the benefit of using a client library is that VS Code enables powerful editing tools, such as IntelliSense, plus the debugging tools you have seen previously.

For example, IntelliSense for Python shows the list of members from the ComputerVisionClient class as you type, as it will do for all the other members. In addition, you can leverage the integrated debugging tools to investigate variables and, more generally, to control the execution flow. Figure 12-15 demonstrates this.

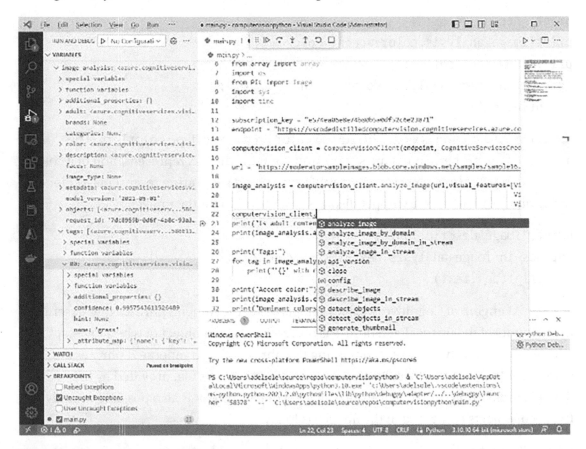

Figure 12-15. *Debugging tools and IntelliSense in action*

As you can see in Figure 12-15, Visual Studio Code enables IntelliSense for JavaScript when invoking types and members from the client library, and it allows you to investigate variable values at debugging time via the VARIABLES window.

Running the Application

Now that you have set up all the code required to perform image analysis based on artificial intelligence, you can see the result by running the application. You can press F5 or choose Run ➤ Start Debugging and you will be asked to specify the debug configuration.

Select the first option, Python File Debug the Currently Active Python File. After a few seconds, you will see the analysis results in the integrated Terminal.

Figure 12-16 demonstrates this.

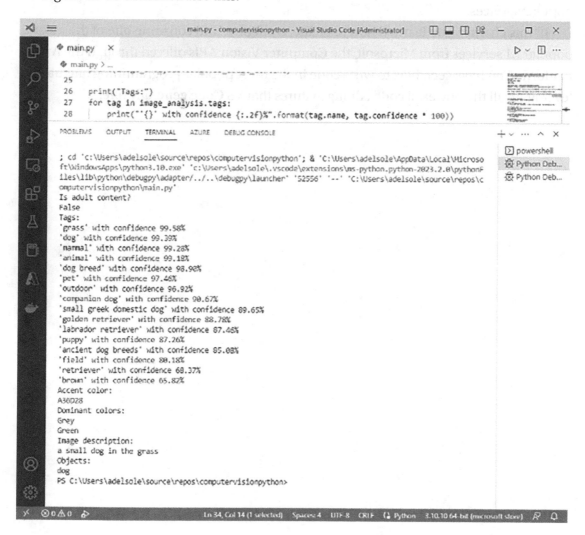

Figure 12-16. *The results of the image analysis via Cognitive Services*

Notice how the list of tags is automatically ordered by confidence (in descending order), and how the description is a complete, human-readable phrase. With a similar approach, you can even combine multiple Cognitive Services.

Summary

With artificial intelligence becoming more and more a part of the daily work of many developers, you can use Visual Studio Code to write code that consumes the most popular services.

In this chapter, you learned how to create, configure, and consume one of the most popular AI services from Microsoft, the Computer Vision APIs offered through the Azure platform. You have seen how to write code in the most popular programming languages, leveraging all the powerful code editing features that VS Code generally offers.

Index

A

AccentColor property, 312, 320

Active editors/open editors, 31, 69, 83, 131, 160, 286

Activity Bar, 19, 23, 24, 26, 33, 36, 37, 43

analyze_image method, 326

AnalyzeImageAsync method, 310

AnalyzeImageUrlAsync, 308, 309

Application development

  creating application

   command-line interface, 215

   Microsoft .NET, 216, 217

   .NET projects, 217–223

   platforms, 223–225

  debugging code

   breakpoints, 230–232

   call stack, 235

   configuration, 227–229

   console path, 236

   Debug Console window, 232

   evaluate expressions, 234, 235

   ru view, 226

   settings, 237

   toolbar, 233, 234

Artificial intelligence (AI) services

  Azure services, 296

  Computer Vision service, 297–299, 301, 302

  JavaScript

   authenticated service clients, 318

   cognitive services client library, 317

command, 316

   image analysis, 319–322

   running applications, 322, 323

   variables/constants, 317, 318

  .NET

   authenticated service clients, 308

   console project, 304

   image analysis, 309–313

   NuGet, 306

   running application, 313, 314

   variables/constants, 306–308

  Python

   authenticated service clients, 325

   image analysis, 326–328

   Microsoft, 324

   running applications, 329

   variables/constants, 324

  retrieving keys, 302, 303

Authenticate method, 308

Azure Functions, 263, 274, 292

  deploy web applications

   extensions, installing, 265, 266

   sigining to subscriptions, 266–268

   web application, 268–271

  Docker images (*see* Docker)

  extensions, 263, 264

  functions

   authorization levels, 276, 277

   configuring VS code, 271–273

   creating project, 274, 275, 277, 279, 280

© Alessandro Del Sole 2023
A. Del Sole, *Visual Studio Code Distilled*, https://doi.org/10.1007/978-1-4842-9484-0

Printed in the United States
By Baker & Taylor Publisher Services

Printed in the United States
by Baker & Taylor Publisher Services